THE BASES

OF THE

TEMPERANCE REFORM:

AN EXPOSITION AND APPEAL.

WITH REPLIES TO NUMEROUS OBJECTIONS.

BY

REV. DAWSON BURNS, M.A., F.S.S.

"The best," said he, "that I can you advise,
Is to avoid the occasion of the ill;
For when the cause whence evil doth arise
Removed is, the effect surceaseth still."
—*Spenser's Fairy Queen*, b. vi. c. 6.

NEW YORK:
National Temperance Society and Publication House,
NO. 58 READE STREET.

1873.

TABLE OF CONTENTS.

PAGE

PREFACE, ... vii

CHAPTER I.—PROPOSITION: THAT THE DRINKING SYSTEM IS THE GREATEST SOCIAL EVIL IN OUR LAND, ... 9

1. *The Production of Intoxicating Liquors*, ... 10
2. *The Circulation of Intoxicating Liquors*, . . . 14
3. *The Consumption of Intoxicating Liquors as Beverages*, . 16
   (1.) Effects upon the *Individual*, ... 17
   (2.) Effects upon the *Family*, ... 19
   (3.) Effects upon the *Nation*, ... 21
   (4.) Effects viewed as *Destructive* and *Obstructive*, . . 23

OBJECTIONS (FOUR) *stated and examined*, ... 26

CHAPTER II. PROPOSITION: THAT INTOXICATING LIQUORS ARE USELESS AND INJURIOUS AS ARTICLES OF DIET, ... 35

I. *Intoxicating Liquors* USELESS, ... 35
   Their supposed uses considered, ... 37

II. INJURIOUS ACTION *of Alcoholic Drinks*, ... 46
1. *Specific Poisonous Nature of Alcohol*, ... 46
2. *Physiological Relations of Alcohol*, ... 47
3. *Testimonies of Medical Authorities*, ... 56
4. *Evidence from Experience*, ... 56

OBJECTIONS (FIVE) *stated and examined*, ... 62

CHAPTER III.—PROPOSITION: THAT INTEMPERANCE IS A TRUE PLAGUE, WHICH CAN ONLY BE EFFECTUALLY SUPPRESSED BY THE EXCLUSION OF INTOXICATING DRINKS, ... 74

OBJECTIONS (TWO) *stated and examined*, ... 89

PAGE

CHAPTER IV.—PROPOSITION: THAT VIOLENCE IS DONE TO THE WILL OF GOD AND THE WELFARE OF MAN BY APPROPRIATING THE FRUITS OF THE EARTH TO THE PRODUCTION OF INTOXICATING DRINKS, ... 85

OBJECTIONS (THREE) *stated and examined*, . . . 93

CHAPTER V.—PROPOSITION: THAT THE SACRED SCRIPTURES DO NOT AFFORD SANCTION TO THE USE OF INTOXICATING DRINKS, BUT GIVE ENCOURAGEMENT AND SUPPORT TO THE TOTAL ABSTINENCE PRACTICE, ... 99

I. *Scripture does not Sanction the Use of Alcoholic Liquors*, . . 102

1. *Cautions given*, ... 104

2. *Supposed Forms of Sanction considered*, . . . 106

II. *Scripture gives Support and Encouragement to the Practice of Total Abstinence*, ... 115

OBJECTIONS (SIX) *stated and examined*, ... 128

CHAPTER VI.—PROPOSITION: THAT THE TRAFFIC IN ALCOHOLIC LIQUORS EXERTS A PERNICIOUS INFLUENCE, CALLING FOR ITS LEGISLATIVE SUPPRESSION, ... 138

1. *In the Production of Intemperance*, ... 140

2. *In the Development of other Social Evils*, . . . 146

3. *In the Diminution of Trade and Commerce*, . . . 152

4. *In the Growth of Insecurity and Local Burdens*, . . 153

REASONS FOR SUPPRESSION BASED ON

1. *General Benevolence*, ... 155

2. *Social Self-Interest*, ... 156

3. *Enlightened Patriotism*, ... 156

4. *Christian Civilization*, ... 157

OBJECTIONS (FIVE) *stated and examined*, ... 159

CHAPTER VII.—PROPOSITION: THAT THE EXCLUSION OF INTOXICATING DRINKS FROM THE DIET, THE ENTERTAINMENTS, AND THE COMMERCE OF SOCIETY, IS A PRINCIPLE APPROVED BY SCIENCE AND CHRISTIANITY; AND IS THE ONLY EFFICIENT CURE AND PREVENTIVE OF INTEMPERANCE . 169

OBJECTIONS (TWO) *stated and examined*, . . . 176

APPEALS TO VARIOUS CLASSES, ... 181

PAGE

APPENDIX—A. *Benjamin Franklin's Experience*, ... 183
B. *Waste in the Production of Fermented Drinks*, . . 184
C. *Adulterations of Intoxicating Liquors*, . . . 187
D. *Nature of the Traffic in Intoxicating Drinks*, . . 188
E. *Responsibility for the Continuance of Intemperance*, . 189
F. *The French Experiments in Alcohol*, . . . 192
G. *Medical Declarations*, ... 196
H. *Cases of Longevity and Abstinence from Drink*, . 207
I. *Testimonies of Distinguished Men*, ... 216
J. *Effect of Abstinence in Prisons and Workhouses*, . 223
K. *Views of Archbishop Fenelon, etc* , . . . 224
L. *Effects of no Liquor Traffic on Social Conditions*, . 226

PREFACE.

THE design of this work is to set forth, with clearness and succinctness, the principal grounds of the Temperance Reform, with the hope that, by securing the reader's enlightened assent, a stronger public sentiment may be called forth against all the causes—personal, social, and legalized—of Intemperance.

There are many opponents who, if better informed, would be converted into friends. There are many inquirers to whom an Essay like the present will be acceptable, as furnishing, within a brief compass, answers to questions by which they have been perplexed. There are also many personal abstainers, who, having become such from benevolent impulse, will be confirmed in their course by an acquaintance with the argumentative bases of the Temperance system.

The mission of this work is in the highest degree *practical,* since nothing can be more eminently practical than the promotion of perfect and universal sobriety—one of the most important of all conceivable ends in reference to the material and moral interests of mankind. How this end can be reached most surely and speedily, is a subject of transcendent and urgent moment; and the writer makes his confident appeal to those who are prepared to conduct this inquiry in a candid spirit, and to carry into effect, faithfully and resolutely, the line of action best contributive to the highest good of the individual and of society at large.

THE BASES
OF THE
TEMPERANCE REFORM.

CHAPTER I.

PROPOSITION: THAT THE DRINKING SYSTEM IS THE GREATEST SOCIAL EVIL IN OUR LAND.

A FAMILIAR adage tells us that the knowledge of a disease is half its cure; but this proverb must be taken with due qualification, or it will lead to false security and folly. To know something about an evil may still leave unknown what is essential to its successful treatment. Neither will simple knowledge insure a remedy, for the passive contemplation of great evils often deadens a suitable anxiety for their removal. It is when full-orbed knowledge rouses the moral forces of a man or a community that hope may be entertained of efficient exertion. Partial knowledge, leading to inadequate or ill-advised action, will tend to little but waste of energy and grievous disappointment. And it is not too much to say that for want of a larger knowledge—in connection, in some quarters, with an indifference calling for the severest censure—the drinking system has continued, down to this time, the weakness, the burden, the curse, and the shame of the British people.

In everyday language, drunkenness is the greatest evil of our social life; but who does not feel, on reflection, that "drunkenness" is a term at once too narrow and too lax for the subject of such a predicate? To speak even of "intoxication" or "intemperance" as our master-curse would be to employ language superficial and misleading; for drunkenness in all its degrees, intoxication in all its stages, intemperance in all its shifting forms, these, each and all, do but indicate the rank exuberance of the evil we deplore; they only mark the brimming channels fed by higher fountains—social arrangements, institutions, and habits—the whole constituting what has been fitly denominated the DRINKING SYSTEM. The phrase may be new to some, but its convenience and expressiveness are its merit. General terms may be compared to the camera-obscura, which depicts miles of scenery on inches of space; and such a term as the DRINKING SYSTEM will preserve the social student from confusing effects with causes, and will enable him to apprehend by what means and in what manner we are misled by the drink curse, the saddest and darkest evil of our age.

The drinking system comprehends whatever is concerned in the production, circulation, and consumption of intoxicating drinks, with all the consequences, direct and indirect; and of this system, so viewed, we affirm that it stands forth as a colossus among the degenerating and mischievous factors of our social state. To see how this proposition is sustained, it is necessary to enumerate some of the more pregnant facts in relation to the several points.

1. THE PRODUCTION OF INTOXICATING LIQUOR.—The genesis of strong drinks, and therefore of all future evils from their use, is effected by the conversion of sugar into alcohol. "When a moderately warm solution of cane-sugar or grape-sugar is mixed with certain albuminous matters, as blood, white of egg, flour paste, and especially beer-yeast, in *a state of decomposition*, a peculiar process is set up, by which the sugar is resolved into ethyl

alcohol and carbon oxide (carbonic acid). In the case of glucose (grape-sugar), these products result from a single splitting up of the molecule: $C_6 H_{12} O_6$ (glucose) = $2 CO_2$ (carbon oxide) + $2 C_2 H_6 O$ (alcohol). Cane-sugar is first converted into glucose by assumption of water, and the latter is then decomposed as above."* In wine-making, "the vegetable albumen of the juice absorbs oxygen from the air, runs into decomposition, and in that state becomes a ferment to the sugar, which is gradually converted into alcohol and carbonic acid gas."† Fermented liquors are those in which the sweet liquid has undergone this change; distilled liquors consist of the alcohol and water drawn off from the fermented mass. The art of distillation (which dates in Europe from about the twelfth century) has rendered possible the use of beverages alcoholically very strong. In fermented liquors the alcohol varies from 3 to 15 per cent., but most of the wines used in this country are branded, or "fortified," as it is termed, up to 25 per cent. Distilled spirits (fitly called ardent, from *ardens,* "burning") contain from 40 to 60 per cent. of alcohol. Rectified spirits consist of 75 parts alcohol and 25 water. Pure or anhydrous (waterless) alcohol is rarely used. A knowledge of these facts will dissipate two vulgar errors, but errors held by many otherwise highly-educated persons. The one error is that "alcohol is *in* sugar," or "*in* everything," as some comprehensively phrase it. It might as well be affirmed that there is blasphemy in the Lord's Prayer, because the words or letters composing it can be so arranged as to express profane ideas. The other error—that fermentation resembles the process of cooking or baking—is equally absurd. Cook-

* Fownes' "Chemistry," p. 601. It is a theory received by many scientific men that nitrogenous substances are not changed into ferment by the action of oxygen, but by the presence of animalcula invisible to the eye, which abound in the air, and which, according to their own nature, impart a specific character to the decomposing action they assist to carry on.

† Ibid. p. 602.

ing makes no change in the substance of the article cooked, but simply renders it more digestible or palatable, whereas fermentation radically alters the constitution of the thing fermented.* What has to be particularly noted, however, in the production of the intoxicating liquors in common use is that fermentation on so extensive a scale involves the appropriation of corn to an enormous amount, which *thereby ceases to be available for food.* In the United Kingdom the grain annually used in distillation is about ten million bushels, and in the manufacture of malt liquors fifty million bushels—a total of sixty million bushels. But in distillation not a trace remains of the nutritious parts of the corn employed, so that the waste is complete. Hence, in times of scarcity, distillation has been repeatedly prohibited by the British Legislature. Paley on this ground condemns the production of spirits;† and the *Times* newspaper has, for the same reason, described their manufacture as an "infinite waste." Nor can it be denied that in the processes of malting and brewing a similar waste occurs. The notion that beer "is liquid bread" could not be retained were it remembered that the whole object of brewing is the production, not of a thick, soup-like solution of the barley, but of a clear, attenuated, and exciting drink. Franklin acted upon this discovery when a journeyman printer;‡ and an accurate study of the brewing process, and an analysis of the liquors produced, concur in exposing the superstitious esteem in which malt liquors have been held from the darkest ages.§ Beer is the British fetich, and the sooner the ridiculous idolatry is overthrown, the

* In baking with yeast, part of the sugar of the dough is changed into alcohol and carbonic acid gas, but the former is entirely dissipated by the heat of the oven. The latter, whose struggle to escape makes the bread porous and light, is alone of any service, and means have been applied for obtaining and using it for this purpose, apart from the employment of yeast.

† Moral Philosophy, book ii. chapter 11.

‡ See Appendix A. See Appendix B.

sooner will the tremendous waste of food, now annually repeated, be arrested. The 60,000,000 bushels of corn thus lost as nutriment would supply some millions of persons with wholesome food; and it is no defence to assert that the void thus created is filled with imports from abroad. Destruction of food is not rendered less criminal because more remains behind; the food fund of the world is, of necessity, reduced by the quantity thus wasted; and foreign imports raise the price of corn in our home markets beyond the actual standard. To this must be added the loss of the labor of all kinds in bringing about a waste of valuable aliment. If he who makes a grass-blade grow where one did not grow before is a benefactor of his species, what name shall be bestowed upon the system which causes the yearly loss as human food of 2,000 square miles of strengthening grain? The same objection lies against the liquors imported, all of which have been produced by the waste of substances sent by Providence for the sustenance of man. It will be observed that this effect is bound up with the very production of alcoholic liquors, which could have no existence but for the conversion of that which is nutritious into that which is not.

It may also be remarked that in the production of intoxicating liquors, more than of other articles of consumption, forms of adulterations can be practised, and are known to be so, extremely pernicious to the consumer. Complaints are made that such practices are almost universal, and the temptations to this abuse are too powerful to permit the hope that they will be very sensibly reduced while the manufacture of the liquors is continued.*

The plea that "very much capital and labor are embarked in the production of alcoholic liquors" is no justification, unless it can be shown that capital and labor so

* See Appendix C.

applied result in a public benefit. But in reality the plea recoils on the system it is advanced to shield; for, compared with the cost to the purchaser, the production of alcoholic drink gives extremely limited employment to capital and labor. A quantity of spirits or beer costing the buyer a pound sterling can be distilled or brewed for about two shillings in wages, while a pound spent in furniture and clothes will yield to the workman from twelve to fourteen shillings. But it is certain that if the drinks were not produced a large portion of the money spent on them would be spent on articles of personal wear and family comfort, the increased demand for which would stimulate the labor market of the country.* Hence the production of intoxicating liquors may be pronounced not only necessarily destructive of the people's food, and conducive to noxious adulterations of every kind, but also incompatible, in proportion to its extent, with that healthy development of native industry which would relieve the public distress and increase the substantial wealth of the community to an unprecedented degree.

2. THE CIRCULATION OF INTOXICATING LIQUORS.— These liquors are circulated by way of public sale or private distribution. The public traffic is wholesale and retail, and it is chiefly by means of the retail sale that the great bulk of the liquor produced is diffused among the people. This sale is licensed, and all unlicensed sale is illegal and subject to heavy penalty, because the state assumes a special control of a traffic found, by long experience, to be dangerous and hurtful to society.† But as

* This point has been treated with unanswerable ability in Mr. W. Hoyle's work, "Our National Resources, and How they are Wasted." The Caledonian Distillery, which sends out spirits valued at £1,500,000 yearly, employs 150 men; the same money spent on cotton goods would employ 10,000 workmen.

† By the "Intoxicating Liquor (Licensing) Act" (35 and 36 Vict., cap. 94), the penalties for selling by retail any intoxicating liquor without being duly

the licensed vendors derive all their profits from the extent of their sales, it is also found that the legal control claimed is mostly nominal, and that the evils which that control is intended to avert flourish with fatal luxuriance wherever the traffic is allowed. As public circulation of the drinks is the means of private profit, the circulation is cultivated by the vendor at all risks and consequences to society; nor need this conduct excite surprise. It is too much to expect that the dealer in strong drinks, who makes money by provoking and gratifying an appetite for them, should be solicitous to curb the appetite or refuse to satisfy its demands. By a fiction of law he is supposed to be able and willing to solve the problem—how he shall traffic in intoxicating drink, and not assist in creating and confirming the love for such drink; but it is a problem which he could not solve, however willing; and, being neither able nor willing, the ruinous results are visible on every hand. The traffic in alcoholic liquors has confessedly become a system of solicitation and seduction to drinking, issuing in the formation and strengthening of tastes, habits, and customs, destructive to health, morals, and the social good.* The circulation of intoxicating liquors is also greatly favored by many trade usages and convivial customs; by free gifts of liquor to servants and others; by the festal, hospitable, and dietetic exhibition and and recommendation of drink; by

licensed to sell the same, or at any place where a person is not authorized by his license to sell the same, are a sum not exceeding £50, or imprisonment with or without hard labor for a term not exceeding one month; for a second offence, a sum not exceeding £100, or imprisonment with or without hard labor for a term not exceeding three months; for a third offence, a similar fine, or imprisonment with or without hard labor for a term not exceeding six months, and the offender may be disqualified for ever holding a license. If a license-holder, he shall forfeit his license on a second conviction; and, in the case of any conviction, all liquor found on the offender's premises may be forfeited.

* See Appendix D.

injudicious medical advice, and other private means.* It may be laid down as axiomatic that this circulation of alcoholic beverages, however brought about, is attended with innumerable dangers and evils; and that upon all who assist in this circulation, and more especially upon persons of public and social influence, a great weight of responsibility rests, which cannot be shaken off by any avowal of good intentions or regrets for the miseries that ensue. Ignorance cannot be pleaded of the tendency of alcoholic liquors to entice, corrupt, and destroy; and no one can be released from that share of accountability for the aggregate effects, which is incurred by helping to circulate the drinks that operate thus injuriously on the personal, domestic, and national state.† But both the production and circulation of intoxicating liquids are subservient to—

3. THE CONSUMPTION OF THESE ARTICLES AS BEVERAGES.—They are produced to be drunk; they are circulated to be drunk; and that they are very generally and copiously drunk is a matter of statistical demonstration. They are drunk to such an extent that (looking to their alcoholic quality) above two gallons of alcohol would be the yearly portion of each person in the nation, did every person drink and did all drink alike; but, as millions drink little or nothing, the average consumption of alcohol for each drinker cannot be less than from three to four gallons per annum. The question, then, presents itself—whether this aggregate consumption be a good or an evil? and what is the kind and degree of good or evil, or both, resulting from the system of drinking?

If any good arises from strong drink, it must be derived

* Mr. Dunlop, in his "Philosophy of Drinking Usages," enumerates nearly 300 trade and other usages associated with drinking. Many of these (especially the compulsory forms) are extinct; but the reform is yet incomplete.

† See Appendix E.

from properties which it possesses in common with other articles of consumption, or from properties peculiar to itself. But good of the former kind would be no reason for using strong drink, when the same good is so plentifully and innocently provided elsewhere; and, indeed, the universal reason for using alcoholic liquor is its possession of some special virtue not present in other articles of consumption. But this special virtue can reside in nothing but the alcohol, the intoxicating element, which distinguishes fermented and distilled liquors from all other articles of diet, whether solid or fluid.

In the investigation of the effects of alcoholic beverages it will be desirable to consider them, first of all, as related to the individual, the family, and the nation.

(1). *The individual is affected by his own use of these drinks, or by the use of them by others.*

Are the effects of intoxicating liquors on the consumers *salutary or otherwise?* Here it is to be remarked that rarely any advantage is claimed from them except of a physical kind, and that even this advantage is invariably restricted to their use "in the strictest moderation." Any "excess" is confessed to be an evil—an evil also allowed to prevail very extensively both in the form of drunkenness and in less repulsive forms. Since, then, any transgression of the rule of "moderation" is pernicious, it is important to know what this rule is, and how it may be applied. It cannot be altogether a rule of quantity, for the liquors greatly differ in alcoholic strength, and even liquors of the same class have never the same amount of alcoholic ingredient. To say that there is no general rule, and that each must discover or frame a rule for himself, "as in eating," is, in truth, no direction at all; for (1) in eating there is, at least, an approximation to a general rule as to quantity; (2) occasional excess in food does not create a habit of gluttony; and (3) no excess in food is followed by results like those which attend even a slight excess in drink. Besides—a point of primary importance—nature imposes a restraint on eating when hunger is satisfied, so that the individual appetite for food becomes its own protection against excess, whereas the effect of strong drink is to beget an appetite for itself, and, therefore, no such safeguard is provided; and hence the need of some other rule, plainly perceived and easily applied, is the more urgently demanded. Especially is this the case in view of the admitted tendency of alcoholic drink to strengthen desire, while it weakens the power of restraint, and even the power of perception that restraint, at each removal from the line of strict sobriety, is more and more required. Proceeding upon the assumption that some portion of intoxicating liquor is good for him, the consumer should be able to satisfy himself first as to how much alcohol it is safe and good to take at one time, and, next, as to how often in the day this amount may be safely taken; for, though the quantity may be small at one time, the times may be so numerous, in any given period, as to render the daily or weekly quantity excessive. Sir Henry Holland warns wine-drinkers against "a dangerous plenitude," which they are apt mistakenly to think consistent with moderation; and as an error of this kind will, it is acknowledged, turn the drink used into an unmixed evil—(not so in the case of excess in food—another broad distinction)—every user of alcohol is bound, before he can claim to be deriving good from the quantity he takes, to have established for himself some rule of "moderation" by which he strictly and constantly abides, and so avoids the excess which he condemns. It is needless to ask how many—rather how few—"moderate drinkers" adopt and carry out such a precautionary rule. The facts of society render such an enquiry superfluous, and demonstrate, on the consumer's own ground, how little security he can have for the virtue or even innocuousness of the alcoholic liquor he consumes day by day and year by year.

In the following chapter we shall examine whether the use of alcohol, in any measure, is ever a benefit, and whether it be not in all cases a means of physical injury instead of good; at present we are content to ask the candid reader whether any supposed benefit to the individual derived from its very careful use is to be compared for an instant with the amount of evil—bodily, mental, and moral—caused by indulgence which even stops short of habitual and gross excess? To this must be added the loss of personal health, character, prospects, and life itself, induced by notoriously intemperate habits. If there are 600,000 distinct persons in the United Kingdom who deserve the name of "drunkard"—and the estimate is not too high—the number of persons below that black line who take, as the phrase goes, "more than is good for them," must be very much greater—opening up to view a magnitude of individual suffering perfectly appalling. We have been referring to the user of strong drink; but individual wrong, and loss, and even death—nay, worse than death—may rise quite independently of a person's own relation to intoxicating liquor. A man or woman may lose work; may be put in peril of limb and life, or forfeit both; may be compelled to see and hear what is odious and revolting; may be heavily taxed and burdened; may be made to undergo for years exquisite suffering, not from personal drinking, but from the drinking of neighbors, associates, friends, relatives, or even strangers. And what is here said to be possible is a real infliction in countless thousands of cases, and oftentimes, as with the wives and children of the intemperate, without any power of self-protection or escape.

(2.) *The family effects of using strong drink are not visibly beneficial, but are very visibly and painfully injurious.* The families of abstainers may claim to enjoy as much health and happiness as the families of any who use alcoholic drinks; while the families of those who deal in intoxicating liquors share with others in the evils that attend their circulation.* There are between five and six million families in the United Kingdom whose average expenditure on strong drink annually is nearly £20; with many families it is much more; and, as the families of the working class are to be counted by millions, we may judge what is involved in the abstraction as drink-money of so large a proportion of the wages earned. If but forty of the hundred millions annually spent in alcoholic drink flow from the working class, this will form about a tenth of their aggregate wages; and even where drunkenness is not doing its fell work, what can this abstraction of money signify but less food, less furniture, less clothing, fewer innocent pleasures, smaller provident investments, and more limited educational advantages for the little ones? Then, too, tippling is awfully prevalent, and this, sooner or later, settles into sottish dissipation. Should the wife and mother prove a victim, as she often does, the fate of her family is dire. An unprejudiced observer has vividly said, "It would not be too much to say that there are at this moment half a million homes in the United Kingdom where home happiness is never felt, owing to this cause alone—where the wives are broken-hearted, and the children brought up in misery. For the children what hope is there, amid ceaseless scenes of quarrelling, cursing, and blows, when, as Cassio says, 'It hath pleased the devil drunkenness to give place to the devil wrath,' and the two devils together have driven from the house all that peace and sweetness which should be the moral atmosphere of the young"?† Family purity,

* The late Rev. Dr. McLeod has pathetically described the loss of health and virtue by twenty-two families of drunkenness known to himself; and similar instances are of common observation.

† The late Mr. C. Buxton, in the *North British Review*, on "How to Stop Drunkenness" (Feb. 1854).

family happiness, family prosperity, and family piety are sacrificed to the drinking system with a prodigality that must alarm while it humiliates the honest, patient, and ardent philanthropist; and most of all worthy of commiseration are those tender branches of the family stock which have their vital sap poisoned by the parental devotion to alcohol, and which, if they resist the nipping frosts of parental neglect, survive only to yield the bitter fruit upon which society, though disgusted and diseased thereby, is compelled to feed.

(3.) *The national effects of drinking* include those named above upon individual and family welfare, all of which assist to mark and mould the character and destiny of the whole people. On the maintenance of physical stamina and virtue, on the development of the national resources, on the wise application of time and talent, and on the education (in the best sense) of the youthful population must depend the national greatness and glory. What influcnce the use of strong drink has upon these conditions and elements of national prosperity every one can judge. Drink (as commonly used) produces weakness, disease, and death; it impedes the accumulation of capital and the remunerative employment of labor; it induces idleness, dislike of steady work, absence from employment, and consequent disorganization in business affairs; it hinders and makes practically impossible the effective education of vast multitudes of the young; it renders excess, crime, poverty, and vice prolific, and adds a stimulus to every form of evil; and all this it is doing *without intermission,* and on a scale of national amplitude.

Bearing these things in mind, it is reasonable to enquire —*What is there to set over against these disastrous effects?* It may be said—(1.) There are the capital invested in the liquor traffic, the money spent upon it, and the persons supported by it. But the capital and money come out of the public resources, which are otherwise impoverished by this kind of expenditure, while a different expenditure would enable a far larger number of persons to be supported without suffering to the state. (2.) There is the notion that health and strength are promoted by "the proper and moderate" use of drink—a rule of use which has never been defined; and a notion which will be shown, in future pages of this work, to be founded in delusion. (3.) We may be reminded of the "pleasure" excited by the use of alcohol, whether as a means of personal gratification, or of social and convivial entertainment. But in this species of pleasure lies the source of the moral peril against which all philosophy and religion warn; the pleasure and peril increasing with equal pace. The pleasure arises from the abnormal excitement of the nervous system, and, therefore, when it is keenest, insures a corresponding reaction. It is a pleasure, also, which is only obtained by rendering the senses less susceptible of delight from natural objects, so that, even physically speaking, the abstainer, as compared with the non-abstainer, has a larger sum of "pleasure" during life.* It is a pleasure, too, which, in the case of multitudes, is dearly bought at the loss of pure and permanent happiness which, by a different outlay of drink-money, might have been derived from intellectual and moral sources.†

* Dr. James Johnson, physician to William IV., and original editor of the *Medico-Chirurgical Review*, has said—"There can be no question that water is the best and only drink which nature has designed for man. The water-drinker glides tranquilly through life, without much exhilaration or depression, and escapes many diseases to which otherwise he would be subject. . . . The balance of enjoyment turns decidedly in favor of the water-drinker, leaving out his temporal prosperity and future anticipations; and the nearer we keep to his regimen, the happier we shall be."—(Civic Life and Sedentary Habits. 1818.)

† Dr. Samuel Johnson, who owned that he found relief from mental oppression and gloom by abstinence of wine, said, "Wine gives us light, gay, ideal hilarity"; and he observed, on arguing on wine-drinking, "Wine makes a man better pleased with himself, but the danger is that while a man grows better pleased with himself, he may be growing less pleasing to others." The

Taking the drinking system collectively, *i.e.*, the production, circulation, and consumption of alcoholic beverages, we may sum up its effects under the twofold division of DESTRUCTIVE and OBSTRUCTIVE:

1. DESTRUCTIVE in the following respects:

(1.) *Economically*, by wasting the alimentary products of the earth, by causing destruction and theft of property, by weakening the power and desire of productive labor, by entailing loss on commercial and mercantile undertakings, by eating up savings and capital, and by creating three-quarters of the national poverty and criminality, and much of the disease, all of which become a necessary and oppressive burden upon society.

(2.) *Physically*, by engendering and aggravating bodily ailments which impair the corporeal stamina both of the present and future generations, raising the national rate of mortality, inflicting intense suffering, particularly on children, and giving to epidemical disorders a fatality they would not otherwise exert. Mental diseases dependent on congenital malady or physical malformation are also thus fearfully increased.

(3.) *Intellectually*, by indisposing to thought, study, and the acquisition of useful knowledge—by the deterioration and perversion of the mental powers — by rendering adults brutish and animalized, by disabling and disinclining parents from supplying their children with school instruction, and by reducing many intelligent and educated persons to a sensual state, till "the light that is in them becomes darkness," and not unfrequently the reason is lost beyond recall.*

Rev. Sydney Smith has amusingly described, in letters to his daughter, Lady Holland, his improvement in spirits by abstinence from wine.

* Callimachus of old sang that "wine shakes all the reason out of men"; and Butler, in his poem on "Drunkenness," puts this quaintly, where he says that "man with raging drink inflamed"—

"Lays by his reason in his bowls,
As Turks are said to do their souls,"

(4.) *Morally and religiously*, by the depraved tendencies and propensities called into exercise, by the temptations to vice elicited and encouraged, by the exclusion from myriads of families of moral and spiritual influences, by the weakening of the will-faculty and loss of moral control, by the callousness of conscience produced and the reckless wickedness to which alcohol impels its votaries.* To the depraving effect of alcoholic drink every minister of religion, every Sunday-school teacher, every town missionary, every district visitor, every prison chaplain, bears the fullest witness. This corrupting power of alcoholic liquor is, in truth, something astounding and unparalleled, and is incapable of being more fitly symbolized than by the image of the Serpent, full of guile and fascination in its approach, but armed with fangs charged with deadly poison. A Cochin-Chinese proverb gives the same idea with a local coloring—"As a tiger in a wood, so is wine in a man." Lord Bacon's saying is full of weight; "Wine is the most powerful of all things for exciting and inflaming passions of all kinds, being, indeed, a common fuel to them all." There was more than symbolic teaching in the ancient association of Bacchus with every species of debauchery and vice.

2. The OBSTRUCTIVE effects of the drinking system are innumerable, universal, and all-pervasive. It has been powerfully said, "Intemperance is the mightiest of all the forces that clog the progress of good. It is in vain that every engine is set to work that philanthropy can devise,

Until it has so often been
Shut out of its lodgings, and let in,
At length it never can attain
To find the right way back again."

* "Wine is a *mocker* (scorner), strong drink is *raging*"—(Prov. xx. i.)—epithets which, by being applied to the drinks used, indicate their characteristic effects in disposing to a contempt and violent disregard of all things good and sacred. Dr. Adam Clarke caustically remarks, "Strong drink is not only man's way to the devil, but the devil's way to man."

when those whom we seek to benefit are habitually tampering with their faculties of reason and will—soaking their brains with beer, or inflaming them with ardent spirits. The struggle of the school, and the library, and the church, all united against the beer-house and gin-palace, is but one development of the war between heaven and hell."* With human nature, weak always, depraved often, the issue of this contest is too often certain. But the drinking system makes such a condition chronic in our midst. The institutions formed to elevate and bless the people are impeded and half paralyzed by this common foe. What they attempt to do is imperfectly performed, or half undone again, by this one agency of evil. The persons to be acted upon are made by it either incapable of appreciating the efforts for their good, or indisposed to co-operate with their friends. "A sound mind in a sound body," is the condition of great success in all benevolent and educational and religious enterprise; but the drinking system is incessantly operating to increase and confirm unsoundness both of body and mind. Then, again, it reduces the number of workers in all good works, diminishes the pecuniary support they would receive, and tends to discourage the most zealous laborers. While the drinking system remains, the obstructions it causes must continue, and those who would desire to give free play to every noble movement, and to ensure a glorious success for each, should energetically aid in putting the drinking system out of the way. It is emphatically the great "stone of stumbling, and rock of offence," and its removal is imperative, if moral, social, and spiritual reforms are to advance and triumph.

To sum up— the benefits of the drinking system are, at best, questionable and infinitesimal; its evils are ubiquitous and tremendous, and, because directly involved in

* Mr. Charles Buxton, in *North British Review*, Feb., 1854.

the system, or emanating from it, the system itself may be truthfully described as the GREATEST SOCIAL EVIL OF OUR AGE.

OBJECTIONS.

To this conclusion some objections may be taken, and it is our duty to examine them with care.

1. It may be said "*that the charges made are marked by rhetorical exaggeration, and that many of the evils named are due, at least in their darker forms, to other and less proximate causes—bad food, bad dwellings, bad training, and surroundings.*"

(1.) The *charge of exaggeration* cannot proceed from any one who has made this subject his earnest study. The statistics arranged and the inferences drawn, as to the extent and virulence of the evils of the drinking system, do not proceed from total abstainers exclusively or mainly. Every Parliamentary enquiry, every independent and local investigation, teems with evidence refuting the assertion that things are not so bad as they are represented. Nothing is easier than to raise the cry of "exaggeration," but where no proof is given the cry may be disregarded. The difficulty, indeed, consists in getting at *all* the facts of this tragedy; they are literally innumerable. It is simply impossible to find the bottom of the mischief. How few are the families into which drink has not put, within living memory, "a skeleton"—one or more mournful evidences of the power for evil incessantly exercised by the drinking system! Occasionally, no doubt, ill-instructed speakers may use figures without authority or discretion; but no official data have ever yet been collected setting fully forth the baneful operations of the drinking system. What is seen is but "through a glass darkly," and vast realms of evil endured and done lie unexplored and undetermined. The exaggeration, if any, lies at the door of those who have no bias in favor of total abstinence. What say the Committee of the Lower House of Convocation in their Report on Intemperance? "The results of intemperance, as portrayed in the evidence before your Committee, are of the most appalling description. To this cause may be traced many of the crimes and miseries which disturb the peace of states and poison the happiness of families; while it depraves the character, impairs the strength, shatters the health and nerves, and brings thousands to an early death. It is found to fill our prisons, our workhouses, our lunatic asylums, and penitentiaries, and, more than any other cause or complication of causes, to frustrate the efforts and baffle the hopes of all who have at heart the elevation and welfare of the people. . . . As to the evils inflicted on society and the nation at large by intemperance, these, in their nature and amount, as attested in the evidence before your Committee, are not only harrowing and humiliating to contemplate, but so many and widespread as almost to defy computation. It may be truly said of our body politic 'that the whole head is sick and the whole heart faint.' "*

The latest Parliamentary Committee on the subject of intemperance (to enquire into the best plan for the control and management of habitual drunkards) state in their Report (1872)--"There is much evidence to show that in large towns and populous districts the great evil of drunkenness is on the increase. That drunkenness is the prolific parent of crime, disease, and poverty, has received much additional confirmation. That it is in evidence that there is a very large amount of drunkenness among all classes and both sexes, which never becomes public or is dealt with by the authorities, but which is probably even a more fertile source of misery,

* See "Report of Convocation," pp. 7-11, with corroborative evidence in the Appendix to the Report.

poverty, and degradation than that which comes before the police courts."

(2) The attempt to foist these evils upon *bad social conditions* is both absurd and futile. Absurd, because those conditions, however sad and lamentable, could not induce drinking and the effects of drinking, if the drink were not made, circulated, and consumed. If it be allowed that they cause many to fly to strong drink for a temporary though delusive relief, it must also be allowed that this could not happen if the liquor were not manufactured and placed (and often in alluring forms) within sight and reach of the lowest of our poor. But the attempt to make "bad social conditions," and not the drinking system, responsible for the evils deplored is perfectly futile, when it is borne in mind that it is drinking which is perpetually reducing great numbers from good social conditions to bad ones; and that all the bad conditions that could proceed from unavoidable poverty are multiplied and made worse by the drinking system. These very conditions are invariably amended or banished whenever the drink is excluded; and to seek to drain off the effects of the drinking system while intoxicating drink is made, sold, patronized, and generally consumed is to convert the fable of Sisyphus into a fact.

2. It may be said "*that the evils alleged against the drinking system are, in reality, its abuses, and have no necessary connection with that system when properly conducted and controlled.*"

Certainly, the abuse of a system is no legitimate argument against it; but this plea of "abuse" is notoriously a common resort in defence of systems inherently vicious; and, when it is adduced in defence of the drinking system, justice requires that evidence should be given (1) that the system has practically been free, or can be made free, from the "abuses"; and (2) that it has uses which compensate for the "abuses" while they remain. The evils—or "abuses," as the objector styles them—are patent and appalling—*can they be separated from the system?* Let this be proved, if proof is procurable; but where is the proof? Can it be proved, for example, that the *production* of alcoholic drink is separable from the waste of nutritious food, and from a great loss to industrial labor? Can it be proved that the *circulation* of drink is separable from much temptation, much seduction, much ruin? Can it be proved that the *consumption* of strong drink is separable, while human nature remains what it is, from a-long catalogue of appalling miseries, sins, sorrows, crimes, and other social calamities? It is easy to theorize, and to draw pictures of "might be"; but reasonable men have to do with experience and facts; and all these go to show that what are softly called the "abuses" of the drinking system are, in truth, either inseparable elements of it, or irrepressible tendencies and evolutions of it in connection with human temperament, appetite, and habit. All the evils do not always appear in all persons; the effects of the worst systems of error and vice are never absolute and universal; but the specialty and frequency of the evils, even when all the previous conditions have been favorable to their repression, make it evident that the so-called "abuses" (when not inherent in the drinking system) so naturally spring out of it as to render them fairly chargeable upon it. Especially is this the case when it can be shown that the very nature of intoxicating liquor, as alcoholic, is the initial and efficient cause of the subsequent evils or "abuses" by its action on the nervous system. In the light of this distinction, to talk of "abusing the drink" is a manifest inversion of the fact, which is that the drink abuses the drinker, and therefore that the production and use of alcohol as an article of beverage is in itself an abuse, because inconsistent with the welfare of man. The only question, then, that remains is, *Whether the benefits out-*

weigh the evils, and whether it is wise to endure the evils for the sake of the benefits? Those who would maintain the affirmative impose a formidable labor upon themselves—one which no advocate of the drinking system has ever seriously attempted to perform. When or from what quarter is evidence forthcoming that abstainers from strong drink suffer from the absence of it as much as society suffers from its use? What testimony or inductive reasoning can justify the proposition that, if intoxicating liquors were to cease from the world, more injury would result than now results from their circulation and use? Conceding (for argument's sake) that some good attaches to the drinking system—nay, very considerable good—what sober observer can contend that the good is equal to the evil, either in kind or measure, in quality or bulk? Yet an equivalent ought to exist, or society is the loser, and the drinking system is maintained contrary to the dictates of wisdom and of the supreme law of the public good. A heathen philosopher, Pliny the Elder, supplies to Christians a memorable lesson and admonition in the words—"So vast are our efforts, so vast our labors, and so regardless of cost, which we thus lavish upon that [*vinum*—wine] which deprives man of his reason, and drives him to frenzy and the commission of a thousand crimes."

3. It may be said "*that the same evils would reappear under other circumstances, and that, if the drinking system did not produce them, they would revive in some different way.*" This assumption is so entirely improbable in itself that, to render it in any degree accepted, a powerful array of testimonies ought to be adduced. But of evidence in its support there is none. Who can believe, as this objection assumes, that the effects of strong drink are really no effects of it at all, but results of other causes that would operate just the same if the alcoholic drink were absent? Who can believe that it makes no difference to

any family, any district, or any people, whether intoxicating liquor is used in any measure or to any excess? If alcoholic liquors do no harm, abstinence from them can do no good, and the greatest drunkard would be no better were he to abandon his vice. Who can credit *this?* Trace the objection to its root, and it comes to this—that a certain amount of evil will always exist, and that all means for its diminution are of no avail. To state this opinion is to consign it to the contempt of every mind elevated above the grossest fatalism. Were it universally credited, it would extinguish all hope of progress, and fulfil its own dark prophecy by arresting all endeavor after a better future. The heathen Romans were proud of the man who did not despair of the republic; and are we, who profess Christianity, to sanction a dogma which would compel us to despair of humanity? Some writers who ought to be better informed, and more capable of juster reasoning, point to the vices and crimes of pagans and Mohammedans, who do not use intoxicating liquors, as a proof that the evils connected in this country with drinking are possible without it. But certainly, drunkenness is not possible without intoxicating drink; and though many kinds of evil may have various causes, what reason is there to suppose that, with the removal of one cause, some other cause or causes will, sooner or later, spring up to bring the old evils back? If pagans and Mohammedans are vicious and criminal without drink, would they be less so—would they not be more so—with it? Is it not the fact that the heathen and Mussulman populations referred to are as vicious and cruel as we find them, because they do not strictly observe the rule of abstinence from intoxicants, but either use alcoholic drinks or similar substances of a narcotic or inflaming character? Is it not notorious that many of the worst outrages of the Sepoys during the Indian Mutiny—cases cited to show what horrors the sober can commit—were perpetrated by the men who had first stimulated their passions by draughts of arrack or doses of bhang? Abstemious persons and communities may, indeed, be guilty of vices and crimes, but these are committed in spite of the abstinence; whereas intoxicating drink, besides giving rise to the peculiar vice of intoxication, aggravates every form of evil, and leads to crime and violence and recklessness more specifically its own. It would be as rational to argue that, if we got rid of the indigenous causes of ague and small-pox, we should be visited by yellow-fever or the plague, so that the national mortality would still be kept up to a given point, as to represent that the removal of the drinking system would be followed by an influx of the same or equal evils from other sources. Every known fact, in every quarter of the globe, cries out against this dismal conclusion. When Ireland had abandoned whiskey-drinking, did poverty and criminality retain their former level, fed by other streams? In places where the sale of strong drink is suppressed, are the vice and misery due to other causes greater than elsewhere? It has been the habit of some opponents to charge the spread of total abstinence with an increase in the consumption of opium, but it has never been shown that any coincidence, much less a casual connection, has existed between the two events; while it must be evident that the persons who abstain from alcoholic liquors from a conviction of their injurious influence on health and character will be generally led to abstain, for similar reasons, from all narcotic agents. The use of Alcohol may physiologically lead to the use of opium, and any dietetic use of opium by abstainers must be so rare and exceptional as to confirm the rule of an ordinary and natural separation.

4. It may be said "*that there are benefits conferred by the drinking system of which notice should be taken before any just decision can be pronounced.*" To this objection refer-

ence has previously been made, and to what is there advanced, it may be added that the force of this objection must depend upon the following considerations: 1st, that the benefits pertain to the drinking system *as such;* 2d, that they are benefits clearly established to be so; 3d, that as benefits they bear some proportion in value to the evils that attend them. But on none of these points is there evidence that can satisfy the honest enquirer. On the first, it is true that both the production and circulation of alcoholic drinks are a means of employment and wealth to many persons; but it is demonstrable that the money spent on drink, if spent on other articles, would yield employment to many more persons, and would distribute a larger amount of wealth over a larger surface of society—besides extinguishing the evils now springing from the drinking system. On the second, there is good and sufficient reason for believing that the health and happiness of society would be increased, and not lessened, by the abolition of the drinking system.* Tried by every test that can be applied, it is made apparent that health does not suffer by abstinence, while there are considerations (to be afterwards assigned) that go to mark an injury to health in proportion to the quantity of alcohol used. No doubt there is a peculiar gratification experienced in drinking, else it would not be so common; but a gratification is not necessarily a benefit, and in the case of strong drink the gratification is keenest where, by universal admission, no benefit but lasting and largest injury is the result. Gratifications, too, are relative, and whatever may be lost in this respect by abstinence is more than replaced —in the judgment of those who have made trial of both sides—by the more varied and the higher gratifications flowing from another application of pecuniary means, and

*This is asserted in the great Medical Certificate of 1847. (See Appendix G.)

from the consciousness of aiding the removal of the drinking system and all its evils. On the third point, it may be remarked that comparison there is none between the benefits claimed for strong drink and the calamities inflicted by it. What food does it furnish in return for the harvests wasted? What wealth for the poverty caused? What virtue for the vice? What intelligence for the ignorance diffused? What happiness to set over against the boundless miseries inflicted? What life saved to compensate for the numberless hecatombs made up of guilty and innocent alike? What assistance to religion as an equivalent for the irreligiousness, sensuality, and apostasies it is unceasingly producing? There is but one reply to these interrogations—a reply which confirms the judgment laid down as the proposition of this chapter—that of all the evils unhappily distinguishing the present age, none can compare with the drinking system, whether regarded in the extent, diversity, duration, or virulence of its effects. In the race of mischief, it is without a rival: the palm of infamy it bears away without appeal.

CHAPTER II.

PROPOSITION: THAT INTOXICATING LIQUORS ARE USELESS AND INJURIOUS AS ARTICLES OF DIET.

It is a common belief that alconolic liquors are useful, and even necessary to a good state of health and to long life; and though this belief may not absolutely regulate the personal or social consumption of those liquors, it is of the first importance that this opinion, if erroneous, should be disproved. Health and strength are blessings of a very high order; to the multitude they are invaluable as the means of manual work and industrial support; and although, in countless cases, health and life itself are sacrificed at the shrine of some custom or pleasure, it is very evident that ignorance concerning strong drink, joined to a laudable concern for the maintenance of health, has much to do with the daily use of some alcoholic liquor, especially among the more respectable and thoughtful of all classes.

I.—INTOXICATING LIQUORS USELESS.

In maintaining that alcoholic liquors are useless, it is not necessary to show that they contain nothing which is useful to the consumer. It is practically sufficient for the argument that they contain nothing of any sensible utility which does not exist in other articles of diet, free from objectionable combinations, and purchasable at a cheaper rate. The superstition of ages has attached to fermented drinks properties not residing in other dietetic substances; but scientific analysis and widespread experience have exploded this superstition—one which will, in due time, come to be as generally discounted as the belief in witchcraft and the evil-eye. Scientific analysis proves that distilled liquors, when pure, consist only of alcohol and water, the service rendered by the water being to qualify the potency of the intoxicating spirit. In fermented liquors the nutritive elements are of the smallest quantity and lowest type of quality, as can be proved by any housewife who boils a pint of ale till all the watery and alcoholic parts have evaporated, when the residuum, a waxy and distasteful deposit, represents all the solid and "feeding" particles of the ale. The residuum of a glass of wine is almost imperceptible to the naked eye, and though in some high-priced wines, inaccessible to the mass of the people, there are more useful fixed ingredients, these are derived from the grapes employed in the manufacture of the wines, and are not the product of the fermenting process. There is, in short, nothing in any alcoholic liquor except the alcohol which does not exist elsewhere in abundance, and capable of being purchased at less cost, and with an assurance of freedom from those adulterating acts by which the ordinary intoxicating beverages are made still further unsuited for daily use. There is in this country no real guarantee against adulteration of the liquors bought; and the wines of commerce, like the beers and ales of the public-house, are "doctored" to an extent that renders it absurd to attribute to them any marked sanitive effect. Such adulterations would neutralize any benefit derivable from them did they contain specially nutritive properties; but, on the contrary, these properties are deficient in such a degree that nourishment costing shillings or pounds to procure in the shape of such liquors can be obtained for pence and half-pence in the form of grain, flesh, and fruits. What analysis exhibits to the eye, experience has made clear to the reflection of mankind. Instead of alcoholic liquors being necessary, as some have asserted, or useful, as others have more cautiously contended, it is conclusively made evident by the experience of millions of persons that men and women are nourished and strengthened, can enjoy health and live long, without any alcoholic drinks; and so little can this conflux of personal testimony be questioned that it is now customary with political economists to class alcoholic beverages, not with necessaries, but with luxuries, and even to set them apart by themselves as "stimulants" that have no pretence to the consideration which articles of utility may demand when fiscal impositions are in debate. In truth, the defenders of strong drink have ceased to use the language once accredited as firmly as Gospel truth. They know that, nutritively tested, intoxicating liquors have nothing to recommend them, and they therefore confine all their praise to the alcohol—of which the unlearned drinker of beer may never have heard, but the effect of which he has mistaken for the nourishment of which he has really stood in need. It is now conceded that whatever special virtue there may be in alcoholic fluids must proceed from the alcohol, whence they derive their distinctive odor and strength; and that, if alcohol be not useful, the controversy is at an end. When enquiry is made after the special uses of alcohol, we are referred, 1st, to its use as fuel to the body; 2dly, to its use as an arrester of waste; 3dly, to its use as a promoter of digestion; 4thly, to its use as a stimulant in the performance of daily or unusual work.

1. *The use of alcohol as "fuel to the body,"—in other words, the production of heat by the oxidation or combustion of the spirit*—was a theory first promulged by Professor Liebig, who included alcohol under respiratory food, while admitting that it had nothing in common with nutritious or plastic food. But the learned professor, who was induced to make this classification from purely chemical analogy, also furnished a scale showing "ap-

proximately how much of each respiratory material must be taken in the food in order, with the same consumption of oxygen, to keep the body at the same temperature during equal times"; and in this scale, placing fat and oil at 100, as a standard, starch was placed at 240, cane sugar at 249, grape sugar at 263, alcohol at 266; so that, as a warmer of the body, the value of alcohol was but a little over one-third that of fatty and oily substances, and inferior to the sugar by whose destruction it was called forth. "The effect of fat is the slowest in being produced, but it lasts much longer. Of all respiratory matters alcohol acts most rapidly;"* so that, besides the effect being sooner spent, the greater affinity of alcohol for oxygen was calculated to retard the removal, by oxidation, of those waste matters whose retention in the blood is always attended with danger, if not positive injury to the health. It is obvious that this theory could never justify the use of alcohol so long as the other and better kinds of respiratory food were procurable, as they always are, and at less expense; but the theory itself, after yielding unreasoning satisfaction to the opponents of total abstinence, was scientifically assailed by the experiments of Drs. Lallemand and Perrin, and M. Duroy, as recorded in their great prize treatise on the "Action of Alcohol."† In this work, published in 1860, a minute account is given of numerous carefully conducted experiments, resulting in the discovery that alcohol is eliminated unchanged from the body by the various excretory organs, for many hours after it has been consumed.‡ These experiments were repeated by Dr. Edward Smith,

* See "Familiar Letters on Chemistry," by Justus von Liebig—Letters xxvii. and xxix.

† See Appendix F.

‡ That alcohol is present in the blood and brain for many hours after being consumed, and in a quantity sufficient to kindle a flame, had been previously shown by the researches of Mr. Hare, M.R.C.S., Dr. Ogston, Dr. Kirk, and especially by Dr. Percy, in his prize thesis on Alcohol, published in 1839.

F.R.S.; and though, both in France and England, exception has been taken to the conclusions drawn by the original French experimentalists, because a large part of the alcohol swallowed was not accounted for, the scientific mind of this country generally accepts the experiments as conclusive against Liebig's theory, which taught that alcohol is more rapidly burnt off than other respiratory food, and that all the alcohol imbibed is disposed of in this mode. Seeing that for a period of eight and ten hours alcohol is eliminated unchanged by the lungs, the proof of any combustion (oxidation) within the body rests upon the supporters of Liebig's theory. Against that theory there are several powerful facts: first, the catalogue of well-established cases where alcohol has been found in the blood and brains of persons who have died under its influence, and in such quantity as to kindle on the application of a flame. Secondly, the inability to trace any of the derivatives of Alcohol, which ought to be discernible if alcohol is oxidized as the theory requires. Thirdly, the incontrovertible lowering of the animal temperature after the imbibition of alcohol, a result quite irreconcilable with the doctrine that alcohol, by its rapid combustion, helps sensibly, though briefly, to warm the human body. The utility of alcohol as a heat-producer may, therefore, be denied—first, because it is highly probable that it undergoes no decomposition in the animal economy; and, secondly, because, if it does so to any extent, it is much inferior to other substances which (1) are also nutritious (while alcohol is not); (2) do the work of warming more gradually and permanently; (3) are more cheaply procured; (4) and are entirely free from those irritant and other injurious effects of alcohol to which we shall afterwards advert.

2. *The use of alcohol as "an arrester of waste"* is a plea which, if founded on fact, would make strongly in favor of its general disuse. Waste of tissue is necessary to its

renewal, and without such renewal there is death and not life ; so that if alcohol does arrest the process of natural waste, it must so far act in opposition to the law of life. Dr. King Chambers says, "The most active renewal of the body possible is health ; the cessation of renewal is death ; the arrest of renewal is disease." Dr. Markham says decidedly, "Alcohol does not prevent the wear and tear of the tissues." It is further impossible to harmonize with this tissue-saving theory the other theory, that alcohol stimulates to increased physical action, an effect which must carry with it a corresponding waste of tissue. The unfortunate phrase of Dr. Moleschott, that alcohol is "a box of saving," has done much to popularize the notion that in some mysterious way alcohol both saves tissue—which is only possible by lowering vital tone—while it develops physical energy—which is only possible by facilitating the more rapid conversion of tissue. Some experiments showing an increase of weight while alcohol has been used, as compared with periods of abstention, have been cited in evidence of the "savings" theory. But what really happens seems to be this: that in small and less frequent doses, when the irritant action of alcohol predominates, there is no diminution of the waste process, while in cases where larger or more frequent doses have seriously weakened the principal organs the natural waste process is interfered with, thereby aggravating the diseased bodily condition of which it is a leading symptom. A free use of alcohol undoubtedly causes an accumulation of waste matter in the blood, but such an internal conservation of animal rubbish is anything but conservative of corporeal health and vigor.

3. *It is urged that "digestion is improved by moderate supplies of alcohol, which in this way conduces to man's physical welfare."*

Undoubtedly a sound digestion is a great blessing, and

if the view just stated could be sustained, a point would be made on strictly physical grounds for the utility of alcoholic drinks. But it does not seem reasonable to suppose that the all-wise Creator would have left the soundness of digestion—an act so essential to the health of the living being—to depend upon the use of a substance whose production is the result of a twofold process of decay—first of some nitrogenous matter, and then of sugar acted upon by this decaying agent—a substance, too, of whose very existence mankind might conceivably have remained in utter ignorance, and from whose use millions of men have, in all ages, been debarred by want of knowledge or by deliberate choice. Again, if the function of digestion is aided by alcohol, we might expect this aid to be most required in the case of the very young and tender; whereas, by universal consent, its use in any degree by these is treated as unnecessary and unwise. Further, if the theory were well founded, persons using alcohol would be free from indigestion, or suffer less from this ailment than persons abstaining from its use. But the reverse of this is the patent fact. The use of alcohol is prevalent, and so is indigestion among the users, proving that the supposed assistance is very inefficient and equivocal; while the lesser prevalence among abstainers of this same complaint not only refutes the notion of some special virtue in alcohol, but is calculated to excite suspicion whether a mischievous delusion does not inhere in the traditional belief. This suspicion, we think, would be deepened into conviction if enquiry were directed to the action of alcohol within the stomach. Were the process of digestion at all assisted by alcoholic fluids, they must act by increasing the functional activity of the stomach, or by augmenting the secretion of the gastric fluid, or by rendering the food received more digestible than it would otherwise be. But it has been made clear that alcohol acts in none of these ways. Dr. Carpenter has ably exposed the fallacy of supposing that any good can arise from increasing the natural activity of the stomach, the sure consequence being that "the organ thus 'assisted' will gradually *lose* its own independent vigor."* If it is pleaded that the alcohol is useful in giving temporary activity to an enfeebled organ, the folly of habitually using an agent which increases the feebleness complained of must be transparent. Far better will it then be to adopt some proper medicinal treatment from which real and permanent relief may be obtained. To expend pounds yearly in alcoholic medicines, and then, like the woman in the Gospel, to be no better, but rather worse, is not a proceeding attesting either the value of the medicine or the wisdom of the patient. As to an augmented supply of gastric juice, it is sufficient to state that the presence of food in the stomach is always followed by a sufficient supply of gastric juice; and, as will be shown hereafter, the only effect alcohol exerts upon that important fluid is to deteriorate its digestive quality and power. The notion that food is rendered more digestible by its association with an alcoholic liquid is overthrown by the well-known antiseptic property of alcohol, and by a variety of recorded experiments, making it plain that in precise proportion as it acts at all, alcohol renders food more difficult of digestion, so that its removal from the stomach is a condition essential to the completeness of the digestive process. Sometimes alcohol may mask a morbid state of the stomach, and sometimes it may give relief by helping to pass on portions of semi-digested food, but these are "aids" dearly bought, and which the intelligent owner of a disordered stomach would be only too happy to dispense with.† Hippocrates long ago had anticipated

* "Physiology of Temperance and Total Abstinence" (Prize Essay).

† To apply to alcohol the name of a "tonic" is to pervert the just signification of terms. A tonic is that which gives tone or firmness to an organ, and therefore is the opposite of that which, by exciting an organ to extra action, is certain to impair its tone.

and opposed the fallacy here combated, for two of his aphoristic remarks are that "water-drinkers have keen appetites," and that "hunger is abated by a glass of wine."

4. *It is often urged that "the stimulus to the general system administered by a moderate quantity of alcohol is beneficial by the warmth it occasions and the strength it develops."* As to warmth, it has been previously explained that, on the theory of Liebig, alcohol is fuel, but of a very costly and needless kind, while, on the more recent theory of its elimination unchanged, it has no claim at all to the title of a heat-producing substance. Indeed, Liebig's theory did not explain the *sudden* sense of warmth experienced after the imbibition of alcohol; and, to account for this, recourse is had to the more rapid action of the heart, thus inducing an accelerated circulation of the blood. But unless this excessive action of the heart is sustained by repeated doses of alcohol, it must soon subside, and be followed by reaction, and, in any case, habitually to drive the heart beyond its normal beat is to incur grave risk of diseased complications, both from the direct effect and the consequent reaction. All experience in the severest climates proves beyond a question that alcohol neither warms the blood nor enables the body to resist the cold; and scientific experiments have established the reality of a lowering of the vital temperature from the consumption of alcohol, however diluted or diminutive the dose. This important point will be reintroduced further on. That strength is evolved and used up by alcoholic drink is true, but this is wholly different from any development of strength in the system—as different as expending money is from its acquisition. Nothing is gained by eulogizing (as some have done) natural stimuli, and then adroitly applying the eulogium to alcohol because it, too, is a "stimulant." The language of some distinguished men in exposure of this verbal but dangerous fallacy may here be cited, not so much because of the authority of

their names, as because of the cogency of their reasoning. Dr. James Johnson, physician to the late King William IV., thus meets the objection of a conscious benefit from the excitement induced: "Every substance, medicinal or dietetic, which is applied to the stomach induces a physiological action in the nerves, blood-vessels, and fibrous structure of that organ which we call excitement. If the substance applied be of a healthy quality and proper quantity, it produces insensible or salutary excitement; that is, an action of which we are unconscious. But let the substances introduced be of improper quality or an improper quantity (as ardent spirits or acrid medicine), and the action produced thereby will be raised from insensible to sensible excitement; that is, we shall be conscious of something going on in the stomach. Here the agent introduced becomes, in fact, an irritant, and the action introduced is irritation rather than excitement. . . . It is not very material whether the sensible excitement be of a pleasurable or painful kind; the final result will be the same—irritability or morbid sensibility. If the excitement be pleasurable, as from wine, we are spoiling the stomach as we spoil a child by indulgence; we are educating the organ improperly, and laying the foundation for morbid irritability. . . . In proportion as we rise in the scale of potation, from table-beer to ardent spirits, in the same ratio we educate the stomach and bowels for that state of *unnatural sensibility* which in civilized life will sooner or later supervene."* We thus see how entirely fallacious is the vulgar test of sensation, by which many are perniciously misled into attaching value to intoxicating drink, when, if better instructed, they would perceive that the sensations induced are witness to an agency incompatible with a perfect state of health. So, too, with the feeling of increased

* "Essay on Indigestion."

strength after the use of alcoholic liquors. That feeling, it may be observed, increases up to the point of visible intoxication—a clear indication of its radical delusiveness and of the source of the delusion—nervous irritation. But nervous irritation, so far from giving strength, uses up strength by increasing muscular exertion, or by bringing about a more rapid change of nerve-tissue without corresponding nutrition. Baron Liebig says: "Spirits, by their action on the nerves, enable him (the underfed laborer) to make up the deficient power at the expense of his body; to consume to-day that quantity which ought naturally to have been employed a day later. He draws, so to speak, a bill on his health, which must be always renewed because, for want of means, he cannot take it up; he consumes his capital instead of his interest; and the result is the inevitable bankruptcy of his body."* Dr. B. W. Richardson, in his Fourth Report on the Action of Organic Compounds, presented to the British Association for the Advancement of Science (1867), remarks: "All alcoholic bodies are depressants, and although at first, by their calling injuriously into play the natural force, they seem to excite, and are therefore called stimulants, they themselves supply no force at any time, but take up force, by which means they lead to exhaustion and paralysis of power." Alcohol, in short, no more gives strength than does nervous shock, and the delusion by which men have for ages been cheated into fancying that they are gaining strength when they are actually losing it, will be hereafter numbered among the most remarkable of the impositions perpetuated at the expense of credulous human nature. The high authority of Dr. Parkes, of Chatham, puts the relation of alcohol to strength in this conclusive form: "If we look upon the body as an agent of work from which we desire to

* "Letters on Chemistry," Letter xxix.

obtain as much mechanical and mental as is compatible with health, we can consider the effect of alcohol, *per se,* as simply a means of *preventing the development of force.*" Dr. Richardson, in discussing the "Physiological Position of Alcohol" (*Popular Science Review,* April, 1872), decisively affirms: "The evidence is all-perfect that alcohol gives no potential power to brain or muscle. A fire makes a brilliant sight, but it leaves a desolation, and thus with alcohol."

II.—Injurious Action of Alcoholic Drinks.

That intoxicating liquors operate injuriously by reason of the alcohol they contain, even when the quantity consumed is not regarded as excessive, is attested by the following considerations:

1. Pure Alcohol is classed by all Toxicologists among Poisons.—Orfila and Christison place it in the catalogue of narcotic-acrid poisons—poisons, that is, whose primary effect is of an acrid or irritant nature, and whose secondary effect is that of narcotizing or paralyzing the organism with which they come into contact When the application is very strong, the narcotic effect is hastened, and may altogether supersede the irritant symtoms. This has often been done when, by swallowing a large dose of ardent spirits, instant death has been produced. This fact proves—what might have been presumed—that dilution makes no essential difference in the character of the alcoholic action—the less water there is, the less alcohol is needed to produce toxic results; the more water that is mixed with alcohol, the larger or more frequent is the dose required. But in no case is the antagonistic relation between alcohol and the living system altered; any difference observed is one of degree only. It is incredible that its poisonous action can be transformed into an innocent one, unless—to speak para-

doxically—the dose is so small, or the dilution so great, as to prevent any specific action whatever. But if intoxicating drink produced no characteristic effect as a beverage, it would not be consumed; and the retention of the epithet "intoxicating"—*i.e.*, poisoning—to all alcoholic liquors in common use is a tacit confession that, in proportion to their strength and amount, they act toxically (poisonously) on the human system. The vulgar idea of a poison, as of something that *must* kill if not speedily ejected, blinds many to the true poisonous quality of of alcoholic drinks when freely used without causing immediate death. It is forgotten that in all these drinks the poison of alcohol is rendered less potent by its combination with water, but that the combination being mechanical, and not chemical, the alcoholic virus is not destroyed, and that, so far as it can act, the action will exhibit the distinctive features of the poisonous agent. This principle is in accordance with our knowledge of all poisonous substances, none of which lose or change their specific properties by dilution or admixture. That alcohol should be an exception to this rule would require the plainest evidence, and from no quarter has such evidence been adduced.*

2. Evidence in support of the view that the action of alcohol is always injurious HAS BEEN FURNISHED BY PHYSIOLOGISTS OF THE HIGHEST REPUTE, writing, not as

* Dr. Wilson, in his "Pathology of Drunkenness," writes (p. 192): "All these diversified proofs have pointed unchallengeably to the conclusion that alcohol is the most widely and intensely destructive of poisons. In large and concentrated doses there are few which are more promptly and inevitably fatal. In more moderate and diluted potions, continuously repeated, it is, with its own peculiar modifications of action, obviously one of those so-called accumulative poisons of which science possesses other well-known examples in corrosive sublimate, foxglove, and arsenic." Dr. Carpenter and Dr. E. Smith have expressed the same opinion in terms equally explicit. The latter says: "For all medicinal and dietetic purposes, the dose only affects the degree, not the direction, of the influence." ("Philosophical Transactions," 1859.)

advocates of a traditional bias, but as diligent searchers after truth.

(1.) Evidence exists that *alcohol is not in any sense a food, and that it is not assimilated with the vital structure, but eliminated from it unchanged; and the presence of such a foreign substance cannot fail to be pernicious.* The doctrine here stated rests for support upon the numerous experiments of the French *savants* before adverted to (page 38), and repeated by Dr. Edward Smith, F.R.S., with very interesting additions. These experiments prove that immediately and for hours after swallowing even weak alcoholic drinks the spirit passes from the excretory organs unchanged. The objection raised by M. Baudot in France, and by Drs. Anstie, Dupré, and Thudicum in England—that the major part of the alcohol imbibed cannot be re-collected—is inconclusive. To gather up the whole or chief part of a volatile fluid, after circulating through the system, and while in course of elimination for many hours by the skin, lungs, and other organs, is obviously a task next to impossible. That some sensible and not inconsiderable portion has been collected is presumptive evidence that the substance, as such, is not changed within the body; for there is not an instance on record of a substance being partly ejected unchanged, and partly transformed in the living organism. If any part of alcohol is changed, its derivatives (such as aldehyde) would be discoverable, but they have never been detected. Were alcohol oxidized so as to supply heat, according to Liebig's theory, the quantity of carbonic acid emitted would be increased, but a diminution instead of an increase is invariably perceived.* As it therefore

* Besides the directly irritant effect of alcohol on the nervous system, the stimulating effect ascribed to it may probably arise, in a large degree, from the effort put forth by the organism to eject it as rapidly as possible. Voluntarily, however, to bring about and sustain a state of intestine war is not an indication of wisdom on the part of bodies corporate or corporeal.

serves no use in the animal economy, its introduction there (except under very rare and exceptional circumstances) must be regarded as a blunder and abuse. Dr. Parkes, in a letter to Dr. Anstie (*Practitioner*, Feb., 1872), while acknowledging that the more recent experiments make the destruction of some of the alcohol taken very probable, denies that this proposition is proved, and pertinently adds: "Even if the complete destruction within certain limits were quite clear, this fact alone would not guide us to the dietetic value of alcohol. We have first to trace the effect of that destruction, and learn whether it is for good or for evil. You seem to think that the destruction must give rise to useful force, but I cannot see that this is necessarily so."

(2.) *The fall of the temperature at once or soon after the imbibition of alcohol, however moderately, is an evidence of injury sustained.* Dr. Prout was one of the first of modern enquirers who noted this important fact, which has been corroborated by most subsequent experiments. For a time the irritant effect renders the subject unconscious of this result, but it is soon made apparent by a chilly feeling and an increased susceptibility to external cold. Every Arctic voyager bears witness to the injuriousness of spirits on this very account, when used in high latitudes to any extent. Vierordt says ("Physiology of Respiration"): "The expiration of carbonic acid after the use of fermented liquors is considerably diminished, and does not return to its normal quantity for the space of two hours." Professor Binz, of Bonn, carried out a course of experiments upon this point, and discovered, to his surprise, as he confesses, that in both small and large doses alcohol lowered the temperature. "Experiments on man, made with small quantities of alcohol, led to very similar results. Half a glass of light hock, or a small glass of cognac, caused a fall of from 0·4° to 0·6° (centigrade) in a very short time." The explanation offered, viz., that alcohol obstructs oxygen in its combustive operation, is reason sufficient why nature treats alcohol in the body as an intruder which cannot be too quickly expelled. An agent which hinders the natural generation of heat—one of the great manifestations and conditions of life—is prejudicial to the physical constitution. "The well-proven fact," says Dr. W. B. Richardson, "that alcohol reduces the animal temperature is full of the most important suggestions."*

(3.) *The influence of alcohol upon the blood is seen to be injurious wherever it is traced.* Experiments upon the blood of dogs were made with rectified spirits as far back as 1679, by M. Courten, of Montpelier: and in the experiments of Sir Benj. Brodie and Dr. Percy, the action of *diluted* alcohol upon the blood was invariably seen to produce unhealthy darkness of color and evident impurity of the vital fluid. The more recent researches of Dr. Böcker and Dr. Virchow unite to show that both the *liquor sanguinis* (blood-fluid) and the red corpuscles are impaired by alcohol even when the users of it appeared in good health; and Professor Schultz has observed "that alcohol stimulates the blood discs to an increased and unnatural contraction," inducing their premature decay, and rendering them less capable of absorbing oxygen and carrying away the carbon with which it is loaded. The microscope shows that dark oily specks are formed in the blood from this cause, and in 1,000 parts of a drunkard's blood Lecanu found 117 parts of fat, instead of two or three parts, the normal proportion. These observations

* In the experiments made by Dr. Parkes and Dr. C. Wollowicz upon a healthy young man (Proceedings of Royal Society, No. 123, 1870), the effect of red Bordeaux wine, in quantities of a half-pint per diem for five days, and of a pint per diem for the next five days, was but slightly marked upon the mean temperature, which stood in the water period of ten day at 97·726, and in the wine period at 97·560. In this case the use of the wine at dinner, its comparative alcoholic weakness, and the state of the subject's health, may have co-operated to render the effect less than was apparent in other experiments.

show the tendency of alcohol, whenever present in the blood, to deteriorate the element on whose purity all health depends. "By experimenting on the blood (drawn from the body) with sherry wine, or diluted alcohol, the blood disc becomes altered in shape, and throws out matter from its interior; minute molecular particles also fringe the circumference. Some of these molecules separate from the blood discs, and float about in the fluid; others elongate into tails which move about with a tremulous motion in a very remarkable manner."* Dr. Smiles, in his Life of George Stephenson, relates an anecdote to the effect that the great engineer, who was exceedingly fond of microscopical observations, submitted to this test blood taken from several of his friends, and pronounced the blood of one, who was a teetotaler, to be "the most lively of the whole." This might be a simple coincidence, but it was in accordance with the principle that, other things being equal, blood unaffected by alcohol will be the purest and "most lively" of all.

(4) *The powers and process of digestion are weakened and impeded* by the action of alcoholic liquor. Dr. Gordon, of the London Hospital, in his evidence before the Parliamentary Committee of 1834, said, "Dyspepsia has become the common disease of the poor class, produced entirely by the practice of sipping constantly and habitually small quantities of spirits." That the use of alcoholic fluids hinders the process of digestion is also demonstrated by direct experiments. Dr. Beddoes relates that, after giving two young dogs, of the same litter, equal quantities of food, three drachms of the spirit of wine of commerce, mixed with a drachm of water, were poured down the throat of one of the animals. On opening both, five hours afterwards, the stomach of the dog to which the alcohol had been given, was found nearly twice as full as

* "The Physiological Action of Alcohol," by Dr. Monroe.

its fellow's. "The bits of flesh were as angular as immediately after they were cut off by the knife at the time of feeding; they were also as firm in their substance. In the other dog, these angles were rounded off, and the pieces throughout much softer."* A similar experiment was made by Dr. Figg, who says, "To each of two mastiffs, six months old, five ounces of cold roast mutton, cut into squares, were given, the meat being passed into the œsophagus without contact with the teeth. An elastic catheter was then passed into the stomach of one of them, and one ounce and a quarter of proof spirit injected. After some hours had elapsed, both animals were killed. In the case where the meat had been administered by itself, it had disappeared. In the other the pieces were as angular as when swallowed."† The remarkable observations recorded by Dr. Beaumont, of America, upon the appearance of the stomach of Alexis St. Martin, who had an opening in his side, and put himself under the care of Dr. Beaumont, throw much light upon the state of that organ, when subjected to various kinds of diet. When spirits had been freely used, inflammatory and ulcerous patches appeared on the surface of the stomach, and the gastric juice was diminished in quantity, and was manifestly unhealthy. Yet though St. Martin did not complain of feeling ill, Dr. Beaumont remarks: "The free use of ardent spirits, wines, beer, or any intoxicating liquor, when continued for some days, has invariably produced these morbid changes."‡ That the digesting fluid, the gastric juice, is acted upon prejudicially by alcohol by precipitating one of its principal constituents, pepsine, is incontrovertibly proved. Dr. Dundas Thomson, in a lecture on "Digestion" (1841) pointed out this fact, and Drs. Todd and Bowman, in their

* Hygeia, vol. ii., Essay 8.

† Report of International Temperance and Prohibition Convention, p. 255.

‡ Beaumont's "Experiments and Observations," etc., p. 237.

great work on "Physiology," after remarking the same phenomenon, instructively add: "Were it not that wine and spirits are rapidly absorbed, the introduction of these into the stomach, in any quantity, would be a complete bar to the digestion of food, as the pepsine would be precipitated from the solution as quickly as it was formed by the stomach." Raw beef immersed in spirits for twelve hours loses a fourth of its weight, owing to the abstraction of the water, and is covered with a brown deposit, due "to the caustic influence of the alcohol on the albuminous element of the beef." Dr. Monroe, F.L.S., having placed equal quantities of finely-minced beef in three phials—one containing gastric juice and water, the second gastric juice and alcohol, the third gastric juice and pale-ale—the temperature being the same as that of the stomach, 100 degrees, the results at the tenth hour were as follows: the contents of the first phial were dissolved like soup, *i.e.*, thoroughly digested; the contents of the second and third were found to be solid, with the pepsine precipitated. It thus appears that alcohol can only act on the digestive process by retarding it, and that it is only by the absorption of the alcohol imbibed that the process of digestion can be completed. So long as alcohol is present in the stomach, the first grand condition of alimentation is arrested.

(5.) *By the deteriorating effect of alcohol on the blood, and its irritant effect on the nervous system at large,* many diseased states of important organs of the body are set up or fostered, and the whole body becomes more easily susceptible of zymotic diseases. (*a*) *Fatty degeneration*—a very common complaint, as Dr. King Chambers testifies—is one of slow but certain formation from the impure alcoholized state of the blood, even when no intoxication is visible; and to the same cause all experienced physicians ascribe diseases of the lungs, liver, and brain, the healthy discharge of whose functions is impossible unless the purity of the blood is maintained. (*b*) It is also clear that blood impurities *must increase the tendency to "catch" diseases of zymotic origin*, such as fever, small-pox, cholera, etc.; and it is also plain how readily the violence of these and of all other diseases, when present, is augmented, both by the bad condition of the blood and by the lessened capacity of the body and its various organs to "shake off" the particular *virus* in operation. The weakened walls, so to say, yield to a pressure which, had they been better cemented, they would have successfully resisted. Dr. Lionel Beale, F.R.S., physician to King's College Hospital, observes: "Alcohol does not act as food; it does not nourish tissues; it may diminish waste by altering the consistence and chemical properties of fluids and solids. It cuts short the life of rapidly-growing cells, or causes them to live more slowly. The remedies which act favorably really seem to act, not by increasing vital power, but by decreasing the rate at which vital changes are proceeding. This view accounts for the shrivelling of the hepatic cells, the shrinking of the secretive structure, and the increased hardness and condensation of the entire liver which result from the continual bathing of the gland-structure in blood loaded with alcohol. It accords with the gradual shrinking and condensation of tissues which have long been accustomed to excess. The tendency to increased formation of adipose tissue may be explained upon the same view, and the stunting which follows its exhibition to young animals is readily accounted for,"

(6.) *The nervine stimulation* following the use of alcoholic drinks, so far from supplying or inducing increased strength, is an inevitable cause of weakness. Sudden nervous shock, more or less severe, must lead to loss of power; and all scientific enquiry tends to assign alcohol a place, not among the true stimuli—such as air, light, food, and water, which act calmly and soothingly—but with anæsthetic agents like chloroform and ether, whose short excitant effect is succeeded by a depressing or deadening influence upon the nervous system. Dr. King Chambers, in his "Renewal of Life," challenges the right of alcohol to the title of a true stimulant: "What *is* a stimulant? It is usually held to be something which spurs on an animal to a more vigorous performance of its duties. It seems doubtful if, on the healthy nervous system, this is ever the effect of alcohol, even in the most moderate doses, for the shortest period of time. A diminution of force is quite consistent with augmented quickness of motion, or may it not be said that, in involuntary muscles, it implies it? The action of chloroform is to quicken the pulse, yet the observations of Dr. Bedford Brown on the circulation in the human cerebrum during anæsthesia clearly show that the propelling power of the heart is diminished during that state." Dr. B. W. Richardson, in his Sixth Report to the British Scientific Association, reproduced in a lecture entitled "Physiological Research on Alcohols,"* discountenances and repels the idea that alcoholic excitement is strength: "As soon as the alcohol makes its way into the organism and diffuses through the fluids, so soon there is depression, so soon respiration falls, carbonic acid gas from respiration decreases, and muscular strength, consciousness, and sensibility decline. . . . Speaking honestly, I cannot admit the alcohols through any gate that might distinguish them as apart from other chemical bodies. I can no more accept them as foods than I can chloroform, or ether, or methylal. That they produce a temporary excitement is true; but, as their general action is quickly to reduce animal heat, I cannot see how they can supply animal force. . . . To resort for force to alcohol is, to my mind, equivalent to the act of searching for the sun in subterranean gloom, until all is night." That the

* Delivered Dec. 7, 1859; reported in *Medical Times and Gazette*, Dec. 18.

brain, the centre of nervous sensibility, should be disturbed by alcohol, when used in any quantity, is a sign of the facility with which injury is done to the seat of thought. The action of the heart is injuriously increased by the alcohol used, and in proportion to the amount. The very interesting experiments made by Dr. Parkes and Dr. Wollowicz ("Proceedings of the Royal Society," No. 120, 1870) showed in the case of a healthy young soldier that "the heart during the alcoholic period did daily work in excess equal to lifting 15 tons and 8-10ths per foot; and in the last two days did extra work to the amount of 24 tons lifted as far!" (Instead of daily work, equal to lifting 122 tons one foot, the daily work done was equal to lifting nearly 138 tons, and even 146 tons!) In commenting on this fact, Dr. Richardson observes (*Popular Science Review*, April, 1872): "Little wonder is it that, after the labor imposed upon it by six ounces of alcohol, the heart should flag. It is hard physical work to fight against alcohol—harder than rowing, walking, wrestling, carrying heavy weights, coal-heaving, or the treadwheel itself." Yet people—and educated people—mistake this exaction of work and loss of vital strength for an increase of vigor!

3. It is impossible to enumerate a tenth of the MEDICAL JUDGMENTS ADVERSE TO THE USE OF ALCOHOLIC BEVERAGES, but a selection of some of the more striking is furnished elsewhere;* and it ought to be remembered, as adding peculiar force to these professional opinions, that, in a great majority of cases, they are those of men who might say, with Dr. Richardson, that their "prejudices in regard to alcohol are, by moderate habit, but confessed inconsistency, in favor of it."

4. *Experience, both general and comparative, declares that the use of intoxicating liquors is not useful, but injurious.*

(1.) *Nations and tribes* who have lived without any alco-

* See Appendix G.

holic drinks have not only equalled in health and vigor others that have used them, but have been remarkable for their freedom from numerous species of disease. The early Persians and Romans, the Saracens for centuries, the aborigines of North America and New Zealand when first discovered, a large portion of the present inhabitants of India, including the Himalayan tribes, and the rural population of the Turkish Empire, supply examples of a high average state of health, and of the strongest powers of physical endurance, without any recourse to the liquors supposed by many in this country to be the sources of both.

(2.) *Scriptural history* furnishes us with corroborative evidence, in the sojourn of the Israelites in the desert for forty years without strong drink ; in the life of Samson, "strong above compare," to whom all intoxicating drink was forbidden (not, surely, because it would have made him naturally stronger !) ; in the experience of the Nazarites, who were famed for their personal beauty and vigor ;* in the case of the Rechabites, who had been gainers by centuries of abstinence ; and in the lives of men like Samuel, Elijah, Daniel, and John the Baptist, whose habits of abstinence proved serviceable, and not a hindrance, to the execution of their laborious missions.

(3.) There is the evidence procurable as to *the health* of persons living surrounded by users of the drinks from which they themselves abstained, and attaining, in many cases, *years "long-drawn out" and a hale old age.*†

(4.) Appeal can be made to the testimonies of *persons exposed to severe labors and protracted strain on body and mind*—philosophers, poets, generals, divines, philanthropists, travellers, and the like.‡

* "Her Nazarites were purer than snow, they were whiter than milk, they were more ruddy in body than rubies, their polishing was of sapphire" (Lam. iv. 7).

† See Appendix H. ‡ See Appendix I.

(5.) Legitimate and striking deductions can be drawn from the *statistics of health and longevity among abstainers and others.* There are statistics in regard to the army of very considerable value. A division of the British Army in Egypt, sent from India in 1801, was left without ardent spirits; but, though the fatigue and heat were excessive, Sir James McGrigor, M.D., states: "At no time was the Indian Army in so healthy a state." Sale's Brigade in Affghanistan, when stationed in Jellalabad, was "without spirits" and "without either sickness or crime." The Rev. G. B. Gleig (Chaplain-General), in his history of that war, states: "Their beverage was only water, yet they drank it to the health of many far away, and were happy with a sober joy." When a temperance society was established in the Cameronian Regiment, the annual deaths in the regimental hospital, which had been for 14 years 72 per thousand, sank to 26, and the next year to 22. Liver-complaints sank to half their former amount. The hospitals received 4 per cent. of abstainers, and of others 9½ per cent. In six months of 1838, the sick among the abstainers averaged 3·83, and among the others 9·39. Six European regiments stationed in the Madras Presidency, in 1848–9, were tested with the following results:

	Sick.	Died.
Teetotalers.........	130·88	1·11*
Moderate drinkers..	141·59	2·31
Intemperate........	214·86	4·45

In regard to "fever only," it was found that the teetotalers had suffered at the rate of 31·30 per cent.; the moderate men, 17·78; the intemperate, 20·16; and this solitary apparent advantage was paraded by some writers who

* "Or, to put it," says Dr. Carpenter, "in another form, only one in ninety of the teetotalers dies annually even in India (and this rate would be extraordinarily low for a similar body of men in this country), whilst one in forty-two and a half dies among the temperate, and one in twenty-two and a half among the intemperate."

wished to discredit the total abstinence cause ; but it was discovered, on enquiry, that the 84th Regiment, which furnished to this comparison a large proportion of the abstainers, was, during this year, stationed at Secunderabad—a most unhealthy station—but where, in 1848–9, the 84th lost 22 per one thousand, in place of the usual average of 70 per one thousand. Improved ventilation conduced, with enhanced sobriety, to moderate the fierceness of the fever-laden exhalations.* The experience of the American armies during the civil war attested the physical advantages of total abstinence when exercised on either side by officers or men. Captain Huyshe, in his narrative of the Red River Expedition, which consisted of about 1,200 soldiers and several hundred assistants, bears the most emphatic testimony to the value of the abstinence regimen carried out. (See pages 92–3, 113, etc., of his stirring story.) One extract will suffice : "Not a man of the Red River force touched a drop of alcoholic or fermented liquor the whole way from Shehandowan to Fort Garry, except he was ill and received it from the store of medical comforts ; and there was positively no sickness, and a total absence of crime, combined with the utmost cheerfulness and good-humor, while the work performed stands wholly unrivalled for its unusual nature as well as its severity." Captain Huyshe strongly advocates the abolition of the spirit-ration to the British Army in the field. In the American Navy, the exclusion of grog was followed by none but the best results, and the thousands of ships that navigate the seas with crews that are without any ration of grog or other liquor, add corroborative evidence to the worth of total separation from strong drink. Temperance benefit societies—such as the Rechabites, Sons of Temperance, etc.—show a rate of sick-

* During Sir John Moore's retreat to Corunna, the army was found to improve in health as soon as the usual allowance of spirits was unattainable.—*Dr. Carpenter.*

ness and mortality below that of similar institutions; but the most comprehensive and conclusive evidence upon this point is afforded by the books of the Temperance and General Provident Institution, which, after existing for ten years (1840–1850) as a strictly Abstinence Insurance Society, and exhibiting a very low rate of mortality, began, in 1850, to receive as members very sober persons not abstainers; but the two classes were kept in distinct sections, in order that the profits might be respectively apportioned. Since then, four bonuses have been declared—viz., in 1855, 1860, 1865, and 1870. Comparing the reversionary bonuses in the Whole Life Department of the Temperance Section with those in the General Section, the results were as follows:

Date.	Temperance Section. Per cent.	General Section. Per cent.
1855.........	35 to 75	23 to 50
1860.........	35 to 86	24 to 59
1865.........	23 to 56	17 to 52
1870.........	34 to 84	20 to 49

In the five years ending December 31, 1870, the expected claims in the Temperance Section were 549, for £100,446; the actual claims were 411, for £72,676. In the General Section, the expected claims were 1,008, for £196,352; the actual claims were 944, for £230,297. Comment is needless, except by way of remark, that the Temperance Section is weighted with the policies of many reclaimed drunkards whose constitutions have suffered irreparable injury from their previous habits. Despite, however, of this drawback, the superiority of the Temperance Section has been five times consecutively maintained—a result with which chance can have had nothing to do. A similar superiority is shown in the reports of other life assurance companies where the total abstainers are insured in a separate section. The general health of abstainers, as compared with that of non-abstainers, and as compared with their own state of health before abstinence, is a further vindication of their distinctive regimen; and it is constantly remarked that in all cases of severe contusions, fractures, woundings, fevers, and epidemical disorders, the restorative powers of abstainers exceed those of other persons—the reason of which lies in a sounder condition of the vital organs, and a greater measure of that natural reserve-force which moderate drinking insidiously, but surely, drains off. Where total abstainers addict themselves to athletic and other exercises, they acquit themselves with singular credit, other conditions being equal; as witness Mr. Angus Cameron, who has made the highest score yet reached at Wimbledon, and has been twice winner of the National Rifle Association's Gold Medal and Queen's Prize. The "training" for muscular feats is, in most cases, conducted either on the abstinence plan or with a near approach to it; and so it was in ancient times with the competitors in the Grecian games.* Even the figment that sudden abstinence is dangerous is refuted by the daily experience of more than twenty thousand prisoners (amounting in the course of a year to several times that number of persons) who are instantly deprived of alcoholic drink when committed to jail. It might be expected, apart wholly from the question of abstinence as a general rule, that these individuals (most of whom are free drinkers when out of prison, and not a few of whom find their way to jail through indulgence in drink) would suffer, temporarily at least, by their sudden exclusion from alcoholic liquors; the opposite, however, is the fact, and, in the Appendix to the Convocation Report on Intemperance, eighteen pages

* In a work on "Athletic Training and Health," J. Harrison, M.R.C.S., states (p. 93) that the conviction that "alcoholic drinks are not admissible into a training dietary" "has been forced upon the writer by much observation and reflection."

of selections are given from the written evidence of governors of jails and masters of workhouses, declaring that the consequences flowing from this peremptory interdiction are of a salutary kind.* If, at all and to any, intoxicating liquors are a necessity, or an aid to health and strength, it must be to those who are deprived of that liberty and social intercourse by which the spirits are cheered and the animal vigor sustained; yet, if prisoners can live and thrive on a dietary into which alcohol does not enter, it may be inferred that other persons, with so many advantages of life, do not stand in need of it, but would be better without it, if they had the wisdom to adopt, and the courage to continue, the abstinence plan.

The conclusion, then, to which we are drawn by a candid consideration of medical principles, and a wide induction of facts, past and present, in great abundance, is adverse to any use of alcoholic beverages, and in favor of the judgment which treats them as essentially injurious to the physical health and vigor of our species.

Objections.

1. It may be said that "*intoxicating agents of some kind have been used in all ages and by all nations, and that this universal usage constitutes a defence of the practice and a reason for believing that it always will be continued.*"

But this argument from universality is both historically and morally unsound. It would be impossible to prove that in any age of the world even a majority of the persons then living had been users of some kind of intoxicating substance. The highest moral utterances of the most ancient historical religions—Judaism (in its Nazarite institution), Brahminism, Buddhism, and Mohammedanism—have been distinctly on the side of separation from

* See Appendix J.

strong drinks, and have attracted to that rule numberless millions of our race. But if it could be shown—as it cannot—that indulgence in alcoholic or other intoxicants has been the common habit of mankind, the inference that the prevalence of such a habit involves its own vindication would be utterly false. It would not even tend to show that man has a natural instinct for such drinks and drugs, since there is a flood of present evidence that they are never craved until they have been first supplied, and that there is no sign of suffering from their absence where they are never given. Surely it needs no proving that acknowledged evils may be very common in every age, and almost or quite universal in some ages, yet without ceasing to be evils—evils not to be extenuated or cherished, but as speedily removed as can be. Slavery, despotism, superstition, violence, fraud, and every form of sensuality, are not novelties on the globe, nor has the empire of any vice been limited to a section of the human family. To assert, also, that any indefensible usage "must" continue because it is ancient and general is to resign all hope of human advancement. Is drunkenness necessary and good, and is *it* always to endure because it can plead hoary antiquity and a widespread rule? Why, then, should a plea of virtue or perpetuity be set up for the liquors out of whose use, and from whose intoxicating quality, all this drunkenness has sprung? If the many go astray and suffer thereby, no one can find in these facts a vindication for his own sanction of the error, or of his own refusal to seek the introduction of safer and better habits.

2. It may be said that, "*however suited total abstinence would be to an ideal state of society, we live in so artificial a state that deviations from a rigidly wholesome dietary are not only excusable, but unavoidable, and even useful.*" This argument or apology—one often heard—is a fair specimen of the confusion of thought under which

men love to hide the weakness of their case. Social life in itself is not artificial in any unnatural sense, for "it is not good for man to be alone," and from the social sentiment are derived the family, the tribe, the state; nor is there any reason, intrinsically, why artificial arrangements, arising out of the complexities of civilization, should be injurious to the human constitution. Labor, either of hand or brain, is not unhealthy, but a means of health, unless excessive; and though undue labor, impure air, mental anxiety and suffering, and other things (many of them not limited to an artificial state of society), do conduce to bodily weakness and decay, how can it be shown that resorting to alcoholic drinks is wise and useful? To say that "we live artificially, and therefore must use artificial diet"—*i.e.*, brandy, wine, or beer—is a mere play upon words; for if the artificial life be in itself an evil, and if the use of alcohol be also an evil, how can the conjunction of the evils result in benefit to the subject of them? The excuse that so much work "must" be done, and that alcohol must be used as a forcing-pump, whatever damage may ensue, is not a plea which can be sustained on the ground of morality; and it has but a limited application in a physiological sense. If alcohol draws upon the reserve strength of the system, and uses it up, this plan, like that of living above one's income must come to an end by-and-by, and premature weakness will set in. The physiological offence will be avenged in due course, to say nothing of the collateral losses and injuries sustained, or of the affront offered to him who has made us, and who has given us our physical powers to use and not abuse. No doubt the struggle of life is keen and wearing, and critical periods may occur when alcohol, opium, even arsenic and other poisons, would supply the temporary aid so earnestly desired; "but the prudent man foreseeth the evil," and he knows that to keep the blood, muscles, and nerves free from noxious agents is the best preparation for times of pressure; and he also knows that during periods of pressure it is the wisest, on the whole, to trust to Nature's own resources rather than to those illusory aids which, like the secrets of the black art in tales of magic, cannot be employed without ultimate and heavy retribution. The gifts which alcohol proffers even to the harassed and overworked are always to be feared; and many are there who, like the Trojans of old, have had reason to rue that the tempting offering was not resolutely rejected. Scientifically regarded, the very fact of so much strain being nowadays put upon all classes is an argument, not for the using, but disusing alcoholic liquors, seeing that they possess no really sustaining properties, and that their seductive tendency is calculated to encourage their use in increasing quantities, and at diminished intervals, when once they are taken into the confidence of the toiler. "Fire," says the proverb, "is a very good servant, though a very bad master"; but of the fire-waters it can be truly affirmed that, while they only render apparent service, they often end by securing a mastership fatal to the welfare of those whom they enslave.

3. It may be said "*that nearly all, if not all, the injury produced by intoxicating drinks would be prevented by great moderation in their use.*" There are doubtless degrees of injury inflicted by strong drinks; but if, as we have shown, the benefit they yield is insensible, and their habitual use in any quantity pernicious, it is trifling with both language and facts to enter an appeal on behalf of "extreme moderation." No "moderation" can be so extreme, where the drinks are used at all, as to render them neutral in a physiological sense; if they act, they act for good or ill; and if for ill, they ought not to be consumed. "Do thyself *no* harm"—not "a little harm only"—is the mandate of reason and religion; and the law of temperance cannot be tolerant of indulgences that rest

for their defence upon the smallness of the evils they entail.*

4. It may be said that "*all constitutions are not alike, and that there must, after all, be some flaw in the case for total abstinence, because not a few, having honestly tried to carry it out, have failed and been compelled to return to the dietetic use of intoxicating drinks.*" That constitutions are often dissimilar, and that what suits one will not suit every one, are unquestionable truths; but extreme differences are not common, and those that exist are always found amenable to adaptations of the same general hygienic conditions—food, air, and water. Nature is elastic within certain bounds, but nature will not make new elements for the sake of those who think they cannot support existence on the old. Certain kinds of food may be more adapted to some than to others, but the instances are

* Dr. Anstie is the only man of science who has attempted to define, by alcoholic measurement, the limit of "moderation." He makes it to consist in not more than one ounce and a half of absolute alcohol daily for an adult male (or two ounces in case of unusual exertion), and three-quarters of an ounce daily for an adult female. The latter would represent two glasses of port or sherry. Judged by this rule, it may be said that "moderation" is unknown in the case of multitudes who use strong drink, and never known in convivial circles. Dr. Parkes has justly said of Dr. Anstie's daily allowance for men, "This would be contained in one and a half pint of beer with five per cent. of alcohol, or in fifteen ounces of claret with ten per cent. Is is not quite correct to say that most men would consider these quantities absurdly small?" Yet Dr. Anstie admits that all excess "acts as a narcotic poison to the nervous system"; and hence the conclusion is irresistible that millions of people, who flatter themselves that they are "moderate drinkers," are seriously deluded, and habitually poison themselves by the alcohol they consume. Even could it be shown that a particular quantity of alcohol might be taken daily without physical injury, yet the difficulty of applying the test, and the injury arising from error, would be sufficient to stamp abstinence as the wiser plan; added to which are all the extra-physiological reasons which make abstinence preferable. The Latin word *moderatio* (whence our "moderation") signifies, in a moral sense, the regulation of the passions; and we contend that the virtue of moderation finds higher expression in the abstinence which renders any evil from alcohol impossible, than in the use which is checked by the desire [often inefficient] of guarding against this evil.

rare and abnormal where substances, generally poisonous, are innocuous and even useful to any. In all main points men are made alike, or they would not all be men; and the man has yet to be born on whose constitution alcohol can be shown to act as a food, or as assisting, instead of retarding, the vital functions of the physical system. It is true that many who have tried the abstinence plan have abandoned it, but from the ranks of these seceders great deductions must be made. First, there are those *whose trial has been plainly inadequate*—a few days or weeks only. A mere change of habit might be expected to cause temporary inconvenience; much more when the change has been from the use to the disuse of an article characteristically exciting to the nervous system. Secondly, there are those who, having become really ill, *have been easily persuaded by their friends that their abstinence was the cause*, but who have often been ill before and since without ascribing their ailments to strong drink. Thirdly, there are those who, having become abstainers from benevolent motives, but without any knowledge of the action of strong drink on the body, *have magnified the "sacrifices" made*, and have looked upon themselves as martyrs in the cause of humanity. That the imagination has an astonishing effect on the bodily state is known to all physiologists, who will agree that an expectation of ill-health is expressly adapted to predispose to it, and even to provoke it. Instances are known where persons who have abstained, and have suffered in health from the fancy of having resigned a physical good, have regained their spirits and health when they had become convinced that intoxicating liquors possessed no power of benefiting the users. Fourthly, there are those who, having been consumers, daily or more frequently, of bitter beers and ales, *have accustomed their stomachs to the bitter ingredient in these liquors*, and it is not improbable but that in their case sudden abstinence from this tonic constituent has been followed by a sense of stomachic weakness and symptoms of indigestion. But these effects would have followed the discontinuance of any similar beverage destitute of alcohol, and have no relation to the question of the influence of alcohol upon health and life. It should be remembered that tonics, properly so called, cannot be *habitually* used with impunity, and that, when the stomach flags from their abandonment, the evidence of their abuse is palpably disclosed. The proper course, then, to be adopted is not to resume the use of an alcoholic drink which has a tonic united with it, but to take some tonic apart from the alcohol, diminishing the quantity and strength of the dose till the stomach regains its natural digestive power and can dispense with the misused tonic infusion.* Where the stomachic debility is chronic, enlightened medical advice should be procured, but all alcoholic compounds strenuously declined. After abstracting from the list of failures these four classes of failing abstainers, the remnant of other cases will be found exceedingly small, and will consist of two kinds: persons who have relied so much and for so long on alcoholic excitement as to require *medical treatment* in connection *with* abstinence—not *apart* from abstinence; and persons who are suffering from some ailment whose symptoms are *masked by alcohol*, but the unmasking of which by abstinence is a real service to the individuals so affected. Forms of hysteria come under this description, though it is well known that hysteria is never cured—frequently it is caused—by the use of alcoholic drinks.

That total abstinence really injures any one adopting it is a notion confuted by the voluntary experience of

* The fashionable taste of late years for bitter beer has been exceedingly prejudicial; the appetite may be improved for a time by the greater quantity of hops used, but all medical testimony condemns the use of bitters as an article of diet.

millions, of all ages, temperaments, constitutions, and employments; by the effects of compulsory abstinence upon the inmates of prisons and workhouses; and by the scientific researches that have proved that every specific action of alcohol on the vital organism is to injure and not to aid it. There is one other argument, of no small force, on this very point. Individuals who go to gross excess can only be reclaimed by total abstinence, which is their one means of safety, and imperative, immediate duty; all confess this; but such individuals are of varied constitutions, and they are the persons who, if long use and habit create a need for alcoholic drink, are most of all incapable of existing without it. Either, then, such persons can or cannot totally abstain without injury to health; if they cannot, to urge them to abstinence is inviting them to seal their earthly doom; if they can (and that they can is seen by the reclamation of tens of thousands who have lived more healthfully than before), it is made clear, by the most powerful form of *a fortiori* reasoning, that all other users of alcoholic liquors can abstain with safety, and that those who have failed to persist in their abstinence, on the ground of injury to health, have fallen into an error which longer experience and better information would have effectually dispelled.

5. It may be said that "*alcoholic preparations are useful and even necessary at times in the treatment of disease.*" If so, there is no reason that they should be taken in health, or for the preservation of health. On the contrary, their utility in disease must be impaired by such a customary use as renders the system less susceptible of their influence at critical periods. If benefit is ever to be received from their medicinal application, the daily consumer is less likely to derive it than he who is a total abstainer from their use as a beverage. This is a universally recognized principle as to the action of all medicines, and constitutes, therefore, a cogent reason

why alcoholic compounds should be removed from diet etic use, and why, when medicinally prescribed, the strength and frequency of the dose and the period of use should be strictly defined by the medical adviser. Yet, even as medicines, there are some weighty considerations for reducing their application to the lowest point, or renouncing them entirely.

(1.) The long-established use of alcoholic drinks in this country makes their *strictly medicinal employment exceedingly difficult,* as much so as would be the simple medicinal use of opium in Eastern countries where opium is smoked and eaten daily. Under such circumstances, to maintain a sharp distinction between food and physic is next to impossible with the multitude, who will be only too glad to prize and apply as food that which can only be of value as a drug.

(2.) The large number of persons who have contracted a craving for alcohol, and to whom its taste, even as medicine, brings *moral danger*, makes it much to be desired that it should never be prescribed where other articles will be of service. That it should never be given on any account to reclaimed inebriates seems the dictate of common sense; yet it is a dictate frequently violated by medical men, who never enquire into their patients' habits, or who recklessly ignore the moral consequences almost certain to arise.

(3.) The special evils likely to flow from *patients acting as their own doctors* in regard to strong drink, when once they had been advised to take it for any ailment, is not to be overlooked. Of all "medicines," there is none that people (if at all encouraged by medical opinion) are so ready to prescribe for themselves as alcoholic liquor, however trivial the complaint. They make the wine or spirit merchant or the publican their apothecary on any pretence, and without any concern for the purity of the draught or its specific adaptation to their condition of health.

(4.) The *promiscuous* recommendation of alcoholic liquors by members of the medical faculty is *an abuse wholly indefensible,* whether or not alcohol has medicinal virtues in particular cases. Dr. Carpenter has not hesitated to affirm, "Nothing in the annals of quackery can be more empirical than the mode in which fermented and distilled liquors are directed or permitted to be taken by a large proportion of medical practitioners." Since this was written, Dr. Todd's system of treating fever with heavy doses of brandy has been pursued, and, after causing an awful excess of hospital mortality, has met with the condemnation it deserved from some of the leading organs of the profession. Dr. S. Wilks, of Guy's Hospital, has severely censured the sanction, by many medical practitioners, of the popular opinion that patients who are "low" need "supporting" by wine and spirits.*

(5.) A variety of authentic testimonies and facts are on record, tending to the conclusion that *a diminished use of alcohol, and even its entire disuse, in the treatment of disease is attended with a decreased mortality and more rapid recovery.* The most eminent members of the faculty are generally agreed that the alcoholic treatment of cholera and *delirium tremens* is a complete mistake; and the statistics supplied by Drs. Gairdner and Russell, with respect to the City of Glasgow Fever Hospital, have shown a reduction of the mortality from 17·5 to 11·9 per cent., and, later still, to 9·05 per cent., a reduction keeping pace with a lessened consumption of wine and spirits by the patients. To the same effect are the testimonies of medical men in large practice, who have, with striking advantage, discontinued for years all use of alcohol, whatever the nature or type of disease under their care.† If, then, there is rea-

* See also Dr. Wilks's Letter in *Lancet*, May 18, 1867; also in *Lancet*, January 8, 1870.

† See "Medical Experience and Testimony in Favor of Total Abstinence" (Tweedie, Strand.)—Dr. Munroe, of Hull: "It is now seven years since I

son to believe, that diseases would be less fatal, and more successfully overcome, were alcohol less patronized, or even excluded from the *materia medica* ; and if it is obvious that when prescribed it should not be carelessly used in the form of ordinary liquors, but carefully furnished in the form of a chemical preparation ; and, if it is further apparent that any benefit by alcohol in sickness must largely depend upon abstinence from it in health—no argument can be other than intrinsically invalid which infers its advantage as diet from its supposed utility in disease.

From all that has been advanced, we may reasonably conclude that intoxicating beverages are of no advantage, and that their alcoholic property, so far from rendering them contributory to health and strength, conduces to the injury of those who partake of them, and thereby hinders the attainment of that standard of physical vigor and enjoyment put within the reach of his creatures by the beneficent Creator ; and therefore that, in the words of one great medical declaration, "Total and universal abstinence from alcoholic liquors and intoxicating beverages of all sorts would greatly contribute to the

have ordered any alcoholic drink either as medicine or diet ; and the success attendant upon its disuse is so gratifying as to lead me to its entire abandonment in the treatment of disease." Mr. Higginbottom, F.R.S., of Nottingham, has discontinued the use of alcohol with marked success for forty years. Mr. Bayley, M.R.C.S., of Stourbridge : "I have treated successfully nearly every form of disease without alcohol, and with the best results, for years." Mr. Mudge, M.R.C.S., of Bodmin : "There never has been made a trial of diminished alcohol, or none at all, without good resulting and preponderating." Mr. Collenette, L.R.C.P., Guernsey : "For some twenty-nine years I have banished them from my practice, and I have never had cause to regret having done so." Mr. Bennett, M.R.C.S., Winterton, refers to a treatment of 400 cases of fever, and attendance on 3,000 cases of childbirth, without any alcoholic treatment, with manifest advantage. Dr. Nicolls, Longford : "It is now more than twenty years since wine, spirits, or porter was used in the hospitals under my care, and the result in every way has been most satisfactory."

health, the prosperity, the morality, and the happiness of the human race." *

* Those who are interested in the physiological department of the abstinence question may consult with advantage Dr. Carpenter's Prize Essay, "The Physiology of Temperance and Total Abstinence"; the works of Dr. F. R. Lees, particularly the "Illustrated History of Alcohol," the "Temperance Text-Book," and the "Enquiry into the Prescription of Intoxicating Liquors in the Practice of Medicine"; the Prize Essay, "Bacchus"; the Essay "Anti-Bacchus"; Burne's "Teetotaler's Companion"; the "Alcohol" and "Nephalism" of the late Professor Miller; the "Pathology of Drunkenness," by Professor Wilson; together with admirable dissertations, longer or shorter, by Drs. Monroe, Edmunds, J. W. Beaumont, and Russell, Professor Youmans, and Messrs. T. Beaumont, Mudge, and others. Also, the Parliamentary Committee's Report, 1834; The Committee of Convocation's Report on Intemperance; the Reports of the Temperance Con gress and International Convention of 1862; the *Temperance Spectator* (1859-66); and the *Medical Temperance Journal*, now published quarterly. (Tweedie, Strand.)

CHAPTER III.

PROPOSITION: THAT INTEMPERANCE IS A TRUE PLAGUE, WHICH CAN ONLY BE EFFECTUALLY SUPPRESSED BY THE EXCLUSION OF INTOXICATING DRINKS.

MERE confessions of the evil of intemperance, and of the enormous evils propagated by it, will not suffice for its abatement; sincere but simple sorrow will be equally unavailing; and even much earnest effort may be expended without the desired reward. As there must be a correct diagnosis of disease before it can be effectually encountered, so a just understanding of the origin and nature of alcoholic intemperance must precede that use of counteractive means by which alone success can be secured. In a word, this curse must be conceived of as a veritable plague—a plague in the strict physical sense, and therefore in a sense far different from the vague and rhetorical use of the word by popular orators and writers. Many things are plagues in the general sense of being severely burdensome and injurious; and to speak of intemperance as such a plague is possible without the least comprehension by the speaker of the facts which give to that appellation a scientific significance and force. Not a little confusion, indeed, is occasioned by failing to distinguish between intemperance in the form of any sensuous excess, and intemperance in the restricted and special sense of a craving for and addiction to intoxicating drinks. There are, no doubt, features of resemblance both in the course and consequences of all sensual indulgences, as there are marks of similarity between all forms of disease; yet, just as to treat all disease as one in origin and character is the height of charlatanism—so, to regard alcoholic intemperance as identical with sensual intemperance in general, is an error equally gross and pernicious. The distinction is profound and essential. Sensual excess is the inordinate gratification of natural appetite—a perversion, by exaggeration, of instincts necessary to the existence of the individual or the race; an intemperance, therefore, which must find its correction in the subjection of the animal to the moral nature in man, so that while the physical appetite is gratified (and the connection between soul and body thereby maintained), the supersensuous powers may be developed, and the life of earth be made a fitting prelude to the life of heaven. But the species of intemperance of which we now treat is not the outgrowth or illicit gratification of any natural appetite; it proceeds, on the contrary, from the creation of an artificial appetite; and, therefore, if it is to be cured and prevented—*i.e.*, entirely eradicated from among men—something more and different must be done than is necessary for the subjugation and control of natural desire. An analogy is presented in the distinction between *two classes of disease.* In the one class, disease arises from poorness of blood, or some defect in the due reparation of tissue; in the other class, called zymotic or fermentative, the diseased action is set up by the introduction from without of certain organic germs, which rapidly multiply in the blood, and, by their effect on the circulation and nervous centres, weaken the vital processes, and often bring them to a dead-stop. These latter diseases frequently become epidemical, and in the case of the black death the fatality was so great that one-fourth of the populations visited by that scourge are estimated to have perished. The Great Plague of 1665 was of this species of disease, and, under the name of "pest," "pestilence," or "plague," the world has had to mourn the power of this destroyer. Now, it is of the utmost importance to settle in the mind whether alcoholic intemperance, as a personal and social disease, is produced by a perversion of natural function, or by the infusion of a foreign element into the system. If the former, the remedy must be sought in a readjustment of natural powers, by educational, moral, and religious means operating within; if the latter, no real remedy can exist which does not aim at excluding the *virus* already imbibed, and preventing its further reception. In cholera, fever, and plague, there is no cure till the patient ejects the virulent matter; and could the entrance of that matter be entirely prevented, the existence of these diseases would, under the ordinary laws of nature, be strictly impossible. Now, an examination of alcoholic intemperance in its origin can only terminate in one result—that is, in the conviction *that it belongs, both physically and morally, to the class of fermentative (zymotic) diseases.* No mere depravation of natural appetite will produce it; never does it exhibit itself till alcohol has been consumed; and what is specially to be remarked (as indicating not merely an analogy but a family relation between the plague and drunkenness) is, that alcohol acts, in the production of the intemperate habit, by *poisoning the blood and arresting the healthy operation of the nervous system.** In this manner, and in no other, the craving for alcoholic drinks is produced—which is always a physical malady in its inception—until, by continuous indulgence, it takes a settled and chronic form, not rarely passing into *delirium tremens,* or leading its victim through the stages of so-called oinomania (wine-madness) or dipsomania (thirst-madness) to a miserable

* It is a curious coincidence (if only such) that alcohol, though not a ferment, is, as before explained, the result of a double fermentative process—the putrefaction of albumen, which sets up the saccharine fermentation; and both these processes are allied. Liebig says: "Both fermentation and putrefaction are processes of decomposition of a similar kind—the one of substances destitute of nitrogen, the other of substances containing that element."

death. As, then, the reception of the poison-germs is essential to the appearance of all forms of plague, so the reception of the intoxicant virus is essential to the appearance of all forms of alcoholic intemperance ; and as both are engendered in a similar manner, there is a certain likeness in the methods of propagation attendant on both. Contagion and infection are but other names for agencies by which the poison-germs are transported from place to place, and become more readily introduced into the human system ; and in the transmission of hereditary predisposition to intemperance, together with the influence of example, custom, usage, and licensed traffic, in adding to the consumption of strong drink, we have physical and social forces by means of which the material agent of this terrible malady of intemperance is widely diffused, with its pestiferous influence, on every hand. Other resemblances may be traced, without any resort to fanciful conjecture. Like the plague, the intemperate craving is insidious in its approach—imperceptible in its inception—often deceitful in its earlier manifestations ; but, when fully developed, is imperious, and raging above all common control. If either is curable, it is by the self-same method—the exclusion of the venomous agency. The pest-stricken man can only escape by throwing off and out of him the germs of destruction ; and, failing to do this, an inexorable and terrible death awaits him. With the victim of intemperance the alternatives are the same ; he must either cast forth the alcohol already imbibed, and preserve himself free from its further use, or he must remain diseased, and be consigned to a premature grave.* That abstinence

* Mr. Neison, the eminent actuary, published, in 1851, tables showing that from 20 to 90 the deaths of the intemperate exceed the deaths of the population at large in the proportion of 32 to 10; but that between the ages of 30 and 40 the proportion is 42 to 10.; and that between 40 and 50 it is 41 to 10—fourfold!

alone is the antidote for actual intemperance (drink-disease) is universally admitted—a proof that society perceives one-half of the truth, by recognizing the plague-cast of the malady when formed; so that all that is needed to the full enlightenment of society is a perception of the other half of the truth—that the disease cannot be certainly prevented except by the exclusion of the foreign agent (alcohol) which engenders it. In regard to diseases of the zymotic type, the principal difficulty in the way of prevention arises from the invisibly minute constitution of the poison-germs, and their power of vitality and propagation, except under conditions of heat or cold too severe for human endurance. Could their detection be secured, and means for their exclusion from the human system be devised, science would achieve one of its proudest triumphs and humanity reap one of its most precious boons. Happily, a great contrast is here offered to our view, for the substance by which the alcoholic craving is induced is not too attenuated to be seen, nor is there any danger of receiving it unconsciously into the body. The senses have sufficient indications of this enemy; and if the will issues orders for its rejection, no evil can ensue.

If, however, we contemplate events as they are, not as they ought to be, what do we discern? We see that every year the people of this country, or rather a majority of them (for very young persons and abstainers must be deducted), consume sixty million gallons of alcohol, the physical seed of the drunken appetite; and we see, as we might expect, that the agent of evil takes with it the evil effect; that those who have been smitten grow worse, and that, as they die off, a number as great begin to develop signs of the same terrible malady; that both sexes, and persons of all ages (sometimes the very young, even infants in arms), and in all social conditions, are among the victims; and that from year to year, from age to age, the *tale* of these victims continues to be told, and is never completed. Here, in sorrowful truth, is one broad difference between the Eastern plague and the plague of drink. The one breaks forth epidemically and subsides (in England, there has been no visitation since the seventeenth century—two centuries ago); whereas the alcoholic plague never intermits its ravages, and by the unrelaxing continuity of its infliction occasions an aggregate mortality far surpassing that which pestilence has produced. If plague has slain its thousands, intemperance has slain its ten thousands; and if plague can claim to have hurried its victims more quickly and in vaster masses to the tomb, intemperance may claim not only to have wrought a greater slaughter in the long run, but to have hurried out of life as many of the untainted as of the self-destroyed. The innocent child has died or grown up diseased through the sin of the drunken parent; the wife or husband has been sacrificed to the drunkenness of the sottish mate; and both on land and sea, in peace and war, as the days revolve, accidents of every kind, by which victims' lives are cut short, occur through the effect of alcohol upon those who have duties of importance committed to them.* To have a perpetual plague like this within our borders is, therefore, to suffer a frightful waste of life, compared with which the annual homicides by murder, manslaughter, and suicide, and even by a state of war, would be of inferior account. If these deaths have averaged but 25,000 a year since the Eastern plague disappeared two centuries ago, we have a loss of five million fellow-creatures—a sixth of the population of the United Kingdom at this time—who might other-

* It is probably not true, as roundly asserted at times, that 60,000 drunkards die every year in the United Kingdom; but if to those who die prematurely from the effects of alcohol, in large or often-repeated doses, be added the multitudes who perish as indicated in the text, the host of slain *every year* will probably not fall short of 60,000—5,000 every month.

wise have lived long to enjoy the bounty of their Creator and to bless succeeding generations.

These statistics of destruction would be terrible enough if they stood alone. But they do not. Of the major portion of those who have died directly from the alcoholic plague, it must be feared that the disease attacked the mind and soul not less disastrously than the body; that the poison penetrated where the plague-germs never enter; that mental darkness and weakness—often mental aberration—were the consequences of the love of strong drink; that vice and irreligion brought up the dismal rear; and that when the dishonored body was laid in the dust, charity could drop no word of blessing, and hope could shed no light upon the scene. Who also can estimate the misery of every kind brought upon the family dependents and relatives of the millions whom strong drink has delivered over to ruin? How frequently has not only pecuniary destitution been their fate, but a legacy of immoral influences and associations, which have embittered and poisoned the future lives of wives and children, to whom the domestic relations have brought only sorrow and shame! It may, then, be forcibly asked, *What plague can be compared to this plague? and what can be urged in favor of these beverages,* on which depend its existence, its prevalence, and its power of adding to the ills that man is heir to others of surpassing intensity and sadness?

OBJECTIONS.

The observations above offered may elicit two replies:

1. It may be said that "*The analogy instituted fails in a very important particular, because all who use alcoholic liquor do not take the drink-plague; and that, in fact, those who fall victims to this physical and moral malady form a very small proportion of all who drink.*"

The supposed failure in the analogy cannot be sustained, and if it could the core of the argument would remain untouched. During periods of epidemic plagues, all do not die, all are not seized; nor, in reference to the seeds of zymotic disease in general, can it be said that the same conditions affect all alike. Medical science does not support the theory that all who receive the poison-germs are equally poisoned. The evidence rather tends to show that in various states of the body these germs are neutralized, or exert so partial an effect that the system suffers slightly, and recovers its balance by vigorously ejecting the intruders. To this extent, then, the analogy holds good—that in neither case is the full measure of possible injury generally realized; the worst effects are limited in extent; but in neither case is the connection of the effect with the cause doubtful or obscure, nor can any one person guarantee beforehand his own immunity from the gravest and most fatal results. The plague does not strike all; but who can be sure that it will not strike him? Alcohol does not excite in all who use it the intemperate appetite; but who can foretell that he shall be exempt? Nor can it be pleaded that those affected are so few as to make the danger individually small. A much smaller proportion of seizures spreads intense alarm in a time of pestilence; and were half as much reasonable fear excited by the diffusion of the alcoholic pest, the employment of the best preventive measures would not be delayed.

2. It may be argued that "*The disuse of alcoholic drink is not essential to the security of society; and that with the spread of knowledge, education, refinement, and religion the plague of intemperance will die out, as it has almost died out already in some classes of society.*"

Were this remark much better founded than it is, it would not impeach the wisdom of securing perfect and indisputable safety by excluding the actual originator of this specific disease. In the case of the poison-germs that produce zymotic disease, no doubt personal cleanliness and temperance, wholesome diet, cheerfulness, moderate work, a sound constitution, and dwellings built and held under good sanitary conditions, are of much utility in protecting persons against attack and in diminishing the violence of seizure when it occurs; but who would be content with these secondary measures of defence if the poison-germs could be themselves arrested and destroyed? Why, then, should men trust to subordinate securities against the plague of drink when they can have absolute protection? or why, in other words, should they run the risk which must be run when alcohol is used, and then consider that they have done all that is needful by fortifying themselves with virtuous resolutions against excess? Do they not see that others, once as resolute and as confident as they can be, have proved the vanity of their hopes, and are now blighted in body and soul? That some classes are less deeply tainted than others may be true, but no class, however high, refined, educated, or pious, can be cited as proof against this plague; and it is certain that much of the exultation over a highly improved state in this respect is either wholly fallacious, or is based upon comparisons which prove very little as to the real position of affairs. Gentlemen do not now get drunk after dinner—convivial drinking is not the custom it once was; but to infer that gentlemen do not get drunk on set purpose, do not drink enough to injure them, and are free from all craving for alcoholic stimulants, is a conclusion at variance with all the known facts. The zest with which, both in public and private, respectable persons, even ladies, drink glass after glass of brandied liquors; the incontestable figures that prove an enormous consumption of intoxicating drinks (despite all that temperance societies have directly and indirectly effected); and the testimony of medical men and others to the diffusion of a strongly-marked taste for intoxicating liquors in the highest circles—together with lamentable consequences that cannot be entirely hid from the public eye —all unite to expose the shallowness of the pretence, that the upper and middle classes have learned how to drink without fear of enkindling the alcoholic appetite, and so practically reversing the declaration that "wine is a mocker, and strong drink is raging." Were it possible, however, to bring about this security where all the social circumstances are favorable, it would be chimerical to look for it, in the face of all the predispositions and incentives to indulgence which beset the great multitude of the so-called lower orders. If they drink, they will drink for the excitement strong drink brings, and to separate this from alcoholic intemperance would require a standing miracle for this single purpose. The germs of the drink-plague have but to fall upon this prepared soil, and the harvest of disease and death must be profuse; and those who wish to be regarded as the friends of their species have to choose between letting things take their course (till, at some far-distant epoch, they have in spite of drinking raised the lowest classes to a high educational and moral level) or interfering to banish the instrument of this degradation and ruin. To effect this latter object, they must renounce alcoholic liquors themselves, and thus help to infuse into the masses, so terribly injured, a strength of resolution equal to the greatness of the effort. THE PLAGUE IS RAGING; IT MAY BE SUPPRESSED BY WITHDRAWING THE ELEMENT BY WHICH IT IS ENGENDERED AND FOSTERED; and shall it be said that those who were required to lead in this enterprise, and who were capable if willing to carry it out, were too sluggish and apathetic for the work? If there be any tenderness in humanity, any virtue in patriotism, any inspiration in Christianity, the endeavor to stop the plague of our national intemperance by banishing its cause is fitted to evoke and engage them all. May the reader not suffer this knowledge to be possessed, and this appeal for *his* co-operation to be addressed, as if he had no responsibility in this matter !

CHAPTER IV.

PROPOSITION: THAT VIOLENCE IS DONE TO THE WILL OF GOD AND THE WELFARE OF MAN BY APPROPRIATING THE FRUITS OF THE EARTH TO THE PRODUCTION OF INTOXICATING DRINKS.

If man himself, as to his body, has sprung from the dust, not less true is it that from the dust springs the food by which his bodily life is renewed day by day. The daily (or necessary) bread for which he prays is provided by a divine economy above his control, but with which he is permitted to co-operate, in order that, instrumentally, he may earn the subsistence which gives to labor its sweet reward. There is a profound truth in the narrative, viewed literally or allegorically, which assigns to the first man the care and cultivation of the ground; and the honors paid by early nations to agriculture, and the mysteries associated with the processes of natural production and increase, find their ready explanation in the felt and pressing value of the food with which, at the touch of industry, the wide earth teems. Both Scripture and reason unite to fill the mind with reverence, in the presence of that aspect of nature which, in the form of autumnal affluence, bears the sign-manual of the King of Heaven. Human science, unable to create a single grain of wheat, sees a divine phenomenon in every grain, and in the reproductive energy which makes the buried grain reappear in an increase of sixty or a hundred fold. Inscrutable as the manner of this is, there is nothing dubious as to the purpose of the gift and the will of the All-gracious Donor. It is his will that the produce of the field should be as abundant as the wants of man—enough for his "service" and "gladness"—so richly does he "bless the springing thereof." It is his will that what is so supplied should be applied to its intended purpose—not hoarded for gain, and not wasted by neglect or of evil design. It is his will that the means of nourishment, and health, and life, thus beneficently furnished, should not be changed into the means of impoverishment, disease, and death. If there be aught plain, beyond denial or doubt, in regard to the Divine will, these things are plain.

How, then, does the annual appropriation of sixty million bushels of grain (not to speak of millions of bushels of fruit) in the manufacture of intoxicating liquors, comport with these expressions of the Creator's good pleasure? The leading object of that manufacture is to produce an alcoholic beverage of some kind, which, when produced, bears the faintest resemblance to the substance employed in its production; the nutritious properties almost wholly disappear, and the saccharine element is converted, as far as possible, into a gas (carbonic acid) which it is poisonous to breathe, and a liquid (alcohol) that, but for the water blended with it, would destroy the vital organs with which it is brought into contact. Here, then, we have a triple violation of the Divine will. First—*The supply of food is rendered less abundant than it might be.* Distilling and brewing abstract from the world's store of alimentary sustenance a considerable portion of what Providence bestows. The 60,000,000 bushels yearly thus consumed in the British Isles alone are lost to our food-reserves; and, though Russian or American markets pour in new supplies to make good this deficiency, the corn we destroy is not, and cannot be, restored to us; the world is so much the poorer in solid sustenance, and the price of food is raised to us by the additional cost of freightage and importers' profits. Wealth, the most wonderful of all wealth, the wealth of grain—in more senses than one truly golden—is annihilated—as much obliterated as if it were spilled into mid-ocean or committed to the devouring flames.

Secondly—*The Divine will is frustrated as to the proper application of these mercies.* What God makes good he intends should be received for good—not abused or deteriorated in its transit from the field to the table. If man interferes, his interference should be limited to a better adaptation of the natural growth to the comforts and uses of life. Hence, the corn may be ground, baked, or boiled ; and, hence, the wood of the forest may be turned into the furniture of our rooms or the ships that brave the sea. But to lessen the intrinsic value of the Divine production is a practical reflection on the wisdom and goodness of the Supreme Benefactor. Yet, in distilling and brewing, this is done with the corn of heaven. The vital process of growth—the chemistry of creation—is exchanged for the anti-vital process of disintegration—the chemistry of death. Food has gone, and nothing has taken its place worthy of God to give or man to accept. What is done, and done too effectually, is to reverse the Divine method, and so to make it impossible that the bounties of Providence should be received with thankfulness as "the good creatures" of his power.

Thirdly—*The will of God is still more flagrantly frustrated by the change of this food into an* INTOXICATING DRINK. Food is invigorating—it is the staff of life—but strong drink debilitates, diseases, and destroys innumerable thousands. Food, when employed in the production of alcoholic liquor, is not only limited and lost, but the express objects for which it was sent are contravened, and other effects are substituted—effects which cannot but grieve the Great Father, who desires to see his children flourish and live long in the earth. With food come satisfaction, strength, the power of usefulness, the joys of society, and (in the Christian heart) the thankful sense of God's faithful love. With strong drink come growing want, premature decay, a capacity and love of evil-doing unknown before, offences against the social peace, a defiance of the Most High, and a hideous development of all that is bestial and infernal. The transformation is complete; it could not be more disastrous and revolting to our apprehension; how inconceivably odious, therefore, in his eyes who is too pure to look upon sin! Let no one allege that this is the language of exaggeration because all use of strong drink is not attended with these results. What arises from small quantities of food or strong drink is not the subject of description; the general issues alone are open to observation; and no lover of truth can deny that, in the sum of their respective effects, the corn which is used as food, and the drink which is made by waste of corn, differ as widely as sweet and bitter, as light and darkness, as life and death. It seems impertinent to enquire whether the will of God can be done on earth while this threefold violation of that will is in progress, sanctioned and carried out—be it sorrowfully said—by myriads of those who profess a profound reverence for that will, and who, in many other respects, are found to render to it a cheerful and enlightened obedience. And on man himself descends the penalty of the violation. The corn which, if ground into flour and baked into bread, would feed and strengthen a nation, is diverted from this end, and disappears in the processes which issue in a stream of intoxicating drink, flowing annually at the rate of nine hundred million gallons, sixty millions of which consist of a narcotic-acrid poison fatal to the bloom and beauty of life, physical, mental, and spiritual.* A quantity of breadstuff which

* It has been estimated that this amount of alcoholized fluid (900,000,000 gallons) consumed every year in the United Kingdom, would form, if collected, a lake nineteen feet deep, half a mile broad, and a mile long.

would have stocked the granaries of Egypt, and turned into plenty the seven long years of famine, is, in Christian England, turned aside from the miller and the baker, and made over to the maltster, the brewer, and the distiller; and the fruit of this capital economical and sanitary transgression follows us, through the years, with tireless severity. The crime engenders its own Nemesis, and the punishment keeps pace with the offence. At a period when population was scanty, and the industry of the country was principally agricultural, the consequences were, at times, so sensibly injurious as to call for legislative interference. The use of *aqua vitæ* in Ireland was condemned by a royal act, in the reign of Mary, on the ground that "much corn, grain, and other things is consumed, spent, and wasted, to the great hindrance, cost, and damage of the poor inhabitants of the realm." By the 39th and 40th Elizabeth, c. 16 (1597–8), power was given to the justices of the peace to diminish the number of maltsters, and to prevent, according to their discretion, the buying of barley for conversion into malt. By the 10th William III., c. 4 (1698), a check was given to the "excessive distilling of spirits and low wines from corn"; and in the early part of the next century, when the evils of spirit-drinking called for stringent legislative remedy, it was not the least reasonable of the complaints addressed to Parliament, that the corn used in the manufacture of gin was abstracted from the food of the people. Rutty attributes to the distilleries much of the scarcity commonly attributed to the failure of the crops in 1757; and John Wesley, in his tract (1773), "Thoughts on the Present Scarcity of Provisions," assigns as "the grand cause—because such immense quantities of corn are continually consumed by distilling"; and he speaks of the grain thus used as "consumed, not by so harmless a way as throwing it into the sea, but by converting it into deadly poison—poison that naturally destroys not only the strength of life, but also the morals of our countrymen." In 1795, the eloquent but not always judicious Edmund Burke made an impassioned plea on behalf of ardent spirits and against the stopping of the distillery; but the logic of facts proved too heavy for the light artillery of the orator, and in 1796 and 1797 distillation from corn was prohibited, as a necessary alleviation of scarcity, and with the result not only of saving much food from destruction, but also of rendering the poor "apparently more comfortable and better fed" than when the scarcity was less pressing and the distilleries were in full blast.* Dr. Darwin, the elegant poet and able physician, denounced the whole system of using up corn for intoxicating liquor as "the conversion of the people's food into poison"; and in the Report of the Select Committee of the House of Commons into the subject of intemperance (1834), the wastefulness and injuriousness of this course is vigorously depicted: "Not only an immense amount of human food is destroyed, while thousands are inadequately fed; but this food is destroyed in such a manner as to injure greatly the agricultural producers themselves; for whose grain, but for this perverted and mistaken use of it, there would be more than twice the demand, for the use of the now scantily-fed people, who would then have healthy appetites to consume, and improved means to purchase, nutriment for themselves and children, in grain as well as in all the other varied productions of the earth." Parliament did not profit by these truths when the years of famine in Ireland (1846–9) brought death to tens of thousands and the whole country to the verge of ruin. The policy five or six times resorted to by the English Government within the previous hundred years, and always with success—nota-

* Colquhoun on the Police of the Metropolis (1800).

bly so in Ireland itself in 1758–9 *—was left untried, although the Irish people, who had then been largely made sober by the labors of Father Mathew, would have welcomed the legislative interdiction. It is not too much to say that, through this culpable neglect, enormous destitution and starvation occurred that might have been averted; and nowhere was this let-alone impolicy more glaringly denounced than in an article by the eminent Dr. Chalmers, in the course of which he said: "Had the distilleries been stopped, as they were in 1800 and 1801, and as we believe they would have been now, if the famine, though not greater in amount, had only been general, this alone would have gone far to repair the deficiency. If over and above this the breweries had been stopped, and so for a season all malting had been put an end to, this would have greatly more than covered the deficiency. A humane and virtuous despotism could and would have done it at once. As it is, what between the class interests of our grandees, and the low and loathsome dissipations of our common people, the cry of famishing millions has been overborne." † Some years later, the *Times* newspaper, in commenting upon efforts in Sweden to stop the use of corn in distillation, employed the following remarkable language: "It is a peculiarity of spirit-drinking that money spent upon it is, at the best, thrown away, and in general far worse than thrown away. It neither supplies the natural wants of man, nor offers an adequate substitute for them. Indeed, it is far too favorable a view of the subject to treat the money spent on it as if it were cast into the sea. Yet even so, there is something exceedingly irritating in the reflection that a

* Dr. Henry, in his "Earnest Address to the People of Ireland" (1761), remarks, in reference to the stoppage of distillation in 1758-9, "the salutary effects of which were seen, restoring new vigor to our languishing manufactures, and a visible reformation in the morals of the people."

† *North British Review*, No. 13.

great part of a harvest, raised with infinite care and pains on an ungrateful soil and in an inhospitable climate, instead of adding to the national wealth, is poured in the shape of liquid fire down the throats of the nation that produced it, and, instead of leaving them richer and happier, tends to impoverish them by the waste of labor and capital, and degrade them by vicious and debilitating indulgence. A great portion of the harvest of Sweden and of many other countries is applied to a purpose compared with which it would have been far better that the corn had never grown, or that it had been mildewed in the ear. No way so rapid to increase the wealth of nations and the morality of society could be devised as the utter annihilation of the manufacture of ardent spirits, constituting as they do an infinite waste and an unmixed evil." * What is here so forcibly said concerning the manufacture of spirits is applicable substantially to the manufacture of fermented drinks; for both derive their intoxicating property from the alcohol or "spirit" they contain, and the only superiority the fermented liquors can claim over the distilled ones is that they are richer in water, a pinch of barley extract, and a dash of hops. It must also be remembered that the corn used in distillation is barely a fourth of the quantity used in brewing; and hence the Committee of Convocation, in their Report on Intemperance, make no idle distinction between the liquors manufactured, but say: "It cannot be viewed as of inferior consequence that the drinking habits of the community are gratified at the expense of the annual conversion of fifty [sixty] millions of bushels of grain into spirits and beer—an amount of cereal produce capable of furnishing aliment daily to millions of persons from year to year."†

What more flagrant frustration of the beneficent will

* *Times*, Dec. 7, 1853.

† "Report of the Committee of Convocation on Intemperance, etc.," p. 10.

of God, accompanied in the very act with the greatest evils to mankind, can be imagined than that which is here disclosed? The rain, the soil, the sunshine, join to produce miles upon miles of nutritious grain, rippling like a silver sea under a harvest moon; but the nourishment latent in all this grain, instead of being converted into blood and muscle, vital force and length of days, is disposed of with so much ingenious perversity that the national result is loss of wealth and health, ignorance and vice, violence and bloodshedding, insanity and irreligion, brutal living and hopeless dying. What sadder contrast can be conceived than the corn-field with its potentiality of blessing, and the gin-cask or beer-barrel with its plenipotentiality of physical and moral woe! The art by which this metamorphosis is executed cannot claim to be the philosopher's stone, turning whatever it touches into gold; rather, a fitter object of comparison is the Gorgon head, with its snaky hair, changing into stone everything mortal that gazed upon it. Or, varying the allusion, it may be affirmed that in the substitution of distilled and fermented liquors for harmless and invigorating food, the nation asking for bread receives a stone, and, looking for an egg, clasps a serpent to its breast.

OBJECTIONS.

1. One objector may urge that "*all the nutritious matter in the corn thus used is not lost, a portion remaining in the liquor brewed, and a portion going in the shape of grains to feed animals of different kinds.*" It is, however, a very feeble plea in mitigation of sentence against the brewing process (the distilling process does not admit of even this weak defence), that eight parts out of eighty-eight parts of nutriment are retained in what is brewed, and this rather by accident than by design, since clearness and not thickness is desiderated by the brewer and the drinker

alike. As to the disposal of the grains, distillers' grains, are a danger rather than an advantage to the animals receiving them, and whatever benefit arises from the use of brewer's grains by pigs is to a great extent diminished by the changes effected in the malting process, and the striking deficiency in malt grain of the most nutritive elements of the barley, the hordein of which is diminished from 55 parts to 12.* The pigs have reason to complain that their interests are so little consulted in the expensive and complicated arrangements adopted for deteriorating the "good creature of God," before it is suffered to approach man or beast.

2. Another objector may urge that "*the agricultural interest would be injured by the closing of the markets now open, for the sale of corn for distilling and brewing purposes.*" That this is a very narrow and erroneous view of the question can be demonstrated in a few words. The barley and other grain which the farmers sell to the maltsters and distillers bring them, at most, twelve millions sterling *per annum*; but can they fail to see that, if the hundred millions yearly expended in intoxicating liquors were otherwise devoted, their share of the expenditure would much exceed an eighth of the whole? In the hundreds of thousands of families now pinched by intemperance, the demand for farm produce would not only be doubled, but manifold increased; and, with a sober public to supply, calling for more to eat, and able to pay for it, the farmer would be one of the first to benefit by the happy reformation.

3. A third objector may urge that "*the farmers would be unable to get rid of their barley, and that the rotation of their*

* According to Prout, the changes are as follows, taking 100 parts of each, barley and malt: Yellow resin, 1—1; gum, 4—15; sugar, 5—15; gluten, 3—1; starch, 32—56; hordein, 55—12. In the malt *liquor* scarcely any of the solid elements are retained, every part of the brewing process helping in the attenuation of the article to be produced.

crops would be prejudicially interfered with." But the answers to this objection are conclusive. (1.) *Barley might still be in request, whether for malting or not, as food for bullocks; while its fattening powers have been proved upon horses and pigs.** So with apples now used in making cider. The farmers of America, among whom the practice of total abstinence has made most extensive way, have never found any difficulty in profitably disposing of their produce, either on their own farms or in the open market. English farmers, who have conscientiously objected to sell barley for malting, have not been losers by their adherence to principle. A correspondent of the *Mark Lane Express* communicated the result of an experiment in horse-feeding in these terms: "The keep of the horses upon which the experiment was made had been one bushel of beans, one bushel of oats, and one bushel of bran each per week. The beans and oats were discontinued, and boiled barley supplied instead, of which *one* bushel was found to suffice. In other respects, the food of the horses was the same as they had been used to,

* The long and loud outcry in favor of malt as superior to barley for cattle has been scientifically disproved more than once. In two series of experiments, undertaken in the months of October, November, and December, 1845, by order of the Government, it was discovered that the barley-fed bullocks increased 204 lbs., as compared with an increase of 104·5 lbs. in the malt-fed bullock. Experiments upon milch cows also showed, in the words of Professor Thomson, that "barley is superior to malt, weight for weight." In 1865, a new set of experiments were carried out upon twenty milking cows, twenty fattening oxen, sixty sheep, and forty-eight pigs. The barley-fed cows "invariably showed the higher proportion of cream"; the ten oxen fed on barley gave, during twenty weeks, 408 lbs. more increase in live weight than those having an equal amount of the same barley malted. The agricultural mind must now be convinced of this fact, as the Act of Parliament providing for the making of malt free of duty for the feeding of cattle, has become practically repealed by the almost universal neglect of the farmers to take advantage of it. In 1865 the bushels of malt so made were 55,321; in 1871 they were next to nil! So much for the argument once raised against the malt tax, that cattle would thrive very much more on malt than on barley, and that the tax stood in the way of the better alternative.

and they performed the same heavy work upon the road, travelling a weekly average of 140 miles. At the end of five months the animals were as healthy and active as they could possibly have been upon beans and oats, and were in 'high condition.' In a pecuniary point, the saving effected by the change (including the expense of boiling) was full £1 per week." A Cornish farmer has put the case in this practical shape: "When a laboring man spends 52s. a year in beer, the farmer gets but 13s. of the sum. He (the writer), wishes the farmer to secure the whole in this way: 12s. for a store pig, and 40s. for barley to feed it on; this quantity (12 bushels) would bring the pig to twenty-score weight, and he asks, Which is the best for a poor family, 200 lbs. of bacon or 39 gallons of beer? He puts it to any laborer, whether 2 lbs. of fresh meat a week would not be more beneficial to him than a pint of beer a day; and the answer is generally favorable to teetotalism."* And well it may be.

(2.) *It is absurd to suppose that, if the demand for barley should decline, the farmers of the United Kingdom could not adapt their land to the growth of other crops, for which an equally remunerative demand would arise.* One plan has been sketched by a practical farmer;† but we should be perfectly safe in leaving their own interests in the hands of the men who, whether as landlords or tenants, have proved, within the last quarter of a century, their capacity for conducting with enterprise and judgment the agricultural operations of the kingdom. Let them but know that there is a great increase of custom for farm produce, and they would belie their well-earned reputation if they did not meet that demand, whatever form it assumed, and make it conducive to their own satisfactory remuneration. It is lamentable to see an agitation kept up, from

* "The Farmer's Manual of Teetotalism: A Reply to What will be done with the Barley?" By H. Mudge, Surgeon. Ipswich: Burton. 1841. P. 17.

† "The Farmer's Manual of Teetotalism," p. 19.

year to year, to secure the repeal of the malt tax, in the hope that the farmer would be benefited by an increased demand for his barley, when the agitation, if successful, would either increase taxation in other ways or prevent the reduction of taxes pressing on the real comforts of the people; whereas, with the promotion of total abstinence, the true interests of the farming body would be bound up with the sobriety and prosperity of all other classes. The day will come, if wisdom is not to cry aloud in vain, when the lords and tenants of the soil will recognize the folly of relying for any portion of their gains upon the maintenance and increase of habits and a traffic which diminish the purchasing and consuming power of the community, while poor and county rates are raised to an unprecedented and oppressive degree. No illustration could be apter than the present system of "the penny-wise and pound-foolish" method of business to which the far-sighted trader has a reasonable aversion; and if self-interest alone were to guide the counsels of the agriculturists of the land—and in such a connection self-interest (like self-love) and social are the same—it would prompt them to pray and labor for the hastening of the period when a people, having shaken off enervating indulgences and enslaving customs, should call for larger and yet larger supplies of the really Heaven-sent food, satisfying and strengthening, in the providing of which the husbandman would find a quick and sure reward, so that sower and eater would have good reason to rejoice together. The enlightened Fénelon long ago saw that to stop the manufacture of strong drink was not to lessen, but to augment the wealth of the soil; and the eldest son of the late King of the French had arrived, by observation, at the same legitimate conclusion.* All trade, and not least that which is concerned

* See Appendix K.

in the cultivation of the soil and the satisfaction of man's most imperious wants, must be developed and enriched by the success of a movement which seeks to put the world in repossession of the fundamental virtue of sobriety, and more fully to equip it for that beneficent conquest of nature which Divine Providence has commissioned it to effect.

CHAPTER V.

PROPOSITION: THAT THE SACRED SCRIPTURES DO NOT AFFORD SANCTION TO THE USE OF INTOXICATING DRINKS BUT GIVE ENCOURAGEMENT TO THE TOTAL ABSTINENCE PRACTICE.

It may be confidently asserted, that those who use intoxicating drinks are not led to do so by any supposed sanction to be gathered from Holy Writ; for there are many acts, and courses of action, sanctioned in Scripture which they never think of imitating, and a compliance with which they would regard as irksome or unmeaning. They do not drink, in short, because they think that Scripture approves of drink and drinking; but, since they drink at all, they are glad to resort to Scriptural texts for protection against the persuasions of the temperance advocate. Especially is this their refuge when other refuges have proved too frail; and when hard-pressed with the arguments of the abstainer, drawn from science and experience, some find consolation in the attempt to construct a rampart of texts around the glass of wine, or brandy, or beer which there is no desire to relinquish. This system of defence will generally be found adopted most promptly, and sustained most tenaciously, by persons of religious feeling and profession, whose consciences will not let them be at peace till they have derived, from at least the letter of the Word, a justification of their personal and social habits. Nor is it intended to charge such persons with insincerity, or wilful false-handling of the Sacred Record. It is no new thing for good men of all opinions to seek for, and to discover, in the Bible a support of that which is congenial to their tastes and prepossessions; and there would be no reason to censure so severely this use of Scripture, were the reference to it accompanied by a reverential resolve to accept its teachings in their natural sense, and to walk by the light its precepts and principles reflect. It may be observed, however, that when the Bible is resorted to for the defence of theories or customs that are indefensible by other means, the probability is that a serious error of judgment is committed, and that no real honor is done to the Inspired Oracles by this ostentatious profession of respect. Natural law cannot be opposed to the Written law, unless they have different authors, or the one Author be divided against himself. Questions of experience and science are strictly such as natural law is most competent to decide; and, therefore, the appeal to Scripture against natural law is not only a confession of weakness, but is indicative of a wish to take the case into a court whose decisions the appellant may more easily succeed in construing to his supposed advantage. Yet neither his real advantage nor the cause of true religion can be concerned in the result of this effort when most apparently successful; for the ultimate effect can only be to make the Bible-revelation contradict the revelation of God in the laws he has impressed upon the visible works of his hands. Infidelity may exult in the imagined contrariety, but piety must resent the mischievous inference that has produced it. Let it, for example, be proved that total abstinence is better than the use of strong drink for the individual man in all his capacities, and for society in all its relations, and what is done for the Bible, or to increase man's faith in it, by the endeavor to show that the Scriptures either teach two contradictory doctrines, or that its teaching is contrary to the verdict of nature on the subject? No way can be found so sure as this to shake confidence in the inspiration and authority of the volume of heavenly truth. The wise words of Galileo, if pondered and digested, would avert such evil-meddling: "In these [natural sciences] we must not begin with the authority of the Bible, but with the observation of our senses, and the necessary proofs, because Nature and the Bible alike owe their existence to God. . . . Before all things, therefore, we must make sure of facts. To these the Bible cannot be opposed, else would God contradict himself; we must consequently expound their sense accordingly, and the capacity of making such researches is also a gift of God. . . . It is setting the reputation of the Bible on a hazard, to view the matter otherwise; and, as our opponents do, instead of expounding Scripture according to facts surely proved, rather to farce nature, to deny experiment, to despise the intellect." * Similar is the judgment of the *British Quarterly Review:* "In pure science, in physics, in psychology, in medicine, in the several departments of the social economy, jurisprudence, and politics, there are principles and facts for working out the problems with which men, as philosophers, are conversant; and we are content that, in all such matters, man should be left to the function of analysis, and to the inductions and analogies of practical philosophy." † The proper use of Scripture in all such questions is to show, where necessary, how apparent discrepancies can be explained, and to trace how in its narrative and didactic parts Scripture is in accordance with the laws of the natural world.

When, therefore, it is objected that—let the verdict of science and experience be what they may—the Bible is on the side of intoxicating drink, we are impelled, from our profound reverence for the Sacred Word, to scrutinize the alleged proofs of this position, and to enquire, in our turn, whether the opposite conclusion may not be

* Letter of Galileo to Madame Cristina, Granduchessa Madre.

† *British Quarterly Review*, January, 1846.

derived from a study of the Old and New Testament writings.

I.—SCRIPTURE DOES NOT SANCTION THE USE OF ALCOHOLIC LIQUORS.

The irrational notion on which some persons appear to proceed, that the bare mention of wine and strong drink is equivocal to a divine sanction, would be ridiculous if it did not border on the profane. Two principles of interpretation must be followed if unreason and confusion are not to reign supreme: First, *allusions to customs and usages, and to the habits of pious men, in ancient times, do not involve a divine sanction of those customs, usages, and habits.* The Bible is a storehouse of facts, remarkable for nothing more than for the fidelity with which local lineaments and coloring, and individual characteristics, are represented. But to attach God's sanction to the things and persons so represented is truly absurd, even when men of virtue and renown are the subjects of the portrayal. The wisest and best men in all ages have done many things neither wise nor good, yet things not stamped as unwise or evil in the historic record. Neither the drunkenness of Noah nor the deceit of Jacob is expressly condemned; and these extreme cases will show how necessary is the rule just laid down. It might be, or not, that holy men of old used intoxicating drink; yet it would not follow, as some imagine, that the practice was rendered holy, or was a proof of their holiness, or was other than a remnant of the imperfection adhering to them. Secondly, *Divine permission is not to be regarded as equivalent to divine sanction.* It was not God's pleasure (for reasons sufficient to his wisdom) to lay down minute injunctions providing against all wrong doing, even when he designed to prepare the enslaved race of Israel as a people for himself. Practices were tolerated consistent with the moral perfection neither of individuals nor the nation; and some of these permissions take the form of distinct arrangements and regulations. Slavery, polygamy, facility of divorce, a visible monarchy, together with much ignorance of the more spiritual elements of religion, were permitted, age after age; and what was said of one question was true, doubtless, of the rest, that this was done on account of "the hardness of their hearts." It need not surprise us, therefore, that they were also permitted to use intoxicating drinks, nor are we warranted on account of this permission to infer a divine sanction from the imputation of which every one would shrink in the other cases. As this point will afterwards recur, in regard to New Testament times, we shall proceed to consider those marks of divine sanction which are supposed to be conferred in Scripture upon the use of intoxicating drinks. One remark it is necessary to premise—that the words "wine" and "strong drink," which occur so frequently in the English version of the Bible, and which have certain fixed significations in our common speech, must not be considered as necessarily conveying the proper sense of the original terms. Excellent as is the current translation, it cannot possess the authority of the original Hebrew and Greek; and the present movement in the highest quarters for a revision of this version is a sufficient rejoinder to those who quote it, on this question, with a confidence that could not be surpassed if they held in their hands the autographs of the sacred writers. The argument, as we shall sketch it, is not an elaborate one, and with a little candor and patience it can be mastered by those who have never been trained in Oriental or classical erudition.

1. A sanction is claimed for intoxicating drink *because wine and strong drink are associated in Scripture with the temporal blessings promised to the Jews in their possession of the land of Canaan.* So Isaac's prophecy concerning Jacob (Gen. xxvii. 28) of "plenty of corn and wine"; so

Jacob's prediction of Judah (Gen. xlix. 11, 12) as to "washing his garments in wine, his eyes shall be red with wine, and his teeth white with milk"; so the promise of a bountiful vintage (Lev. xxvi. 5); so the blessing of the "corn, the wine, and the oil" (Deut. vii. 13, xi. 14); so the prospect of drinking "the pure blood of the grape" (Deut. xxxii. 14); and so numerous passages in the prophets, where the corn and the wine are associated as natural blessings of great value, and their loss deplored as a national calamity.

All this is true, and in a footnote * we subjoin references to all the passages where "wine," and "new wine," and "sweet wine," are associated with temporal good; but in doing this we also name the Hebrew words which are so rendered in the English translation. What, then, are the facts patent to every careful reader? (1) When YAYIN—the generic term for expressed juice of the grape—is described as a blessing, it is never represented as having an intoxicating quality, but as the liquid (in one place, Jer.

* YAYIN.—Gen. xlix. 11, 12; Deut. xiv. 26, xxviii. 39; Ps. civ. 15; Prov. ix. 2, 5; Eccl. ix. 7; Cant. v. 1, vii. 9, viii. 2; Is. lv. 1; Jer. xl. 10-12, xlviii. 33; Amos ix. 14; Micah vi. 15; Zeph. i. 13: Hag. ii. 12; Zech. x. 7.

TIROSH.—Gen. xxvii. 28, 37; Num. xviii. 12; Deut. vii. 13, xi. 14, xii. 17, xiv. 23, xviii. 4, xxviii. 51, xxxiii 28; Judges ix. 13; 2 Kings xviii. 32; 2. Chron. xxxi. 5, xxxii. 28; Neh. v. 11, x. 37, 39. xiii. 5, 12; Ps. iv. 7; Prov. iii. 10; Is. xxiv. 7, xxxvi. 17, lxii. 8, lxv. 8; Jer. xxxi. 12; Hos. ii. 8, 9, 22, iv. 11, vii. 14, ix. 2: Joel i. 10, ii. 19, 24; Micah vi. 15; Hag. i. 11: Zech. ix. 17.

SOVEH.—Is. i. 22; Hos. iv. 18.

SHEMARIM.—Is. xxv. 6.

KHEMER.—Deut. xxxii. 14; Is. xxvii. 2.

AHSIS.—Cant. viii. 2; Joel i. 5, iii. 18; Amos ix. 13.

ASHISHAH.—2 Sam. vi. 19; Cant. ii. 5; Hosea iii. 1.

SHAKAR.—Deut. xiv. 26.

The above are not references to all the texts in which the several Hebrew terms are translated "wine" or "strong drink," but they comprise all the principal passages in which an idea of utility is connected with the substances indicated by the original words. For a complete list of all the passages, and elucidation of them, the reader is referred to the "Temperance Bible Commentary."

xl. 10, 12, as the solid) produce of the vine. (2) TIROSH, often spoken of in connection with corn and oil (*Yitzhar*—orchard-fruit) is represented as growing upon the vine, and was the name for vintage-fruit. It is distinctly spoken of (Micah vi. 15) as trodden, and thus yielding *Yayin*. Only once is it referred to as possibly a liquid (Isaiah lxii. 8), and this apparent exception is explicable as an idiom, as when we speak of "drinking a cup," meaning its contents. The triad of *dahgan* (corn), TIROSH (vine-fruit), and *yitzhar* (olive and orchard fruit), comprehended the whole of that agricultural wealth which Israel held on the tenure of loyal obedience to the Great King. (3) SOVEH was a rich, thick, and probably boiled wine, greatly relished, not for any alcoholic property, but for its luscious quality, being more of a jelly than a liquid. (4) SHEMARIM is, literally, "preserves," and seems to refer (Isa. xxv. 6) to the delicacies or sweetmeats common at Eastern banquets, in succession to the "fat things"—*i.e.* savory food, first served up. (5) KHEMER, in the passages named (Deut. xxxii. 14; Is. xxvii. 2), has obvious reference to natural unfermented wine. (6) AHSIS is the fresh sweet juice as it issues from the trodden cluster. (7) ASHISHAH is admitted by all writers to refer, not to wine, but to pressed cakes of grapes. (8) SHAKAR, translated in our version "strong drink," and once (Numbers xxviii. 7) "strong wine," is the venerable lingual ancestor of our familiar "sugar," and specifically denotes the sweet juice of other fruits than the grape, also the juice of the palm-tree. Sweetness, not alcoholic strength, was its characteristic; hence the point of the threatening (Is. xxiv. 9), that it should become "bitter" to those who drank it. Nothing is more common in the East, at the present day, than for palm-juice to be drunk in its fresh and non-inebriating state. No doubt YAYIN and SHAKAR were often allowed to ferment, and used in that state, and were also frequently mixed with drugs, to increase their intoxicating potency; but whenever they are named in Scripture, in language implying Divine approbation, there is either a direct or tacit reference to them as *natural bounties*, the offspring of vital growth, and no word is ever employed in approbation of them as *fermented* liquors. What is said of them, viewed as intoxicating agents, will be shortly seen.

2. *A divine sanction is claimed for "wine" and "strong drink" because they were appointed as drink-offerings under the law; were allowed to be used at sacred festivals; and were adopted as symbols of spiritual blessings by the Jewish prophets.*

Besides what has been already advanced in explanation of the Hebrew words translated "wine" and "strong drink," it may now be replied—FIRST, and *generally*, that the *burden of proof rests upon those who assert that the original terms signify an intoxicating liquor in the passages referred to.* Mere assertion, however bold, is no evidence, and till evidence is given there is no argument to answer. All that is certainly known is that *yayin* (grape-juice in some state) and *shakar* (sweet juice in some state) were appointed, and that if they were used in a natural unfermented state, the command was obeyed. SECONDLY, *and specially*, as to each of the cases cited—(1) The "*drink-offerings*" were, in reality, libations—liquid offerings to be poured out, not to be consumed; and it is clear, from the letter and spirit of the Levitical law, that unfermented fluids would be in stricter accordance with that ritual than fermented ones. There were repeated prohibitions against leaven, and unleavened cakes were in numerous cases distinctly prescribed. (2) The permission (Deut. xiv. 26) was that of exchanging *tirosh* for *yayin*, and partaking of the latter, with the "household," and so rejoicing before the Lord. The circumstances do not warrant us to infer that the vintage-fruit was to be exchanged for intoxicating grape-juice; and if children were to partake of the

feast, and share in its gladness, the probability would rather be that for their sakes, to say nothing of the sobriety of their seniors, the *yayin* would be of the most innocent sort procurable. There is no hint given that an intoxicating sort was to be preferred; and common prudence would dictate to the fathers and mothers of Israel that if the *yayin* had passed into a fermented state, a liberal dilution (like the three or more measures of water to one of wine used by the sober Greeks) would be expedient. There is not a shadow of reason for the shocking supposition that God desired the heads of Jewish families to provide a liberal supply of inebriating drink for their children in order that they might rejoice before him.*
(3) The passages in which spiritual blessings are symbolized by wine are the following: In Proverbs ix. 2, 5, Wisdom is said to "mingle" her wine; but as the other references to mixed wine, as a curse, ascribe to it an intoxicating quality, there is the strongest reason for supposing Wisdom's wine to be deprived of that specific property. The Song of Solomon, spiritually construed, repeats the metaphor (v. 1) "I have drunk my wine with my milk; eat, O friends, drink, yea, drink abundantly, O beloved;" and (viii. 2), "I would cause thee to drink of spiced wine of the juice of my pomegranate." This is language unequivocally pointing to the natural juices of ripened fruits, of which the largest possible draughts could be taken without danger to health or morals. Who would dare to apply such an unlimited invitation to drinks, a few glasses of which would derange the intellect and fire the passions of all but seasoned topers? The passage in Isaiah xxv. 6, has been adverted to above. The ancient versions give very conflicting renderings of the Hebrew *mishta shemahrim*, "a feast of preserves"; and the com-

* See the "Temperance Bible Commentary" on this passage; also an elaborate Prize Essay upon it, by Dr. Lees.

mentators are equally disagreed. The English translators have supplied the words "wine on the," to give, as they imagined, a suitable rendering. Even retaining their conception of the sense, there is nothing to support the notion that the wine is eulogized because of an intoxicating quality. Wine, well-refined from its albuminous particles, and so preserved from fermentation, would admirably fulfil the conditions of the text. Isaiah's invocation (lv. 1) may be compared with the passage in Canticles (v. 1). In Isaiah lxv. 8, the "new wine in the cluster" is the vine-fruit in its ripening state; clearly, it cannot be wine after fermentation. In Amos ix. 13, the "sweet wine" is *ahsis,* which both the Septuagint and Latin Vulgate render by "sweetness"—the idea being that the rich ripe grapes yield their sweet juice to the treader's foot. In Micah vi. 15, the "sweet wine" of our version is not *ahsis*, but *tirosh,* and the real sense of the original can only be perceived by rendering the entire verse—"Thou shalt sow, but thou shalt not reap; thou shalt tread the olives, but thou shalt not anoint thee with oil; and (thou shalt tread) the vintage-fruit (*tirosh*), but shalt not drink wine" (*yayin*). In Zechariah ix. 17, the parallelism of "Corn shall make the young men cheerful, and new wine [shall make cheerful] the maids," would lead the English reader to regard the "new wine" (*tirosh*) as a solid, answering to "corn." This passage is also valuable as showing that in Scripture "cheerfulness" is not related to an intoxicating article. It is the "corn" that makes the youths cheerful, and surely the maidens are not conceived as needing alcoholic wine to make them the same! One Scotch divine is charged with having attempted to restore what he regarded as the proper correspondence by taking "corn" as a synonym for whiskey! The anecdote may be apocryphal, but will serve to point the violation done to the true sense of Scripture by a pro-alcoholic exposition of its really temperance texts.

3. A divine sanction is claimed for the use of intoxicating drinks, *because, it is alleged, the Saviour differed from John the Baptist in using the "wine" and "strong drink" from which the latter was excluded.*

But Jesus differed from John as a non-Nazarite, and John as a Nazarite was interdicted from the use of everything that came from the vine; so that by using the fruit of the vine in any state, the Lord made this difference as clearly marked as it could have been by the use of fermented fluids. The life of John was that of a solitary, waiting till crowds came to him; that of Jesus was as strikingly social, and where men abounded he wended his way to bless and to save them. For this purpose, and not from any disposition to self-indulgence, he visited the houses of all classes, and occasionally went to dine or sup with those who could thus be most intimately reached. Yet, through all, he pleased not himself; he did not gratify, even to the extent he lawfully might have done, his corporeal appetites; he was not the man of sensuous delights, but of sorrows; and his self-denial as far exceeded John's as the greatness of his mission exceeded that of his forerunner's. That "he came eating and drinking" is but another form of stating that he was social in his conduct; and if he was called a glutton and a wine-bibber (*phagos kai oinopotees*, literally "an eater and a wine-drinker"), the accusation implied excessive use of meat and drink, and not the intoxication arising from alcoholic wines. To suppose that the Saviour used any wine *because* it was alcoholic, and therefore sanctioned its use as such, is an assertion without the vestige of proof, nor does the Gospel history supply a fraction of evidence in support of the theory that he used the wine forbidden to the priests in their temple service—the wine forbidden to kings and judges—the wine employed by prophets to symbolize the wrath of the Almighty. To argue that he did so because he speaks of new wine being put into new bottles and not into old, lest the bottles should burst, is to misread the allusion. Fermented wine might have been safely put into old leather-bottles, but new unfermented wine could not, because in old bottles a ferment might exist which would set the juice fermenting, and the carbonic acid gas confined within the bottles would certainly burst them ; but if unfermented wine were put into new bottles, both would be preserved. So, Christian doctrine could not be put into the old bottles of Jewish rabbinism (with which much leaven was connected—against which he warned his disciples), but it must be reserved for other vehicles—the simple unsophisticated hearts which he had selected and consecrated for his service. As to the alleged superiority of old wine over new, of which so much is made, as a proof that the Saviour approved of fermented wine, the inference is destroyed by the three considerations: (1) that he simply alludes to the common taste, without any opinion of his own; (2) that he himself at the supper spoke of "new wine" (symbolically), as the best; and (3) that unfermented wine is more palatable and of finer quality the longer it is kept. As to the miracle at Cana, the whole narrative has been exhaustively considered,* and it will suffice to say briefly in this place, that (1) the narrative gives no other information as to the change of water into wine, beyond this—that the water drawn and handed to the governor of the feast was so transformed. That all the rest of the water, or any other part of it, was also changed into wine is simple inference, nothing more. The evangelist is silent concerning any other change, and the remarkable reply of Jesus to his mother, coupled with the absence of all mention of a provision of wine for the guests, leaves the question of quantity, to say the least, in the utmost doubt. Mr. Law, a century ago, held that only the cupful of water was

* See "Temperance Bible Commentary" on this passage.

turned into wine. (2) The supposition that the Lord supplied twelve gallons of alcoholic wine for a village wedding-feast, after the guests had exhausted a previous supply, is one so gross that reverence for the Redeemer would call for its rejection. If it is pleaded that his presence would guard against excess, the miracle ceases to be an argument in favor of wine-drinking, without such a protection at the present day. (3) The explanation furnished by St. Chrysostom, St. Augustine, and other eminent theologians, that the miracle consisted in doing instantaneously with the water in the firkins what is done, by Divine power, gradually with the water in the grape upon the vine, gives (on the theory of a transformation of all the water) a satisfactory key to the miracle as revealing the Saviour's glory, averts all evil reflection from him as the holy and blameless One, and disposes altogether of the theory that the wine so made must have been of an intoxicating character. It may further be remarked, that the merely external and physical acts of Christ, as to eating, drinking, clothing, lodging, and the like, are never proposed to us as examples for literal imitation. It is even obvious that many of those acts which were suitable to him might be very unsuitable to us; and it ought to require no words to show that to have the spirit of Christ—not to repeat his external actions—is to be really his, and to win his acceptance. The apostle who refused to know Christ "after the flesh," would have stood aghast at the indelicacy which holds up the Saviour as a wine-drinker, in order to justify an indulgence which prevents the rescue of souls from death, and the hiding of multitudes of sins.

4. *The sanction of the apostles is claimed for the use of intoxicating drinks.* It is said that Peter, when he and the rest were accused of intoxication, did not say they were total abstainers; and that Paul inculcated temperance in all things; declared all creatures of God to be good, and

to be received with thanksgiving; and advised Timothy to abandon total abstinence, and use a little wine for his stomach's sake, and many infirmities. In reply, as to Peter, he sought merely to argue with the accusers on their own ground; he did not even say that the apostles were never drunk; but he appealed to the hour of the morning (9 A.M.) as evidence that, if they ever drank, and ever got drunk, they were not likely to do so at that early period of the day. As to Paul—(1) He appeals to the competitors in the Grecian games, who were "temperate in all things," as an example to Christian disciples; but this temperance (or self-restraint) in all things included, as he knew, abstinence from wine and sensual pleasures. (2) The apostle affirms that whatever is good for food is not to be rejected on grounds of ceremonial uncleanness. He does not affirm (how could he?) that whatever exists ought to be eaten; but he defends what is intrinsically fit against superstitious objections. If, in truth, every creature of God good for food is to be received as God madé it, what is to be said of the practice of turning incalculable quantities of corn into an intoxicating drink? (3) Paul's advice to Timothy concerning wine can no more be transferred to every other person than can his advice to him to beware of Alexander the coppersmith. The advice was given to a total abstainer in ill-health, and had respect to a medicinal use of wine; but it is appropriated by those who are not abstainers, who are not ill, who apply it to a dietetic and habitual use of intoxicating drink, and who are utterly ignorant what was the cause or nature of Timothy's ailment, and equally as ignorant of the kind of wine the most fitted for his cure. We may search long and in vain for a more extraordinary abuse of Scripture than is exhibited by this violent wresting of St. Paul's kindly counsel.

5. Sanction is claimed for the use of intoxicating drinks, *because neither Christ nor the Apostle forbade that use, but*

tacitly permitted it. Bishops and others, we are reminded, were warned, not against "all" wine, but against "much" wine. The true meaning of Apostolic testimony on this subject will shortly be examined. On the objection as above stated, it may be remarked that a similar sanction may be claimed for many things which the Christian world has agreed to reject. Neither Christ nor his apostles forbade polygamy,* or gladiatorial shows, or domestic slavery, or Roman suppression of Jewish independence, or an absolute form of government; yet are these things sanctioned in the Scriptures? It was not the intention of Christianity to weave a network of regulations applicable to all possible circumstances, but to breathe into men's hearts a spirit which would, if cherished, lead at length to a correction of all abuses. The early Church was far from perfect in knowledge or practice; and the apostles themselves were too sincerely conscious of imperfection to set up their own lives for imitation, except so far as they imitated the Lord in the spirit of his life. The design of God was the progressive holiness of the Church, and its increasing conformity to his laws, physical and spiritual. The plea that because this thing and the other were permitted, therefore were sanctioned once, and therefore are sanctioned for ever, is an attempt to nullify and reverse the intentions of Providence. All light is light, but not always equally luminous; all goodness is goodness, but not equally free from alloy. The spirit of love in the ancient Church set its brand on the cruelty associated with slavery; and now (with the fuller knowledge of the evils inherent in slavery as such) it sets its brand upon slavery itself. It would be useless to ask why ancient Christianity did not expressly condemn

* A "bishop" was to be "the husband of one wife"; hence it has been argued "other Christians were permitted to have more than one," a mode of reasoning worthy of that which is brought against total abstinence principles.

slavery; it would be worse than useless to allege that therefore modern Christianity ought not to have condemned it. Christianity does not change, but its seminal principles branch forth and bear richer fruit as time goes on. The acorn is not an oak, but the oak springs from the acorn. The apostles, while their positive religious teaching was "with the Holy Ghost and with power," exhorted the whole body of Church members to cherish those spiritual gifts which would more and more open up fields of knowledge and pastures of truth, and ways of righteousness, in which their Divine Leader would guide them, "for his name's sake." We have yet to enquire what the apostles did teach respecting intoxicating drinks; but it is universally admitted that they warned men against the dangers of their use, and condemned intemperance in all its forms. The evil, *as they apprehended it,* they denounced—how much of the evil this was we shall proceed to consider; but, acting in the spirit, and walking in the track of the sacred writers, we are not only authorized, but constrained to condemn whatever we may discern, by means of our increased experience and scientific researches, to be also evil. Unless the apostles are supposed to have had an infallible and universal knowledge of all truth upon all questions—and we know that this knowledge they did not possess, even as to all questions of religion (for example, the period of the Lord's second coming and the final judgment), we may claim, without presumption, to possess upon many questions of physical science, social economy, and political jurisprudence a knowledge greater than theirs, and therefore the right and duty of applying to these subjects those principles of Christian judgment which it was their glory to proclaim. In so doing we do not disparage their work; on the contrary, we render it the loftier homage when we apply to the circumstances of our times the unchangeable canons of Christian righteousness. We deny, then, most emphatically, that the apostles ever extended a sanction to alcoholic drinks; but what they did—as in the case of slavery—was to enunciate a rule of action, and to inculcate a spirit of judgment, carrying with them, in embryo, all that was needful to lead, in the one instance, to the overthrow of the institution and instruments of slavery, and, in the other instance, to the avoidance of all the causes of intemperance, whether residing in the nature of strong drink, or in the drinking usages and traffic of our age.

II.—The Sacred Scriptures give support and encouragement to the practice of Total Abstinence.

1. *They show the consistency of total abstinence with the highest health and vigor.* The sojourn of the Israelites for forty years in the wilderness without wine or strong drink (Deut. xxix. 6); the abstinence rule of the Nazarites, with the picture drawn of their physical vigor (Lam. iv. 7); the prescription of total abstinence to Samson, and, before parturition, to his mother (Judges xiii. 4, 5, 7); the great age attained by men who, like Samuel, were Nazarites from birth (1 Sam. i. 11–25); the physical benefits enjoyed by the Rechabites for three centuries, down to the time of Jeremiah (Jer. xxxv. 7–10); the refusal of Daniel and his friends to take the king's wine, and the results (Dan. i. 11–16): these are so many Old Testament proofs of the greatest strength and longevity without the use of any inebriating drinks. The case of Samson alone is a crucial one; for no one can suppose that, if alcohol had been conducive, in a peculiar manner, to the development of strength, it would have been denied to him. The striking extension of this inhibition to his mother while she bore him in her womb, was also in accordance with all that science has disclosed as to the influence of the mother's diet upon her unborn offspring. The language of the chorus in Milton's *Samson Agonistes*

gives eloquent expression to this temperance testimony:

> "Oh! madness to think use of strongest wine,
> And strongest drinks, our chief support of health,
> When God, with these forbidden, made choice to rear
> His mighty champion strong above compare,
> Whose drink was only from the liquid brook."

That men need a daily portion of intoxicating liquor for daily sustenance, or to preserve them in good health, or to give them long life, is a doctrine contradicted and refuted by the historical parts of the Bible; and when the prophet brings before the people the man of iron sinew, the smith who "worketh in the coals, and fashioneth it with hammers, and worketh it with the strength of his arms," he does not exhibit him as flagging for want of exciting drinks; "yea, he is hungry, and his strength faileth; *he drinketh no water, and is faint.*" * Bread and water, and a few figs and raisins, revived the fainting Egyptian after three days' want of food and drink; † and all through the Biblical record there runs the sound physiological assumption, that nutritious food, with water as a diluent, is alone essential to robustness of health and length of days. When God would threaten Judah with the severest temporal loss, it is "the whole stay of bread, and the whole stay of water," that he determines to take away. ‡

2. *The Scriptures illustrate the pernicious influence of intoxicating drinks upon persons of the highest rank and the greatest advantages of intellectual and moral training.* The modern notion that only ignorant and low-born people are likely to be overcome by wine, is opposed to the whole tenor of the sacred narrative. The men who are described as betrayed by strong drink are the holy Noah, the obedient Lot, the rich sheep-master Nabal, the royal Elah, Benhadad, and Belshazzar; and when the ravages of in-

* Isaiah xliv. 12. † 1 Sam. xxx. 11, 12. ‡ Isaiah iii. 1.

temperance are portrayed in general but appalling terms, it is not said that the classes thus scourged were the ill-educated and the down-trodden, but it is the "priest and the prophet" who stray and stumble;* the luxurious inhabitants of Ephraim who are abandoned to dissipation;† the princes who are sick with wine, and the king who stretches out his hand with scorners;‡ the rich and powerful oppressors, who turn their temples into wine-shops;§ the wealthy sensualist, who debauches his neighbors.‖ And when the Saviour and his apostles would warn against the perils and evils of strong drink, they do not assume that only the ignorant and the worldly are exposed to those perils, but they press these warnings upon the most faithful and pious. "Take heed to yourselves," said Jesus, in warning his followers against "surfeiting and drunkenness;"¶ and it is to believers that the exhortations are addressed, "Be not drunk with wine, wherein is excess" (*asotia*—mental and moral ruin).** "Be sober, be vigilant; because your adversary the devil, as a roaring lion, walketh about, seeking whom he may devour" (*katapiee*—drink down).†† The general fact is that the richest, wisest, and best have fallen, and the general inference is that none can guard too vigilantly against the influence of this betrayer of men. The Scriptures, therefore, do not at all sanction a current opinion that "education," or even moral and religious influences, will secure society against the evils of strong drink, unless the education and moral influence are directed specifically against the formation of the drinking appetite and the exclusion of its causes.

3. *The Scriptures clearly point out that the cause of intemperance and all its mischief lies in the intoxicating and corrupting nature of strong drink.* Alcohol, as such, was not

* Isaiah xxviii. 7, 8. † Isaiah xxviii. 1, 3. ‡ Hosea viii. 5. § Amos ii. 8. ‖ Hab. ii. 15, 17. ¶ Luke xxi. 3, 4. ** Eph v. 18. †† 1 Pet. v. 8.

known to the sacred writers, but they knew that *yayin* and *shakar* when fermented were no longer innocent as before; and instead of the modern epithet of "good creature" bestowed on alcoholic drinks, they used the most powerful terms they could employ to describe the evil character of that property in wine and strong drink by which they seduced and demoralized mankind.

(1.) In Proverbs xxiii. 31, the *phenomena of fermentation are described*, and in verse 32 the result is declared—"At the last it (such wine) biteth like a serpent, and stingeth like an adder." Such wine is possessed of the serpent's nature, and instils the serpent's poison.

(2.) *In referring to strong drink there is a remarkable use of "khamah,"* a word translated in the English version "poison," "anger," "fury," "heat"; but the sense of which is lost in two important passages, where the colorless rendering "bottle" is given to it. In Hosea vii. 5, "the princes have made him sick with bottles of wine," should be, by consent of all critics, "the princes have made him sick with poison (or inflaming heat) of wine." And in Habakkuk ii. 15, "that puttest thy bottle to him," should be, "that puttest thy poison (or inflaming drink) to him." The same word occurs in Deut. 32, 33, "Their wine is the poison (*khamath*) of dragons": a text which throws light on Prov. xxiii. 32, where the red bubbling wine is compared to the serpent.

(3.) *The nature of wine and strong drink is displayed by use of epithets with a moral sense.* Prov. xx. 1, "Wine is a mocker, strong drink is raging." So Habakkuk ii. 5, "he transgresseth by wine"—or rather, "the wine is defrauding"—is a defrauder or deceiver. The Vulgate renders it, "wine deceives the drinker." Other translators give, "wine is treacherous." So Doddridge and others consider that in Eph. v. 7, the apostle ascribes "excess" (dissoluteness) not to being drunk with wine, but to wine itself—"in which (wine) is *asotia*." The epithets used by Solomon and Habakkuk are, of course, metaphors, but they would be senseless if they did not indicate the specific character of the object to which they relate. An attempt to evade the only reasonable conclusion—that the article so described is not a good, but baneful thing—is sometimes made by the plea that what is said of "wine" is said of its excessive use; but the excessive use is not "red," and does not "give its eye (bubble) in the cup"; and if such terms as "mocker," "raging," "deceiver," do not mark some causative quality in the substance spoken of, metaphorical language is a delusion. Wine cannot literally be a "mocker" (scorner); but if this epithet is not assigned it on account of its peculiar power of turning men into "mockers," or scorners, for what reason is it assigned? To say that "the effects are meant," is to say nothing, for does not the nature of the effects indicate the nature of the cause? Can a good tree bring forth corrupt fruit? The attempt to find an analogy to such metaphors by alleging that money is called "the root of all evil," and the tongue "a world of iniquity," and "full of deadly poison," is of no avail. Not money, but love of money (one word in the Greek—*philarguria*) is spoken of; and what is said of the "tongue" is plainly meant of the evil disposition which moves the tongue to evil utterances, as wine moves those who consume it to evil in thought, word, and deed. Thus we find that Scripture sustains the temperance doctrine that the evil arising from drinking is to be referred to a perverting quality and tendency in the drink used, and that, therefore, to blame the effects while cherishing the cause is not to act conformably with enlightened religion. Hence we are prepared to find that—

(4.) *Intoxicating drink is employed as a symbol of evil and of divine wrath.* The evil operates within, the wrath from without; but they resemble one another in their disastrous effects, and this resemblance finds fit symbolic expression in the inebriating potion. That Moses had this likeness in view (in Deut. xxxii. 32, 33) is probable; but its recognition is indisputable in such phrases as, "the wine of astonishment;"* "In the hand of the Lord there is a cup, and the wine is red; it is full of mixture," etc.;† "The cup of his fury—the cup of trembling;"‡ "The wine-cup of this fury;" § "Babylon is a golden cup: the nations have drunken of her wine; therefore the nations are mad;" ‖ "The cup also shall pass through unto thee [Edom];" ¶ "I give her cup into thine hand;" ** "The cup of the Lord's right hand shall be turned unto thee;" †† "I will make Jerusalem a cup of trembling." ‡‡ The same imagery recurs in the Book of Revelation, where the spiritual Babylon is said to have "made all nations drink of the wine of the wrath of her fornication;" §§ and the awful image is renewed "of the wine of the wrath of God, which is poured out without mixture into the cup of his indignation" ‖‖ ["poured out without mixture," really, is "mingled, unmingled"—mingled with drugs, unmingled with water], and "the cup of the wine of the fierceness of his wrath." It may be alleged that the "wine," thus used, as symbolical of so much profligacy and punitive fury, was wine made artificially stronger by drugs of maddening strength; and that this complex idea was in some cases in the prophets' mind may be admitted; yet it is not necessary to the force of a majority of the passages, and when included, is only an adjunct to raise the lurid glow of the prophetic symbol. The radical idea is *that the wine is intoxicating*—that the cup is full of intoxicating wine, mixed or unmixed—and that the drinking of this intoxicating draught is attended with terrible evils. Here, beyond question, the liquor is inebriating, yet it is not the symbol of good, but of evil,

* Ps. lx. 3. † Ps. lxxv. 8. ‡ Is. li. 17, 22. § Jer. xxv. 15. ‖ Jer. li. 7
¶ Lam. iv. 21. ** Ezek. xxiii. 31–34. †† Hab. ii. 16.
‡‡ Zech. xii. 2. §§ Rev. xiv. 8, xvii. 1, 2, xviii. 3. ‖‖ Rev. xiv. 10

not of joy, but of woe; and if the intoxicating element is employed to depict such intense depravity and suffering, how can we suppose that it is recognized in Scripture with favor and approval? *

4. *The Scriptures distinctly advise separation from intoxicating drink as a means of protection from its insidious and dangerous effects.*

There can be no doubt that the Nazarites were a body "separated," as the word implies, to exhibit in bold relief a purity of life superior to that of the people at large. Certain signs of this separation were enjoined, and it is not questioned by impartial commentators that the interdiction of intoxicating liquors was adopted to guard them against the moral perils to which, by using them, they would have been exposed. Is such a precaution needless now, when the liquors in common use are much more potent, and the drinking customs much more prevalent, than in those ancient times? How vitally this abstinence was associated with Nazaritism may be gathered from the divine displeasure against seducers, "And I raised up of your sons for prophets, and of your young men for Nazarites. Is it not even thus, O ye children of Israel? saith the Lord. But ye gave the Nazarites wine to drink; and commanded the prophets, saying, Prophesy not."† The Nazarite system prevailed down to New Testament times, and it was a tradition in the early Church that some of the apostles were attached to that venerable institution.

Again, in Leviticus x. 8–11, there is a remarkable prohibition made general and unchangeable in regard to the priests when they ministered before the Lord. On such

* It may also be added that "ferment" or "leaven" was treated by the sacred writers as a sample and symbol of corruption. So Christ speaks of "the leaven of the Pharisees," and St. Paul bids the Corinthians "purge out the old leaven." But without leaven where would be intoxicating drink?

† Amos ii. 11, 12.

occasions they were not to take wine nor strong drink, lest they died. Expositors usually connect this law with the preceding event described—the offering of strange fire by the sons of Aaron, Nadab, and Abihu. But whatever the origin of the interdict, its stringency and solemnity cannot be mistaken, nor can the precautionary object of the Divine Lawgiver be overlooked: "And that ye may put difference between holy and unholy, and between unclean and clean; and that ye may teach the children of Israel all the statutes which the Lord hath spoken unto them by the hand of Moses." Clearness of discernment, and fidelity in the discharge of duty, were the reasons for this command; and when it is pointed out that the command was only binding during the period of ministration, we are constrained to ask whether the possession of a power to see and act aright is not praiseworthy at all times; and whether the security of abstinence (a security enjoined under awful sanctions for a special purpose) may not and should not be embraced perpetually by those who are described as a "holy priesthood" appointed "to offer up spiritual sacrifices acceptable to God by Jesus Christ"? For when, it may be asked, is the Christian desirous of ceasing to be engaged in this sacrificial work? How, indeed, can it be intermitted, when his whole body is to be "a living sacrifice, holy, acceptable unto God"? The principle embedded in this Levitical precept is as applicable to us as to the Aaronic priests; and we shall be but placing ourselves under a divine guard when we follow, in all our way of life, the rule to which they were called upon to render periodical obedience. Again, the command of the wise man, "Look not thou upon the wine when it is red,"* coupled as it is with a description of the liquor named, is not to be toned down into a caution against overindulgence, without setting

* Prov xxiii. 31.

criticism and common usage at defiance. "Look not upon" may not mean "Do not cast your eye upon," but it unquestionably means, "Do not gaze at so as to desire the object looked upon"—an injunction which cuts away by the root the opinion that intoxicating drink is good, and therefore is to be desired and consumed. Again, the admonition addressed to Lemuel, "It is not for kings, O Lemuel, it is not for kings to drink wine, nor for princes strong drink,"* remains a standing rule for all kings and princes; and when the reason is assigned, "Lest they drink and forget the law, and pervert the judgment of any of the afflicted,"† it is manifest that such a reason renders the rule applicable, not to princes and monarchs only, but likewise to all who are engaged in any business which concerns the happiness and interests of their fellow-creatures. The import of the injunction is, "Do not imperil your capacity of benefiting those who depend upon your sobriety of judgment and feeling; and, to ensure that sobriety, hold aloof from the liquors by which it might be subverted or impaired." The following verses (Prov. xxxi. 6, 7), "Give strong drink unto him that is ready to perish, and wine unto those that be of heavy hearts. Let him drink, and forget his poverty, and remember his misery no more," must be taken in subordination to the preceding injunction. To read them as a warrant to "drive dull care away" by the help of alcohol would be to put Anacreon into the Bible, and to turn the Proverbs into a primer of inebriation. What is intended is not to recommend wine and strong drink as antidotes to grief and pain—a proposal at which poverty revolts, and which the Redeemer rejected on the Cross‡—but to point out that the only use to which such things could be put (were such use lawful) is to dull the mind, and to

* Prov. xxxi. 4. † Prov. xxxi. 5.

‡ Matt. xxvii. 34, compared with Mark xv. 23.

blunt the sensibilities, and to drown the memory of past and present sorrows. Where mental activity and self-possession are required, the exhortation is, "Drink not," *lest* you should—not because you certainly will—be less fitted to discharge the duties and responsibilities of your station. An important question now arises, Is there, in the New Testament, anything answering to the foregoing declarations? It must be remembered that the Old Testament retained its sacred authority in the Christian Church on all questions of morality and spiritual truth, and it was one of the points most carefully insisted upon by the apostles that the law of liberty in Christ did not free believers from the law of obedience to that divine law which is always "just and good," and in the observance of which there is a daily and everlasting reward. From the peculiarity of their circumstances as builders of the Christian society, it was not to be expected that the apostles would decide on questions of civil polity, diet, and the like. We know they did not; and it was according to the divine wisdom that they laid down broad principles of moral right and duty, the application of which was to be carried on and out under the enlightening and quickening influence of the Holy Spirit. We find, then, that the apostles did not contradict or in any way contravene the judgment passed upon intoxicating drink by the fathers who wrote as they were moved by the Holy Ghost. But

(1.) *They enforced the virtue of temperance* (*enkrateia*)—the restraint of the appetites and passions—restraint not only as to the degree, but also as to the direction of the desires.*

(2.) *They enforced the virtue of mental soundness* (*sophronismos*)—that calm and judicial state of the faculties, of

* As before remarked (p. 112), St. Paul speaks with warm commendation of the temperance of the Grecian athletes, one feature of which consisted in the exclusion of strong drink.

which, as we have seen, abstinence from intoxicating drink is the appointed guardian.

(3.) *They enforced the virtue of sobriety*—freedom from unnatural excitement; and they selected for this purpose a word (*neepho*), the acknowledged meaning of which, at that time, was total abstinence from wine, or such a sober state of body and mind as is consequent on this abstinence.* This is the very word used in Greek to express the abstinence enjoined upon the priests during their ministrations; and, whether the apostles intended to convey the full sense of the term or not, its very selection intimated their conviction that the sobriety which was based on total abstinence was that which they could most cordially approve. To break the force of this conclusion, attention is often drawn to the passages in which bishops are enjoined "not to be given to wine," and deacons and elder women "not to be given to much wine"; hence it is inferred that some wine was permitted. But (1) cautions against excess can never be held to express approval of the acts referred to. "Let not the sun go down upon your wrath" is not an approval of wrath while the sun is above the horizon. (2.) A general condemnation of all that was comprised under the name of wines (Greek *oinoi*, Latin *vina*), would have included some drinks perfectly harmless. (3.) Bishops were to be "not given to wine" (literally, "not near to wine"), and both these and deacons' wives were enjoined to be "abstinent" (*neephalious*),† a command not to be obeyed by any indulgence in wines capable of exciting the animal nature and deadening the mental and spiritual powers. It may, in conclusion, be affirmed that the New Testament does not contradict, but coincides with, the letter of the Old, while the *ideal* of religious perfection it holds

* See "Temperance Biblical Commentary," pp. 361–5.

† 1 Tim. iii. 2, "vigilant" in English Version, but in the same version, iii. 11, "sober."

up to imitation calls for the exercise of the greatest self-restraint in leading to separation from articles whose influence for evil, on the bodies and minds of men, has been universally lamented. The "moderation" alluded to in Phil. iv. 5 is not moderation in wine-drinking or any kind of drinking, but moderation of mind in the midst of injustice and sufferings from without.

5. *The Scriptures lay down general principles of action, which, without any straining, cover the whole ground of total abstinence practice.*

To "love his neighbor"; to care for the stranger; to build his house with a battlemented roof; to hold the owner of an ox known to push with his horns answerable for any harm the ox might do; to guard against coming or contingent evil; to break down occasions of sinful transgression; to take stumbling-stones out of the way—all these are principles of action prominently adduced and illustrated in the Old Testament: and in the New there is not less earnestly impressed upon all the duty of sacrificing sensuous pleasure (even if a real good, as an eye or right hand) rather than incur spiritual loss; the duty of so acting that others shall not be led into temptation or into conduct by which their own consciences may be defiled; the duty of sacrificing our own pleasure for others' good; the duty of subordinating our present and physical interests to the development of the inner and higher life; the duty of doing all things to the glory of God; the duty of not neglecting any known means of good—all these lines of duty are written with heavenly brilliance in the New Testament scriptures, and ought to be imprinted with equal brightness on the Christian's heart and life.

But how can this be done without a cordial exemplification of the practice of total abstinence?

How are the intemperate to be cured if they do not cast away that which ensnares them?

How can the causes of so much temptation, seduction, and stumbling be removed while drinking customs are sanctioned by the influential and the pious?

How can men effectually guard themselves against danger while they invite it by habitually using the intoxicating cup?

How can the intemperate be assisted to reform, and the young to grow up in habits of abstinence, if the sober and elder portions of society content themselves with advice which their own example does not, to say the least, comport with and confirm?

How can Christian spirituality be realized in its utmost beauty and excellence while the wine which mocks and deceives is consumed day by day? How can Christian self-denial fulfil "what remains of the sufferings of Christ" when it is incompetent to the resignation of "moderate" doses of intoxicating drink? How can Christian benevolence bind up bleeding hearts, and staunch the chief sources of human wretchedness and vice, when the brewery and distillery and drink-shop are afflicting society with every species of vice, every degree of misery, every depth of degradation? How can the believer be blameless concerning the neglect of opportunities of usefulness, while he leaves untried the means of doing good provided in the personal and associated influences of the temperance reform? Whatever in Christianity is pure and purifying, sweet and saving, luminous and light-giving, self-protecting and self-sacrificing, brotherly and beneficent, God-honoring and Christ-imitating, finds in the practice of total abstinence either a congenial assistant or an appropriate instrument for attaining the supreme object of all Christian prayer and endeavor, that God's will "may be done upon earth even as it is done in heaven."

OBJECTIONS.

Many objections have been disposed of in the course of this discussion, but there are several which may be separately reviewed before this chapter concludes.

1. It is said "*that by using wine in the ordinance of the Lord's Supper, the Saviour gave it a special honor inconsistent with the character ascribed to it by the advocates of total abstinence.*" Several points of consequence are overlooked by persons who raise this objection :

(1.) *That the word "wine" does not once occur in the New Testament in reference to the institution and celebration of the Lord's Supper.* The phrase used by the Saviour is "the fruit of the vine," and the apostle Paul simply speaks of "the cup." Those, therefore, who assume, contrary to evidence, that the Greek word *oinos* always meant the intoxicating juice of the grape, gain nothing by the assumption, unless they also show that "the fruit of the vine" is also of necessity an inebriating fluid. Who, however, can pretend to advocate a proposition so utterly ridiculous? Who does not know that the "fruit of the vine," as it exists in its natural state, is not and never can be of an intoxicating quality; and that, when the expressed juice becomes so by passing through the fermenting process, it *so far* ceases to be the fruit of the vine and vital growth, and becomes the fruit of the vat? The wine of commerce can only claim to be considered the fruit of the vine to the extent that it is physically identical with the substance which the vine produces, and this identity can never be so complete as when the expressed juice of the grape is preserved and presented, in the sacramental service, chemically the same as it exists within the uncrushed cluster. Besides, it is notorious that, beyond the change in the grape-juice effected by fermentation, the adulterations of various liquors are so ingenious that the ablest connoisseurs cannot tell fabricated from genuine wines; and are so extensive that very few who purchase even the high-priced sorts can have any real guarantee of their genuine character; hence it is evident (1) that the unfermented juice of the grape is more really the "fruit of the vine" than any fermented wine, however genuine; and (2) that the assurance of using the "fruit of the vine" at all must be exceedingly slender in the great majority of cases where the wines of commerce enter into the sacramental service. It is also forgotten—

(2.) *That as all ferment and fermented things were forbidden to the Jews at the Passover,* when the Lord's Supper was instituted, it is more in accordance with the symbolical meaning of that prohibition (one which the apostle applies to Christians—1 Cor. v. 6–8) to take the unfermented than the fermented juice of the grape. We need not enter into the controversy whether the Jews celebrated their Passover with fermented or unfermented wine: if with the former, they must have broken their law; and whenever they do so now, they break their law; and those who assume that the Lord used such wine must also assume that he broke the law he came to fulfil (as a Jew) to the letter.* Modern science has demonstrated (what careful observation must always have shown) that the fermentation of grape-juice is similar to the fermentation of bread or beer; and, therefore, that whatever spiritual symbolism is conveyed by the absence of fermentation must be expressed more clearly by unfermented than by fermented wine. If it is argued that consistency would require the bread used to be unleav-

* The casuistry by which the modern Jews (who used fermented wine) and their Christian apologists defend this breach of the Levitical law is a striking illustration of the leaven of sophistry which characterized the teaching of the Scribes and Pharisees. Its inconsistency is not less marked, for, while some say that fermented solids only were meant, others assert that the fermentation of grape-juice is not like the fermentation of beer, and some that the grape-juice does not ferment at all!

ened, it may be answereed that partial inconsistency is better than total; and, further, that if the old symbolic meaning should be still conveyed at all, it may most properly be observed by rejecting the fermented substance (wine) which retains the products of the fermenting process (alcohol and carbonic acid), rather than the substance (bread) which has cast off those products while subjected to the heat of the oven. The objector likewise forgets—

(3.) *That as the Lord's Supper is designed to bring before the communicant the redeeming work of Christ as typified by his broken body and shed blood, there ought to be as close an analogy as is possible between the physical elements and the spiritual facts.* The Redeemer himself was "pure, undefiled, and separate from sinners," and his work was like himself, and designed to conform us to his glorious image. Bread is a fitting representative of what is life-giving, for it is the staff of bodily life (and leavened bread does not lose this essential representativeness); but alcoholic wine is in reality wine mixed with an element hostile to health, life, virtue, and Christian excellence—it is wine which by fermentation has become a "mocker" and "defrauder"; and, as soon as this fact is understood, the symbol loses its symbolic beauty and fitness, and the communicant is compelled to think of what the physical element ought to be, and not what it really is. But what need is there for this incongruity to subsist, when "the pure blood of the grape" can be procured, and a true correspondence between the visible substance and invisible reality can be established? The silly charge that total abstainers reject wine and prefer water in the eucharist is one of the idle tales by which ignorance or malice is accustomed to defame a principle unassailable by reason. The head and front of all the offending is that many of the friends of temperance desire to use, and to see used, in the celebration of the

Lord's Supper, an article which is unquestionably "the fruit of the vine," rather than a liquor that is, at best, the fruit of the vine partially perverted, and that may not contain a single drop of the juice of the grape. The reader must judge for himself whether this preference is contrary to the example and will of the Redeemer in the institution of the Holy Supper. *

2. It is said "*that if total abstinence had been a practice universally right and needful, Scripture teaching would have been so plain as to have admitted of no doubt upon the question.*" It might be enough to reply that if the use of intoxicating drink were right and desirable, Scripture (on the objector's principle) would have given a declaration to that effect impossible to have been mistaken. The objection proceeds on the assumption that God will place our duty before us in a form to render misconception *impossible;* but this assumption is contradicted by all experience. In another form this objection is directed against Christianity, the evidences for which it would require to have been made impossible of denial; and it is in replying to this objection that Bishop Butler remarks: "The unsatisfactory nature of the evidence with which we are obliged to take up, in the daily course of life, is scarce to be expressed. Yet men do not throw away life, or disregard the interest of it, upon account of this doubtfulness. The evidence of religion, then, being admitted real, those who object to it as not satisfactory, that is, as not being what they wish it, plainly forget the very condition of our being; for satisfaction, in this sense, does not belong

* It will be observed that the objector is met on his own ground, though it might be retorted fairly on him that as the temperance reform aims to remove the evils of strong drink, taken as a beverage, the occasional use of wine in the Lord's Supper has never been made a bar to temperance association. An earnest desire is, however, prevalent that what is discarded as dangerous from the domestic board should not be retained at the table of the Lord.

to such a creature as man." * What we do know is that God has been pleased in the Scriptures to supply such intimations upon this subject, by narrative, by description, by proverb, and by general principles, as are amply sufficient to guide men to a correct opinion and a wise decision; and it is exceedingly doubtful, had he done otherwise, and had still more precise directions been afforded, whether the world would have been more convinced and more obedient. Do we not see now that the nearest approach to a positive injunction, "Look not upon the wine," etc., is qualified and attenuated by persons professing profound reverence for the Divine Word, but who are unwilling to cast away the wine "when it is red, and when it gives its bubble in the cup"? And, further, may not the same objection be brought against every form of Christian belief, that if God had willed men to adopt it, he would have revealed it so plainly that none could have failed to discern it? Each church replies: "There was good reason, doubtless, for not doing what is thus demanded, and what is revealed is sufficient for the purpose"—and with this reply, the objector against the total abstinence principle must be content, unless he is prepared to maintain that all who differ from him, even upon religious questions, are hypocrites or fools.

3. It may be said "*that had total abstinence been in accordance with Scripture, it is extremely improbable that this accordance would have been overlooked by so overwhelming a majority of good and devout persons from the earliest times.*" But, strange as this may seem, it is not stranger than the indisputable fact, that both the text and sense of many passages of Scripture have been misunderstood by the multitude of believers. How few doubted, until modern times, that Scripture sanctioned slavery and the government of the many by the few, not to speak of numerous

* Analogy, part ii. c. 8.

physical theories which were supposed to rest upon the plainest sense of various Scripture texts! How few are the distinctive principles of any Christian denomination which have not been overlooked or rejected, often for long periods, by the majority of Christians! To argue that God, if he foresaw that there would arise so much error and sin from the misunderstanding of Scripture on the drink question, would have interfered to prevent it, is to say what the objector does not believe in regard to other matters of equal or greater importance. Did not God foresee what different interpretations would be placed upon the text, "Thou art Peter"—yet did he interpose to prevent the variance and the error, with its consequences, which have been tremendous, on whichever side the error lies? Truth may not always dwell with minorities; but the conviction which every reader must have, that on some questions—and those of great religious moment—majorities have been, for ages, egregiously in the wrong, ought to expose the fallacy of the objection which is brought against total abstinence, because so many men of learning and excellence had failed to perceive the testimony for it contained in the Sacred Scriptures.

4. It is said, "*that we are warned in the Bible against doctrines of abstinence and asceticism, and the rejection of things which God has commanded to be received with thanksgiving.*" Doubtless, there is an ascetic doctrine and practice condemned in Scripture, but between this and the total abstinence principle there is no harmony, but a radical repugnance. The asceticism which taught that matter was intrinsically evil, and, therefore, that the soul could only become perfect, and would become perfect, by self-mortifications and "bodily exercises," has nothing in common with the temperance teaching, that intoxicating drink is to be rejected because it is physically useless and injurious, inimical to the highest development of bodily

health and vigor, and, by *diminishing* corporeal tone and energy, is antagonistic to the intellectual and moral life of man. Asceticism sought to enfeeble and degrade the body: total abstinence seeks to invigorate and dignify the body; so utterly unsubstantial is the objection against the latter from its supposed connection with the former. Total abstinence teaches no other asceticism than that mortification of "fleshly *lusts*," which Scripture solemnly inculcates, and that control of the animal nature which the exclusion of alcoholic drinks renders easier and more complete. Christianity has its own asceticism, without which, as Dean Howson has forcibly pointed out, it has never been "really efficient"; * and it is with this asceticism, and not with the heathen or superstitious burlesque of it, that total abstinence has an honorable and noble alliance, teaching all men to avoid the physical agent of danger and seduction, which extends its narcotic and paralyzing influence over both the corporeal and moral powers.

5. It is said "*that the total abstinence principle of avoiding strong drink because of the danger incident to its use is a confession of weakness, and an avoidance of resistance to evil not compatible with Christian courage, and not indicative of reliance upon the grace of God.*" This objection is one urged by some eminent Christian teachers, and in a temper the reverse of amiable and courteous. It is based on the gross misconception that total abstinence is advocated because strong drink, like other objects of sense, may be abused, and may thus become a spiritual snare. If these brethren, instead of constructing this whimsy out of their own imagination, and then calling it by ugly names, had taken the pains to understand the true ground of the temperance objection to alcohol, they would have seen that their method of reply is as much mis-

* Lectures on the Character of St. Paul, p. 131.

applied as was the action of Xerxes in casting fetters into the sea to curb its fury. What the total abstainer asserts, and what we have endeavored in this work to sustain, is that intoxicating drink is intrinsically different from other articles in dietetic use, because unadapted to man's real wants, and because calculated to do him physical injury, and, by creating an unnatural and terrible appetite, to plunge him into evil of every kind; this being so, the abstainer urges that no man has the right to expose himself or others to the danger which the use of such an article carries with it; and that, if he does use it, he is both exposing himself to needless temptation and tempting Providence to leave him to the folly of his ways. The primary question, then, is one of fact; and no Christian man admitting the fact could for an instant accuse the abstainer of either cowardice or a depreciation of divine grace. Nothing is more strongly enjoined in Scripture than the avoidance of needless temptation; and he who, under the pretence of honoring divine grace, subjects himself to such temptation, shows conclusively that the grace has not given him understanding or prudence. The Gospel teaches us to shun evil and danger when they have not to be met and confronted in the discharge of duty; and the grace which both discerns the danger and draws the Christian aside is incomparably more valuable than the rashness which tampers with temptation, and despises each warning against the evil that is braved. Better far is the humility that even overestimates the power of the enemy than "the pride which goeth before a fall."

6. It is said, "*that if total abstinence be in accordance with Scripture, the same cannot be said of the pledge, which binds the conscience, and which seems to imply a deficiency in that Christian obligation which vows of Christian baptism and membership involve.*" But "the pledge," whether regarded as a personal declaration or a bond of association, is

not open to this reproach. A pledge of total abstinence is an avowal of present conduct and a promise of future action; but there is nothing of bondage in this, and no diminution of individual independence. The pledge does not create any obligation; it merely expresses a sense of obligation already felt; and in what other shape could this sense of obligation show itself, except a statement of present fact and future intention? The real bondage would consist in being prevented making or taking such a pledge—the form of which is indifferent, but the substance of which is inseparable from sincerity and candor of mind. If I think abstinence advisable, shall I not practise it? and if I practise it, shall I not avow the practice? and, if I intend to continue the habit, so long as I believe it right, shall I not say I intend to continue it? So, instead of forfeiting independence and Christian liberty by such a pledge, it is by means of it that I assert and express my liberty and independence. That the pledge can have any "binding" force, as distinct from personal conviction, or after conviction has changed, is a notion which never entered into any but an objector's head. As to the supposed slight to baptismal vows, nothing can be more illusory. The temperance pledge is not a vow unless the individual pleases to make it so, as he may please to make any other resolution: and, by "taking the pledge," nothing more is done than to assert that abstinence is included under the general vows of baptism by which the soul entered into the service of goodness against evil—of God against Satan. It would be absurd to charge a man with disloyalty because he specified a certain act as one of allegiance, as to represent the pledge as impugning or overriding baptismal vows If (as the objector asserts), those vows comprehended all possible good, then, says the abstainer, all that I do in the pledge is to affirm that one of the forms of good I adopt and intend to pursue is the practice of abstinence from intoxicating drinks. Considered as a bond of union, all objection to the pledge must be given up, or take a sweeping range; for every benevolent and Christian association involves a pledge, expressed or understood, on the part of those who conduct and support it. Men cannot act together without an agreement, and in the temperance pledge the friends of total abstinence find the form of agreement suited to their principles and object. If the necessity for such distinct pledges is lamented, on the ground that all Christian men should feel committed as such to every good work, the complaint may be accepted as a reflection on Christian inconsistency, and not upon the nature of the pledge. Those Christians who have for the longest period acted upon the pledge of total abstinence are the least able to understand what is meant by the "yoke of bondage" with which some who stand outside are pleased to connect it. Not those who zealously embrace a good work and continue faithful to it are held under any yoke or burden, but rather those who are the victims of delusion on questions of greatest moral and social value, or who are wanting in the self-devotion and courage which would impel them to "do good and to communicate," remembering that "with such sacrifices God is well pleased."

CHAPTER VI.

PROPOSITION: THAT THE TRAFFIC IN ALCOHOLIC LIQUORS EXERTS A PERNICIOUS INFLUENCE CALLING FOR ITS LEGISLATIVE SUPPRESSION.

TRADE or traffic, being a social act, is, by general consent, subject to social control. This control has at times been exercised foolishly and injuriously; but never yet has the man appeared who, admitting that the social state is desirable, has held that the individual—the social unit—has the right to make his own individual inclination or opinion the rule of his social action. It is unanimously agreed that the freedom and even the good of the citizen must not be gratified so as to injure the commonwealth. As society guarantees each citizen the free use of his powers, and puts him into possession from his birth of many advantages of which he would have been otherwise destitute, it has a corresponding right to prevent him turning against society the powers it has protected and the advantages it has secured to him. Society may blindly or apathetically allow its right of self-defence and self-preservation to lie disused, in regard to one or another form of flagrant evil, just as the individual may neglect his own improvement and support; but if, in any important particular, society has thus been remiss, true patriotism will urge those who perceive the error to awaken society to a sense of the neglect, and to the use of such remedial measures as are required by the nature of the case. Long-continued insensibility or oversight may have permitted evils and abuses to become gigantic in dimension and terrible in their strength; but this result is a reason, not for inaction and despair, but for a more energetic endeavor to grapple with the difficulties of the situation. The slave-trade had developed into a great commercial interest, and had gained new vigor from the slave-systems it had implanted in our colonial possessions; but what it was, and threatened to become, was felt to be a spur to the philanthropic labors of the men who sought its suppression by the agency of law. In regard to another and different question, the police arrangements of the country, it was lamented by successive generations of statesmen, that the so-called police-system of our greatest towns was a national disgrace; and it is but of late years that we have endeavored to supply the lack of public service, injuriously prevalent for centuries, in this respect.

In relation to trades of every kind, it may be laid down, as a rule without exception, that they are tolerated and protected solely with a view to the good of society; and no small part of the modern legislation on which we justly pride ourselves has sought to put a stop to incidental and collateral evils arising out of industrial pursuits. Even where those evils do not affect society, or the locality generally, but only persons who are employed in the trades themselves, the law has beneficially interfered to check such forms and degrees of activity as tend to injure health and shorten life. The reason why such trades are not entirely suppressed, is because they are believed to yield an overwhelming balance of benefit, and because it is believed that the abuses complained of are removable without a suspension of the works carried on. The *Edinburgh Review* has put the varied relation of law to pernicious trade in so pertinent a shape, that its words well merit citation: "There are some trades to which the State applies, not restriction merely, but prohibition. Thus the business of coining money is utterly suppressed by the laws of all civilized States; thus the opening of lotteries is a commercial speculation forbidden by the law of England. If it be asked on what grounds the State is justified in annihilating these branches of industry, it must be answered, that society may put down what is dangerous to itself—*salus populi suprema lex*. Any trade, employment, or use of property detrimental to the life, health, or order of the people is, by English law, a public nuisance. And in suppressing it, the State assumes the right of sacrificing private interests to the public good. And this not only when the detriment is physical or economical, but also when it is moral. Thus, unwholesome graveyards are shut up, and noisome vitriol-works pulled down, for their physical noxiousness; private coining is made illegal for economical reasons; slave-trading, lotteries, cockpits, bear-gardens, gambling-houses, brothels, and obscene prints are prohibited on moral grounds."* It now remains that we see what reasons exist for the suppression of the liquor traffic, arising from its effects upon the social state.

1. *Its influence in the production of intemperance is a fact of the gravest significance.* The drinking-habit—whether it shows itself in a frequent use of small quantities of intoxicating liquor, or whether it assumes the form of chronic besotment or raging inebriation—is an evil the prevalence of which is a national calamity. Personal character is damaged, fitness for the duties of life is impaired, family resources are squandered, family education is neglected, and a decay, more or less rapid, of the physical, mental, and moral faculties—in a word, of the whole man—sets in, the arrest of which is always difficult and, at certain stages, utterly impossible. Drinking is both a disease and a vice, and, while cursing the victim in his individual, domestic, and citizen relations, it deprives society of much valuable service which, should he even

* *Edinburgh Review*, July, 1854.

be reclaimed, it never can recover. Obviously, therefore, any commercial system which operates directly and largely in the production of this evil subjects itself to the severest condemnation. DOES THE LIQUOR TRAFFIC DO THIS OR NOT? *To the affirmative answer there is not a dissenting voice.* All Parliamentary deliverances have asserted this in the strongest terms, and the Committee of Convocation's Report asserts what general observation and all available information has made clear: "It appears an unquestionable fact that, in proportion as facilities in any shape for procuring intoxicating liquors are countenanced and afforded, the vice of intemperance and its dismal effects are everywhere increased. That this would be the case has been continually maintained by members of the community desirous of the repression of intemperance, and extensively acquainted with its phases and its workings. This conclusion the evidence before your Committee amply confirms."* The licensed vendors have repeatedly admitted the truth of this position, and profess to found upon it their opposition to all measures for increasing competition and "opening the trade." That the increase of intemperance is related to the increase of drinking-shops is true; but it does not follow from this, as some imagine, that intemperance depends on a given number of liquor-shops, or that the degree of the evil can be estimated by the proportion of public-houses to population. The unit is the commencement of the mischief; for the keeper of one place has a direct interest in extending the sale of the articles by which the drink appetite is created and fostered, and he has no such direct or immediate interest in preventing the promotion of intemperate habits. A few curious instances are on record of conscientious drinksellers seeking to prevent drunkenness by refusing to sell more than a specified amount to a

* Committee's Report on Intemperance, p. 4, and Appendix C.

particular person; but this device could only operate to check drinking on the premises, and would cease to act the moment another licensed house was opened sufficiently near for the customer to resort to both. What may be termed *the permanent and ever-powerful tendencies of the liquor traffic in the promotion of drinking are these:* 1. The seductive character of the drinks sold; 2. The ready access to the liquors presented by their sale; 3. The encouragement of tippling by the accommodation offered; and 4. The social temptations to drinking, from the nature of the company drawn together. Add to all these the interest of the vendor in pushing the sale of his liquors; the extraneous allurements offered, prompted by greed of gain and the spirit of competition; and the special inducements arising out of very favorable positions and lavish decoration—and we have a concurrence of forces in the production of intemperance against which there is absolutely nothing to set, except the wish of the seller not to do harm, and his prudence in trying to keep his house "respectable" by excluding notoriously drunken and disorderly persons without unnecessary delay.* To such an absurd refinement has this view of the law been practically reduced, by magistrates as well as publicans, that a Lord Mayor and a Metropolitan M.P., when deciding a charge of disorderly conduct, remarked that "he knew many respectable publicans who, *as soon as men are*

* A writer in the *National Review* (No. 19), though hostile to total abstinence and the Alliance, observes (p. 134): "The publican has a strong personal interest adverse to the public interest. That which is mischievous to society is profitable to him. No other trade has the same power of making its own interest prevail over that of society. No other article is liable to be used to so great an excess; no other tradesman has equal power of inducing his customers to purchase to excess; no excess in any other article is half so dangerous to the common weal. The peculiarity of the retail trade in intoxicating drink is this, that it is in the hands of a large and influential class, with an interest strongly adverse to the interest of the country at large, and with tremendous opportunities of advancing their own interest at the cost of the country."

drunk, turn them out!" The extent to which the drink-shop acts as the great social factor of intemperance *is not to be tested by the number of apprehensions for drunk and disorderly drunken conduct,* though there are upwards of 100,000 yearly in England and Wales, besides upwards of 90,000 cases of assaults, most of them the effects of drinking; for it is admitted by the police authorities themselves, that to take up all cases of "mere drunkenness"—*i.e.* drunkenness short of incapacity to move along, or disorderly behavior—would overtax all their resources of men and station accommodation, while the mere reporting of public-houses and beer-shops where drunkenness is encouraged or permitted, contrary to the express terms of the license, would be to enter a bill of indictment against the mass of drinking-shops in every district. So inevitable is the association between the ordinary liquor-shop and the production of intemperance that as early as the time of James I. a legislative effort was made to suppress "tippling"—*i.e.,* stopping to drink upon the premises—and confining the traffic of inns and ale-houses to the supply of drink taken away for consumption by neighbors and furnishing travellers with food and lodging. Acting on the same impression—*that promiscuous sale of liquor for consumption on the premises must induce and foster intemperance*—not a few philanthropists of the present day propose to abolish that portion of the drink traffic, and thereby, as they imagine, put an end to drunkenness as a common vice. They forget that to enforce this separation would require a perpetual inspection of drinking-shops, without the possibility of preventing a vast amount of evasion; the necessary exception of "travellers" would form a constant sluice-gate for drinking upon the premises, and even the most rigid enforcement of the law would allow of revelling by persons from a distance, and would keep up that intercourse between the liquor-bar and the private houses of the neighborhood, by which domestic drinking and female social tippling would be sustained. There is, in short, no escape from the conclusion *that, the traffic in alcoholic liquors being what it intrinsically is, no amount of care in the vendor will make it harmless;* while, judging of human nature by its average qualities, it is ridiculous to expect that the sellers of intoxicating drink will subordinate and sacrifice their own pecuniary profits to the maintenance of sobriety in their districts. As a rule, with few exceptions, they will sell to all customers, without any delicate or serious concern as to the present habits of the buyers, or the probable effect of the liquor sold at any given time upon the sobriety of the drinkers and the general temperance of the vicinity. A perception of this fact is revealed by the desire of all social and moral reformers to attract men and women from the public-house, although the licensing of them proceeds on the supposition that no public-house is to be a means of intemperance and demoralization. Experience is more powerful than any legal fiction; and the best men of all classes have learnt that though Orpheus is said to have tamed wild beasts by his melodious music, there is no charm in legal regulations by which the drinking-house can be constituted a temple of temperance. *Police supervision is a lamentable failure,* and not unfrequently the policeman is himself the victim of the evil against which he is principally supposed to guard his neighbors. Police authorities confess that the most active agents in demoralizing their men are the liquor-shops, especially at nights, when their influence in the promotion of general intemperance is the greatest. A world of truth is condensed into the testimony of one witness: "If the policemen inform, magistrates do not convict. Every policeman we have had resident has frequented the public-house himself. The residence of a police-officer in a moral parish has proved more hurtful than beneficial." * The earnest resistance offered by the publican interest to the clauses of the Government Bill of 1872 appointing inspectors, was a sufficient indication of their knowledge of what their traffic is even visibly bringing forth within the public-house itself. It is matter of history that they were successful in this resistance, and the nation will have to suffer from the amount of evil that will thereby escape detection and punishment. The drinking-shops of the United Kingdom are not fewer than 130,000 (excluding unlicensed places, known as shebeens, hush-houses, and by other names); and if in regard to no single place the absence of direct temptations to intemperance can be safely affirmed, some numerical conjecture may be formed—though the mind is unable to apprehend the aggregate—of the intemperance which is bred and developed in all these licensed nurseries of the evil. For the diminution of this vice many thousands of good men are laboring, and numerous educational and temperance institutions are using efforts with marked and visible effects; but *no calculation can be more chimerical than any which is founded on the power of "education" to counteract or neutralize the agency of the drink-shop in the production of intemperance.* How is it credible that the education which is to act by drawing out the better nature, and which must act by slow degrees and in spite of numerous drawbacks and obstructions, should undo the educating work of the public-house in drawing out the more sensual propensities of man? When will the number of schools, mechanics' institutes, etc., equal that of the drinking-shops? When will the same amount of money be expended in their

* Committee of Convocation's Report on Intemperance—Appendix K.—By the New Licensing Act the supply of liquors to constables is visited by a penalty, for the first offence not exceeding £10, and for the second offence not exceeding £20. It is obvious, however, that where the publican and policemen are on the alert, the law may be long evaded with impunity.

furniture and decoration? How can they start fairly in their educational rivalry, when the animal nature is first developed and, in regard to millions, always the most powerfully? How can the education of the school and class-room hope to eradicate intemperance when, as Lord Brougham has said, "it is the common enemy—it attacks even persons of cultivated minds"? When and where has education shown its power to empty the liquor-shop? Yet, as we have seen, so long as the latter acts, it acts adversely to social sobriety. The Beer Bill in one year opened more *new* seminaries of drinking than there were educational establishments in the kingdom. "To rely upon popular improvement alone, and take no measures for removing the great cause of crimes [intemperance, and therefore the drink-shop, the great cause of that intemperance] would be to lull ourselves into as perilous a security as theirs who should trust to the effects of diet and regimen when the plague was raging; or in that confidence, before it broke out, which should take no precaution against its introduction." * The epithet "pest-house," as applied to the drink-shop, may appear to some unnecessarily strong; but if, as we have shown, the seed of the intemperate appetite is the alcoholic drink itself, and if the diffusion of that drink is the sole object for which the liquor-shop, as such, exists, and if the result is seen in the raging of a national "plague"—a name to which our national intemperance is entitled by general consent—the place where so dreadful an evil is systematically produced is a veritable "pest-house," and no legal regulations, or fumigatory process, can give to it a clean bill of health, or ensure society against the deadly contagion.

2. *The influence of the liquor traffic on social evils of the greatest magnitude calls for careful consideration.*

* Lord Brougham's Inaugural Address before the Social Science Congress at Bradford, 1859.

As the consumption of strong drink is stimulated, and drinking habits and appetites are formed, there will not only appear an alarming amount of intemperance; but associated with this, and in large part dependent upon it, and the personal dispositions thus fostered, social evils of the darkest hue become invariably aggravated and extended.

(1.) There is *poverty, deepening into destitution, and sinking into pauperism*—a many-sided evil both to the sufferers and to the state. How this is created and confirmed by public-house influence, and the grounds of the common estimate that three-fourths of the gross amount is due to strong drink, need not be elaborately set forth. A few persons who are in love with paradoxes deny the all but universal admission, and talk of poverty as the cause, and not the effect, of drinking. But the opposite is demonstrated by the testimony of all the authorities who have ever given witness before parliamentary committees and royal commissions, or who have placed their views upon permanent record: and the reasonableness of this judgment will appear when it is remembered that great multitudes spend on drink a proportion of their wages which is thus lost to all savings and investment purposes; that drinking leads to idleness, very commonly to one day's absence from work every week, and often to longer periods of "play"; that money is lost, and good openings missed, by the stupidity or recklessness brought on by drink; that fits of sickness, frequently prolonged, are occasioned by intemperance; that numerous accidents, unfitting for labor, are occasioned by drinking; that the abuse of earnings on drink causes much domestic sickness through want of food and timely medicine; and that the death of the husband or wife from this cause reduces the survivors at once to the paupers' roll. Nor must it be forgotten that many well-conducted sober persons are brought into a similar plight through the intemperance of others with whom they have had business relations, or to whom they have lent money, or for whom they have become legally responsible. If, as the result of these causes, all proceeding from one source, we can explain why we have two cases of general distress instead of one, and four cases of poor-law relief instead of one, we shall perceive why all means for the abatement of pauperism must fail to effect any striking reduction until intemperance and its chief fountain, the drinking-shop, are successfully assailed.

(2.) *There is crime of every degree and form,* from petty larceny to red-handed murder, which could not prevail as it does, did not strong drink and the drink-shop engender, nurse, train, stimulate, and develop it. It is not true, as some would represent, that poverty is the principal cause of the more serious crimes; and, if it were true, the poverty, as we have seen, finds its mainsprings in the bottle and the tap. Every act of Parliament passed for the regulation of the drink traffic has proceeded on the supposition of its crime-creating power; every writer of experience on crime traces the connection between it and intoxicating liquor; and judges, jailers, and chaplains have concurred in this, if in nothing else—in assigning to drinking, and temptations to drink, a predisposing and producing influence on crime the most intimate. From such a chain of testimony, at once authoritative and unbiassed, there can be no appeal; and the inference—that crime cannot be extensively rooted up while intemperance and drinking-shops abound—is simply one application of the axiom that the effect must continue till the cause is abolished. The testimonies of the most ancient judges, from Chief-Justice Hale to Chief-Justice Bovill, would constitute a valuable *catena*;*

* Lord Chief-Justice Hale says (1670): "The places of judicature which I have long held in this kingdom have given me opportunity to observe the original cause of most of the enormities that have been committed for the

and not a month has passed, in the revolution of centuries, which has not given illustrations of the pregnant *dictum* of Mr. Justice Keating, "Some of the saddest cases with which we have to deal are those in which men go into public-houses respectable and respected, and come out felons."* The effect of drink in producing poverty, and thence crime; the connection of drinking and drinking society with misapplication of funds (not the holder's own), and the resort to crime to replace them; the incitement to crimes of violence by the cerebral influence of alcohol; the use of strong drink as a means of deadening the moral sentiments and raising the brutal instincts; the temptation offered to the commission of robbery by the spectacle of drunken persons unable to defend their property—these are some of the modes and means by which drink and drinking facilities are conducive to crime in such a measure that of all the crimes committed two-thirds are usually ascribed to this single cause. In most cases, where persons of previously good character have fallen into crime—and these cases are exceedingly numerous—drink is usually at the bottom of the connection; and though the "criminal classes" are not addicted to drunkenness when engaged in their illegal pursuits, their fondness for liquor goes far to

space of over twenty years; and, by due observation, I have found that, if the murders and manslaughters, the burglaries and robberies, the riots and tumults, the adulteries, fornications, rapes, and other enormities that have happened in that time, were divided into five parts, four of them have been the issues and product of excessive drinking at tavern or alehouse meetings."—(*Advice to My Grandchildren.*) Chief-Justice Bovill says (1869): "I have no hesitation in stating that in the North of England, and in most of the large towns and the manufacturing and mining districts, intemperance is directly or indirectly the cause of by far the largest proportion of the crimes that have come under my observation."—(*Convocation Report on Intemperance*, p. 62.)

* Ditto p. 64.—See also much other valuable testimony in the same section of that Report.

explain their criminal proclivities and the absence of any restraining principle of a moral nature.*

(3.) *There is a vice of every grade, including that which is specially stigmatized as "the social evil."* How strong drink acts as the ally of every species of licentiousness is best known to those who have studied the sins that eat as a canker into our great cities and rural parts. Womanhood is discrowned and degraded by no agency at once so sure, so swift, and so subtle, as that of strong drink. The picture drawn (Prov. xxiii. 33), "Thine eyes"—if thou lookest on the wine that is red—"shall behold strange women," is true to all times. What is said by Bishop Porteous of the "simple youth" may be said more sorrowfully of the inexperienced maid when partaker

> "Of midnight revel and tumultuous mirth,
> Where, in the intoxicating draught concealed,
> Or couched beneath the glance of lawless love,
> Death snares the simple youth, who, naught suspecting,
> Means to be blest, and finds himself undone."

Prostitution, as a public vice and scandal, could not be sustained were intoxicating drink not ever at hand as a means of seduction, a hardener of the moral feelings, and a bar to that repentance which all but the most abandoned never lose some hope of finally regaining. The clause in the license which forbids "the assembling of prostitutes in a public-house" tacitly acknowledges a fixed relation between dissoluteness and alcoholic drink; but, under the plea that "prostitutes must have refresh-

* It is notable that of the indictable offences and summary cases, amounting in all to above half a million yearly, a large percentage (from 20 to 40) have respect to persons of "previous good character," and nearly as great a percentage to persons of "character unknown," giving an aggregate of about three-fourths of the cases as acts of misconduct of men and women who might have been supposed as unlikely to commit crime as the rest of the community. In five cases out of six "the drink" was at the bottom of the offence, or a leading element in the list of causes.

ments," a door is opened for every encouragement which vice need seek.*

(4.) *There is disease,* to an extent far above that which the physiologist assigns as the normal and expected average; and every enquirer refers much of this to drinking habits, which the public-house systematically promotes. Much sickness unquestionably arises from bad dwellings, deficient nutrition, improper exposure of young persons to cold and contagion; but, as these causes are themselves very common effects of drinking, their results should largely be ascribed to the intoxicating cup. As alcohol also impairs the blood and tissues, it invites acute sickness of every kind, and renders chronic disease less curable; while more ailments, such as nervous weakness, liver derangement, and brain affections, are aggravated (where not originated) by a use of strong drink considered to be perfectly moderate, because not connected with conscious or visible intoxication. Mental diseases are in this manner multiplied greatly; and as both physical and mental maladies are transmissible, the germs of the most terrible disorders become the fatal legacy of one generation to another. The influènce of this disease on the national rate of mortality is, of necessity, fearfully impressive. That it has much to do with the excess of town over rural mortality (equal to the loss of nearly 200,000 lives in England and Wales per annum) cannot be questioned; and even the rural mortality is known to be unnaturally raised by the indulgences which find their congenial sphere in the village inn or alehouse.†

* The New Licensing Act (clauses 14 and 15) contains stringent provisions against permitting prostitutes to remain in public-houses longer than is necessary for obtaining reasonable refreshment, and heavy penalties for a violation of the law; and any licensed person keeping a brothel is liable to be fined not more than £20, to lose his license, and to be disqualified from holding another.

† Dr. Lankester, F.R.S., Coroner for Central Middlesex, remarks: "The death from alcoholic poisoning in Great Britain is prodigious; it may be set

3. *The influence of the liquor traffic on trade and commerce is of capital concern to a great manufacturing and exporting country like our own.* How this influence acts will be seen by considering (1) that all trade and commerce must be benefited by the health, sobriety, and regular habits of those who are engaged in them, so that whatever exerts a contrary effect is to be regarded as their enemy; and that this inimical effect is universally attendant on the establishment of drinking-shops all employers of labor and many workmen have unpleasant experience. Again, (2) the expenditure of upwards of a hundred millions sterling on strong drink is a diversion of a large portion of that sum from other productions which would have given labor and remuneration to many times more workmen. The reply that "it does not matter how the money is spent, if it is afterwards re-expended in the country," is akin to the fallacy which represents taxation to any amount as no hardship, because the taxes are returned to the community in the purchase of goods. If money is spent on articles produced within a country, it must surely be of importance to the trade of the country whether the workman receives 2*s.* or 12*s.* in the pound for his labor. (3.) The economical disposition, which is impaired by drinking and attendance at taverns, is a great promoter of trading and commercial enterprise. Let the working classes become investors instead of dissipators of their surplus means, and the permanent and productive wealth of the country will immediately be augmented—a result which every drinking-shop tends to

down at something like a tenth of the whole death-rate of the country." The total mortality of the United Kingdom is about 700,000 annually, which would give 70,000 as about the number who are slain by alcohol every year—an estimate higher than that of any temperance statistician. Could there be a complete investigation, it would probably be found that the annual deaths of supposed "moderate drinkers," hastened by "alcoholic poisoning," equal those of acknowledged drunkards minimize or set aside. No artificial equalization of wealth is possible ; but, with the absence of the drinking system, we should not despair of beholding a more general distribution of the national resources, involving a more equal diffusion of that social happiness which attends the state removed alike from poverty and riches.

4. *The influence of the liquor traffic upon the security of life and property, and the averages of local taxation, is of pressing importance.* Shallow objectors often talk and write as though all the consequences of intemperance rested with the intemperate ; and it is said, with an air of authority, as if all argument must close, "If they don't want to be injured by the public-house, let them stay outside!" But apart from the question of humanity, it is of no small importance to every person in society that houses which deal in drinks that muddle and inflame should not exist for men to go into, whether they are moved to do so by habit, appetite, or fancied good. One intoxicated or drink-excited man may imperil the lives of many ; and, could all accidents on land and water be traced to their source, society would be surprised at the number of casualties and fatalities that have arisen from "a drop too much." A drunken pilot had nearly cast away the ship on which Colonel Wellesley (afterwards the Duke of Wellington) was proceeding to India ; and drunken drivers have exposed eminent statesmen of our own times to serious risk of limb or life. Drinking at home casts herds of "arabs" upon the streets ; and the loss of property thus incurred, amounting to millions yearly, falls upon society, as do all the external results of all the crime and vice, including the corruption of the children of the sober, traceable to this fountain of evil. Local rates, also, to the extent of many millions, are paid, not by the publicans, but by the people ; and where in very degraded districts these imposts press severely upon the industrious poor, who are just above the pauper-line

themselves, the exaction made and enforced has the effect of sensibly reducing their domestic comforts, and of preventing them having either that physical or intellectual recreation, or providing that class of education for their children, which they could otherwise have secured. Ratepayers have a heavy interest in this question which they have not sufficiently realized; for, allowing that many of the charges are permanent, and that a reduction of the rates would not be greater than one-half by the removal of public facilities to drinking, who can estimate the relief which that reduction would impart? Could it be effected by the fiat or device of any statesman, he would become at one bound the most popular member of his class, and memorials in his honor could be raised in his lifetime wherever the benefit of his action was enjoyed. But if to strong drink and the drink traffic two-thirds of our pauperism is due, it is not too much to expect that, with the exclusion of this cause, a relief from one-half of the burdens would be speedily possessed. One other effect of the poor and county rates is not to be omitted—that the exercise of private charity becomes doubly burdensome, and is often felt to be so difficult as to lead to a neglect of the claims of those who are willing rather to suffer unnoticed than to parade their sufferings before the eyes of strangers. Hence two results, each very injurious, arise: the duty of private benevolence becomes needlessly severe, and it is so inefficiently discharged that the most deserving objects of charity—those to whom a little timely aid would be exceedingly serviceable, and whom it would preserve from pauperism—are frequently left to struggle and to perish. It is in vain that the visitor of the public-house is left to take the consequences of his folly; the carelessness or insensibility that leaves him to his fate becomes judicially visited by consequences that weigh upon the neck, and pierce into the vitals of the society that ought to have foreseen, and, foreseeing, should have averted them. The foregoing considerations may be briefly recombined, so as to form an argument for the suppression of the liquor traffic, on the grounds of General Benevolence, Social Self-interest, Enlightened Patriotism, and Christian Civilization.

General Benevolence demands that those who are tempted and ruined should, if possible, be rescued, and that others who will be tempted and ruined, if the drinking-shop remains, should be saved by its removal. To say that such can save themselves if they will is nothing to the point, if true, for humanity impels us to try and save many who might have escaped the danger they have incurred, whether the danger be physical or moral; but the plea can hardly be considered pertinent to the two great classes who are the victims of the liquor traffic—first, because the class that has become so drink-smitten as to have lost by a diseased system the conditions of moral freedom; and, secondly, the other class of the inexperienced, who, acting on the presumption (sanctioned by law) that the drinking-shop is a safe place of resort, or it would not be licensed, commence their acquaintance with it in ignorance of the peril they encounter. No language is too strong in denunciation of the inequity which would throw upon these classes the whole of the responsibility of their own misery and degradation, and which would leave them to sink beyond redemption, heedless of their cry for a shielding and uplifting arm. But were it even conceded—though human nature and Christian charity repel the concession with horror—that these should be left to the darkest fate which can overtake mortal man, General Benevolence may be invoked on behalf of all who are compelled to suffer privation, hunger, cold, cruelty, and the most demoralizing associations, or who are given over to death through the intemperance of those nearly related to them. These, beyond question, cannot help the intemperance which curses them, nor can they deliver themselves from the miseries which overwhelm them. The question is, Shall *they* be sacrificed because the drink traffic must be sustained?

SOCIAL SELF-INTEREST enters its protest against the continuance of a system which is at war with every true interest of the state. It is the interest of society that sobriety shall prevail; that there shall be little or no vice, crime, pauperism, lunacy, and avoidable disease; that there shall be domestic comfort and general education; that trade and commerce shall be encouraged by the demand for good food, clothing, furniture, and books by every family; that the rates and taxes and the demands on private charity should be reduced to the *minimum* consistent with the contingencies of life; and against the whole and every part of this enlightened interest the liquor traffic wages incessant war. All these objects, for the promotion of which society is supposed to use its collective wisdom and power, are largely frustrated wherever the sale of strong drink is licensed—and yet the license is intended to guard society against the evils which are hatched beneath its wing! It may be affirmed with certainty that the moment society awakens to a just conception of what it loses by the traffic in alcoholic liquors, that traffic is doomed. May the awakening speedily come to pass!

ENLIGHTENED PATRIOTISM cannot be blind to the truth that a nation, vitiated, weakened, and burdened by the liquor traffic, must have its vitality lessened, its glory obscured, and its prosperity imperilled. If there is one sign of the times more unerring than another, it is this—that the tendency of science, peace, and commercial intercourse, in bringing nations more closely together, is also exposing each to a severe competition, and will more and more test the capacity of all to retain that relative position which they occupied at the outset. This country, though territorially small, has enormous advantages in entering upon this world-round competition; it has population, capital, skill, mineral wealth, and a vast industrial plant; but it has also some striking drawbacks, first among which is the injury, loss, degradation, and emasculation produced yearly by the drinking system—one of whose chief corner-stones is the licensed traffic in strong drink.

CHRISTIAN CIVILIZATION, which is but another name for the advancement of mankind in all that is good and wise and great, is profoundly concerned in the right settlement of this question. The results of the drinking system in one place are a fair example of the results in every other place. As in all lands water, light, and air are the conditions and vehicles of life, so wherever intoxicating liquors are circulated, they carry on their work of temptation, and ruin, and death. The drinking-shop, licensed or unlicensed, is a common snare and a common curse, nor has the wit of the wisest devised a scheme for making it otherwise. The influences favoring a higher style of civilization are broad, deep, and powerful, and they are affecting the condition of the whole earth, from "Britain to Japan," from Norfolk Island to Nova Zembla; but the "Drink Demon," as the late Mr. Davenport Hill has graphically said, "starts up everywhere," to confront and often to confound the reformer. What is to be done? The Christian evangelist and missionary meet with the same fiery obstruction. What is to be done? This adversary is not passive, waiting to be attacked; he is active, subtle, insidious, and unceasingly attacking every scheme of improvement and plan of reformation. WHAT IS TO BE DONE? How long will the friends of civilization and Christianity decline the challenge thus extended, and seek to parley with this treacherous and insatiable foe? The evil done by it yearly, daily, hourly, is not to be reckoned; the good undone by it is equally beyond computation; and to hope that Christian civilization will be able to effect what it might, and as quickly as it might, with this agency of evil in the field, is to fall into a stupendous and calamitous mistake. Could we personify this civilization appealing to her friends—the friends of invention, of intellect, of justice and religion—we should depict her standing in the midst of all the wreck and ruin which strong drink has wrought from the beginning of time; and as she points to the veil which hides the future from all eyes but One, we should behold her pleading that such wreck and ruin should not embarrass and impede her in her progress through the years to come. Civilization is a precious and splendid heritage, and it is the concern of any one who values it that it should be transmitted in a richer and nobler form to the succeeding ages. How this can be done is for each to ponder. How it will *not* be done is clear, if the love of alcoholic liquor and an organized system of its sale are carried on with the tide of time and with the increasing intercourse of nations. But let the English race—whether in the British Isles or in the "Greater Britain" outside, or in the commonwealths that have cast off the maternal rule—resolve to deal boldly and effectively with the great antagonist of Christian civilization, and this example would form a precedent which other races would be encouraged and proud to follow. Let it be laid down as a position not to be questioned that alcoholic liquor as a beverage is a poison to all civilization, and that common traffic in it is a curse of the greatest magnitude; let all the energies of civilization in the most civilized of nations be directed against its deadliest enemy; and the results of this action would soon manifest themselves in forms of the grandest and most enduring benefit.

Objections.

1. The objection from *free trade* is now seldom put forth, and there are few persons who plainly contend that the sale of intoxicating liquors should be as free as the sale of corn. Perfect freedom of trade is impeded by taxation and by restrictions upon sale; and there is almost unanimity upon the points that intoxicating drink should be taxed more heavily than other articles, and that its sale should be limited by restrictions not applicable to other traffic. In the interests of trade as such, the fewest restrictions are best; but the confession that the liquor traffic ought to be restricted is a confession that is not a traffic to which the principle of freedom (from taxation or restriction) can be safely and legitimately applied.

2. The objection that "*prohibition would be contrary to liberty*" is grounded on the supposition either that the liberty to sell strong drink is a natural or civil right, or that the sale of strong drink is necessary to the exercise of some other liberty which is a personal or civil right. The first theory is contradicted by every license law, and particularly by the License Law of England, which denies the existence of any individual right (whether natural or civil) to trade in alcoholic liquors. The second theory is one which has received the sanction of Mr. John Stuart Mill. The gist of his plea is contained in this sentence, "The infringement complained of is not on the liberty of the seller, but on that of the buyer and consumer; since the State might just as well forbid him to drink wine, as purposely make it impossible to attain it." The liberty thus claimed is the liberty of purchase; yet Mr. Mill is content with asserting the claim, and does not advance a single reason in defence of the proposition that some one ought to be at liberty to sell strong drink because another person wants to use it. The only way of proving this would

be to prove that whatever a person wants the law must allow to be sold; but Mr. Mill admits that sale is a social act, and, therefore, if subject to social regulation, why not, if necessary for the social good, also subject to prohibition? How can it happen that, at one and the same time, society has the right to restrict or forbid the sale of something which a member of society has a right to claim shall be sold? Such "rights" are conflicting, and cannot both be sustained; but the social fabric rests upon the principle that the individual has not a right to demand that anything shall be done which society judges to be prejudicial to the common good. If he reply, "What I wish is something for my pleasure or my good—something that *I* should not abuse" (say, the wine of which Mr. Mill writes), the answer is one and the same: "Supposing your use would be harmless to you (a point which is quietly assumed by Mr. Mill, in regard to the use of wine), what you require to be done in order to that use would not in our judgment be harmless, and therefore cannot be be allowed." And this answer is either conclusive, or there is no conclusive answer to be given to any person who wishes, for the sake of his own convenience or advantage, to have liberty to do, or to cause to be done, something which is prejudicial to the common good. As to the sale of intoxicating liquor, it is plain that if society has a right to stop the sale for public ends, no citizen can have a right to buy—*i.e.* to claim that the sale shall exist—for his private ends; and to identify his claims with liberty is to degrade it into every epicure's drudge, instead of reverencing it as the protector of social rights. The form of this objection, which draws a parallel between personal liberty of conscience and worship, and the liberty of using and buying strong drink, is also too whimsical to need reply. Liberty of conscience is beyond the reach of law, and liberty of worship cannot be compared with the liberty of using, buying, or selling strong drink—

because, in the first place, the things compared are intrinsically different: because, in the second place, society has agreed to treat them differently, as belonging to different spheres; because, in the third place, worship does not depend upon something else which society has a right to forbid (as the purchase does upon the sale); and because, in the fourth place, where even worship becomes so connected with secular affairs as to bring it within secular authority, any injury offered to social law subjects it to social interference and suppression. If, for example, under the pretence of worship, or as a part of so-called worship, conduct was pursued (say seditious plotting or immoral practices), society would have, and would use, the right of putting an end to such "worship," precisely as it has the right, and ought to use it, of interdicting the common sale of intoxicating liquors. Let even belief take the overt form of polygamy, as among the Mormons, or as suttee among the Hindoos, and the law brushes aside the claim to liberty of action, and interposes its stern denial. The religionist is not allowed to make his conscience the justification of a social evil, and neither can the drinker of intoxicating liquor be allowed to make his convenience a reason for the continuance of a traffic which is a curse to the body-politic. If he *will* use his wine or strong drink of any kind, the least that he can do is to obtain it in some way that does not cause ill to his neighbor and to the society of which he is a part.

3. The objection that "*the principle of regulation can be applied to the liquor traffic, so as to bring with it, substantially, all the good results of suppression, without any of its vexations to those who drink,*" is an objection the force of which will be apparent when any instance of the success of regulation has been produced. Up to this time, and in the United Kingdom, nothing approaching to such an event has been witnessed. The experiment at

Gottenburgh, in Sweden—where the council has prohibited the system of private profit in the sale of drink, and where the sale of food in taverns is kept in the foreground, and the sale of liquors in the background—has been found to work well; it is an experiment, however, still in its infancy, and demands a constant inspection and supervision that could hardly be applied on a general scale. The present dealers in strong drink in this country would regard it with scarcely more favor than they do the principle of prohibition; and, as it proceeds on the rule that as far as the sale of drink is checked, so far will be the spread of sobriety and every civil good, it is an argument for the adoption of the fuller rule wherever the public sentiment will uphold it. The failure of "regulation" has been attested by the social history of every civilized country; and, in view of this established fact, the Report of Convocation on Intemperance, having sketched a variety of excellent palliative and secondary measures, concludes with a recommendation that the adoption of prohibition should be made legal wherever the local opinion is ready to embrace it."*

4. The objection that "*the rights of property would be invaded, and the national finances injuriously damaged, were the liquor traffic suppressed,*" is one that proceeds from a misconception of the whole question. The only right of property which the seller of intoxicating liquor can claim is the right of ownership or occupancy, which no one wishes to disturb; but his "right" to sell liquor is derived from his license, which is a yearly grant, liable to be revoked within the year if the terms are violated, and requires to be granted afresh to the year's end, or he is disqualified from selling strong drink. Some insist that

* The new licensing act will produce public benefit in proportion as it diminishes drinking and inducements to it, and no further. Its best friends do not regard it as the "settlement" which successive governments, from 1854 downwards, have promised to the country.

compensation should be given if licenses are withdrawn; but every license is now liable to be withdrawn without compensation; and as suppression would result from a conviction that the terms of the contract had been broken, and a nuisance had taken the place of a supposed convenience, it is not easy to see why the people should (contrary to common law) be called upon to tax themselves for the abatement of this particular nuisance. The vendor has no moral claim to a renewal of the license, unless he observes its terms and spirit; and if the locality agrees that this has not been done, but the contrary, compensation would but add to the wrongs and burdens already endured by the district. The liquor vendor knows from the first the uncertainty of the tenure on which he holds his privilege to sell strong drink; and when he is proved to have abused that privilege, it is rather a question how much *he* should pay society, than how much society should pay him, as compensation for loss sustained. To represent this as a case of "spoliation" and "robbery" is to overlook the gist of the question; it is to overlook, also, the fact that in innumerable cases the tenant is little else than some brewer's agent; and it is to overlook the fact that the house occupied, and much of the furniture, would be available for the adaptation of the premises as a *bona fide* victualling establishment, free from the noxious associations of the past. In every populous district, "British Workman" public-houses would do a thriving trade, and nothing need prevent hotels under good management enjoying a commercial success.

The *derangement of the government finances* is not a contingency possible unless the liquor traffic were simultaneously suppressed over the whole kingdom, or over a very extensive area. This is not contemplated, and would not be attainable, under a permissive prohibitory act; and the Chancellor of the Exchequer who was not prepared to take his chance of raising as large a revenue from a sober people as from a community deeply cursed with intemperance, would be unworthy of his honorable office. His invention would not, at all events, be severely taxed to make good any gradual reduction of excise receipts that would proceed from the diminished consumption of intoxicating drinks.

5. The objection that "*the suppression of the liquor traffic in any district by the vote of a majority would be an act of oppression on the minority, and that, in fact, the people generally are opposed on such a measure,*" is an objection frequently heard, but consisting of two members, the first of which is not correct, and the second not pertinent, while they are reciprocally destructive. The first section is not true ; for, though minorities have undeniable rights, one of them is not a right to compel majorities to endure a terrible social evil in order that minorities may be readily supplied with a physical indulgence.* Indeed, this branch of the objection is a new form of the liberty argument before considered. The second section, if true, is without any pertinence, either as directed against a movement to persuade the people of the wisdom of prohibition, or as directed against the proposal to empower the people of districts to decide whether for drinking-shops or against them. The people might be universally against suppression, yet they might be wrong, and it would be desirable to convince them of their error ; and if, as the objector assumes, the people of all localities are ready to vote against prohibition, to allow them to vote

* The *tu quoque* argument that one part of society has no more right to force another part to go without strong drink than the other has to force the former to use it, is the shallowest of sophisms ; for, first, the question is not as to a right of use or disuse, but as to a right of sale—a social act ; and, secondly, if the non-use of intoxicating drinks produced similar results to those arising from their use, the question of forcing their use upon abstainers would then—and not till then—be a proper subject of comparison and discussion.

is a proposal the liquor interest should desire, not dread. But the two sections are opposed for the first evidently contemplates the probability of prohibition—which the second denies. It is manifest, however, that prohibition cannot both be popular and unpopular at once. To say that the question is not one for localities to decide, but that it ought to be decided for the whole country by a general peremptory enactment, is to assume that the local liquor question is not a local one; whereas it both is so, and has been treated as such for centuries; and, further, the objection assumes that an immediate and universal change would be preferable to a progressive local movement—a proposition which, whether true or not, does not affect the justice of the proposal to allow districts, as soon as ready, to make the change for themselves. The objector also does not bear in mind that a majority of the people might be favorable to suppression, and yet a majority in Parliament opposed to it, for no social question has ever yet decided a general election; and the sincerity of the opponents who make this objection will only be raised above suspicion, when they are ready to support a *plebiscitum* (national vote) upon the subject, and to abide the issue. A permissive prohibitory measure would, in reality, afford the best possible test of the general popularity, or otherwise, of the policy embodied in it, without the risk of making it operative where the public sentiment would be too weak to enforce and uphold it.

6. The objection that "*the experiment of prohibition has been tried and has failed,*" is one of those ready-made assertions which pass current among the prejudiced or ignorant, and among none besides. Since 1851, the "Maine Law" has been on the statute-book of that State (with a short interval sufficient to prove the inferiority of a strict license system); and both there, as well as in every other American State where prohibition has been carried out,

and in proportion to the thoroughness of the experiment, the results have been all that were predicted. Where, as in Vineland, a district of New Jersey (not a Maine Law State), the sale of liquor has been continuously and rigidly excluded for a term of years, the effects have been such as might well excite the envy of less favored regions. But we need not travel outside even our own island to see what the absence of the drink-shop secures in the way of sobriety, order, comfort, and comparative prosperity. A Committee of the General Assembly of the Church of Scotland reported, in 1849, on the causes of intemperance in that country; and in this report it is said: "The returns made to your Committee's enquiries clearly prove that the intemperance of a neighborhood is uniformly proportioned to the number of its spirit-houses: so that, wherever there are no public-houses nor any shops for selling spirits, there ceases to be any intoxication." The Committee of the Lower House of the Convocation of the Province of Canterbury, charged with a similar commission in 1868, extended its enquiries over the counties of England and Wales, included in that ecclesiastical division, and their Report states: "Few, it may be believed, are cognizant of the fact—which has been elicited by the present enquiry—that there are at this time within the province of Canterbury upwards of one thousand parishes [1397], in which there is neither public-house nor beer-shop; and where, *in consequence of the absence of those inducements to crime and pauperism,* according to the evidence before the Committee, the intelligence, morality, and comfort of the people are such as the friends of temperance would have anticipated." No fewer than twenty-five pages of an Appendix (JJ) are filled with illustrative testimonies on this point. The parishes and other places so situated number 1,397, with an aggregate population of 222,258. A large number of places in the province of York, embracing all the North of England, are known to be under the same rule ; and in Ireland, besides scattered towns and districts, a section of the county Tyrone 61½ miles square, with a population of 9,500, is without a liquor-shop of any kind, to the great satisfaction and advantage both of the landowners and the tenants.* What, indeed, is of the greatest value in the consideration of this question, is the unexceptional contentment of the people with this prohibitory regimen, though they have had no voice in its application ; and, along with this, the persistent upholding of this policy by the landowners, few of whom are total abstainers, and who are, therefore, only influenced in their course by its self-evident superiority over the license system. These specimens of prohibition side by side with license are also exceedingly useful in refuting the oft-told objections brought against permissive prohibition, that if adopted, it would lead persons to bring drink in large quantities from adjoining parishes ; or would increase the drunkenness of those parishes ; or would multiply illicit selling ; or would promote domestic tippling ; or would make total abstinence compulsory ; or would give rise to evils as bad as drunkenness or worse ; or would make existence stale, flat, and exceedingly dry—objections which are all freely lavished with as little thought as they embody, and without any regard to their contradictory character. These objections break like bubbles when confronted with the actual state of things which has continued for years in thousands of places within the United Kingdom ; where the predicted evils ought to be evident, but are not ; and where, whatever drawbacks exist, they are so inconsiderable as not to interfere with the general beneficent result.

Blessed will be the day when the legislature of this Empire no longer hinders the people of any district from

* See Appendix L.

weeding out the causes of their saddest sorrows and sorest burdens; and, when that day has dawned, blessed will be the districts whose inhabitants employ this form of legislation to save themselves from calamities which no skill and prudence can avert, where the licensed drink-shop system is retained!

CHAPTER VII.

PROPOSITION: THAT THE EXCLUSION OF INTOXICATING DRINKS FROM THE DIET, THE ENTERTAINMENTS, AND THE COMMERCE OF SOCIETY IS A PRINCIPLE APPROVED BY SCIENCE AND CHRISTIANITY, AND IS THE ONLY EFFICIENT CURE AND PREVENTIVE OF INTEMPERANCE.

IT will be perceived by the thoughtful reader that the proposition now submitted is in effect the only reasonable conclusion to which all the facts, arguments, and illustrations of the previous chapters tend, and in which they converge.

FIRST. It has been shown *that intoxicating drinks are not food, and do not serve any of the purposes of food;* but that, wherever their action can be traced in the human frame, they *are found to diminish vital power*, and to render man less capable than before taking them to discharge the functions of a living being. It irresistibly follows that they are unfit for diet, and that they cannot be introduced as luxuries, or permitted to be sold, under the pretence that they can add to the health, vigor, and longevity of mankind. Submitted to physiological tests, and to the comparative experience of persons in all occupations and of all constitutions, they stand condemned. The plea that they add to the enjoyment of social life is not a plea which science can entertain; and while it may be admitted that hilarity is excited by them, owing to their effects on the nervous system, it is not true that their use is necessary to the greatest amount of rational pleasure, either personal or social.* On the contrary, it is

* Among Sydney Smith's Rules and Maxims was the following: "If you wish to keep the mind clear and body healthy, abstain from all fermented

true that the most sober pleasures are the sweetest as well as the most prolonged, and that they bring in their train none of the reaction and satiated feeling which follow the unhealthy excitement occasioned by alcoholic drinks. In regard to commerce, laws already exist against the sale of tainted meat or adulterated articles of consumption, on the ground that the sanitary interests of society ought to be first consulted and maintained ; and with what consistency, in the face of this proceeding, can any apology be offered for the legal permission given to the wholesale and retail traffic in a thousand million gallons of alcoholized fluid annually, the most characteristic constituent of which is a narcotic acrid poison, whose specific effects on the brain, the blood, the liver, and all the vital organs is one great cause of the sickness and mortality of the nation?

SECONDLY. It has been shown *that intoxicating liquors are not manufactured without a prodigious waste of the material of nutritious food;* that in the process of their manufacture *the amount of labor employed and wages paid to workmen are very inconsiderable;* and that the effect of their promiscuous use is *to weaken the industrial powers and disposition, and to increase beyond all comparison the most oppressive burdens and frightful evils of our social state.* What can political economy have to say to the production of such liquors, but to pronounce it a mistake of the first magnitude? And what can be the relation towards them of the spirit of that social science which seeks the elevation of the people, except a relation of unmixed aversion and relentless repugnance? Wealth in the limited sense of property available for the public and private good, and wealth in the more ancient and comprehensive sense

liquors." Haydon, in his "Autobiography," has the following note: "Dined at dear honest John Sturge's, and spent a very pleasant evening. They were all teetotalers except me and John Sturge. I could not have believed so pleasant an evening could have passed without a glass of port."

of weal or welfare, material or moral, are sacrificed to an extent, year by year, which would be incredible if the evidence were not incontrovertible. That the homely proverb, "Wilful waste makes woeful want," finds an illustration in the drinking system nowhere else supplied, is the more apparent the more fully an examination is carried into the origin, influences, and ramifications of the system. Waste is written upon every part of it, and want and woe are its inevitable and widespread accompaniments. As it is founded on a destruction of the alimentary value of the fruits of the earth, its development is marked at every step by the subversion of what is good in man, and of that which might be the means of greater good in all succeeding time. Capital, industry, frugality, all shrivel beneath its touch, and instead of imparting a golden value to things of inferior worth, it turns to veriest dross whatever is most precious in earthly good and in man, by whom that good is multiplied and enjoyed.

THIRDLY. The *principles of morality which attain their highest and grandest expression in Christianity* can pronounce but one verdict upon the social use and legalized sale of liquors, *which are at war with the physical, intellectual, moral, and spiritual interests of our race.* To make, buy, and use as food that which is not food is a violation of natural morality which could not pass without astonishment if the facts were correctly apprehended; and another Swift might awaken the wonder of another generation were he to picture a nation possessing the purest principles of religion, yet suffering its wealth to be engulfed, its vigor to be impaired, its morals to be defiled, its burdens of every kind to be doubled, its works of benevolence, education, and piety to be thwarted, by the sanction it gave to the production and circulation of articles which had no power to lengthen and lighten a single life among the millions of which it was composed. Christianity inculcates the love of the useful, and the

avoidance of the useless, the dangerous, and the hurtful. Christianity is so much superior to philosophy that while the latter could define temperance to consist in a preference of the profitable over the merely pleasant, the former not only inspires men with a passion for the truly profitable (though to the sensual nature unpalatable), but so extends the application of that term as to include what is profitable to others as to one's self; hence he who, in order to benefit others, abstains from intoxicating liquor which habit may have made agreeable, exhibits the virtue of temperance illuminated with a heavenly charity. The Christian man is such, and is worthy of the name in proportion as he is possessed and ruled by the spirit of Christianity—and no further; hence the Christianity of our times is so imperfect, because this spirit operates so imperfectly in the hearts and lives of its professors. Still, if their profession be genuine, they must desire that this spirit may have its "perfect work," and they must be prepared to "try every spirit" and every system by the genius of their divine religion. We do not unchristianize those who are not acting against the drinking system; but if that system is anti-Christian in all its parts and operations, the true Christian will be best discharging his duty and justifying his name by ceasing his connection with it, and exchanging that connection for an attitude of resistance and opposition. *Every petition in the Lord's Prayer is in contradiction to the drinking system,* and in equal contradiction should be the Christian's spirit, example, and endeavor. "Our Father who art in heaven" teaches us that we should love and do good to one another as children, as our Father loves and does good to all of us. "Hallowed be thy name" is a petition which should inspire all who hallow the holiest name with horror of that system which incites man to blasphemy and vice. "Thy kingdom come, thy will be done in earth, as it is in heaven" is an empty supplication if, through our concurrence or connivance, that kingdom is hindered, that will is disobeyed, and earth rendered more like hell than heaven. "Give us this day our daily bread" is a request partially nullified in the asking if we sanction the waste of bread-corn for that which is not bread, but a deadly bane. "And forgive us our trespasses, as we forgive them that trespass against us" is not a prayer compatible with a careless continuance in trespassing, or a want of tender concern for the happiness of others. "Lead us not into temptation" is a cry of conscious weakness not capable of being answered if we create or seek temptation which (as in the case of strong drink) is superadded to the temptations inherent in human nature and the constitution of society. "But deliver us from evil" is an entreaty which is dishonored when we fabricate causes of evil, or refuse to aid in their suppression when laid bare. "For thine is the kingdom, the power, and the glory," is a sublime doxology which is best embodied in the earnest effort to labor with God, who refuses not the co-operation of the weakest in the advancement of principles and practices which illustrate the nature of his kingdom, the grace of his power, and the glory of his all-glorious attributes in the redemption of the world.

Much has been said upon *the principle of "Christian expediency" as a motive to total abstinence;* but, very unfortunately, this term has been turned aside from its apostolic meaning, and has been applied in a manner which robs is of more than half its force. As commonly used, it is taken to signify something different from or short of *Christian principle,* as if it might be expedient to abstain, though Christian principle would not interdict, but permit of a continued use of intoxicating drinks, their presentation to others at the social board, and their common sale under the sanction and protection of the law. It requires a very short examination of the New Testament doctrine upon the subject to explode so untenable a distinction. It is true that the Apostle Paul speaks of some actions as lawful in themselves which he proceeds to describe as inexpedient; but a perusal of these passages will show that such actions are described as lawful in their self-regarding relation only—*i.e.* their abstract moral character as affecting the individual actor. But when the Apostle proceeds to refer to them in their influence on other persons (not the doers), he affirms in the strongest language that the actions are no longer expedient, but inexpedient, no longer lawful, but unlawful and sinful, because tending to ensnare and destroy those for whom the Saviour died. Both the logical understanding and moral sentiment of the Apostle would have been shocked at the modern interpretation which places Christian expediency on a lower ground than Christian principle and duty; seeing that it is the Christian principle and duty of acting with a regard to others' good which gives to "expediency," as he defines it, all its virtue and importance. If, in addition to what is demanded by the welfare of our fellow-creatures, our own interests call for a certain line of action, such as separation from and hostility to the drinking system, the "expediency" (fitness) of the action becomes stronger; and the sanction of it, and incentive to it, drawn from the law of Christian morality, have then reference to an enlightened self-interest, as well as to an enlightened benevolence, and a conformity to the Redeemer's example.

As to the CURE OF INTEMPERANCE, who that understands the nature of that evil, when it is not the concomitant of dissipated associations, but the expression of the appetite for alcohol, can imagine that the present race of intemperate persons can be made sober unless they are separated from strong drink, either by their voluntary resolution to abstain, or by being placed where drink is not within reach? Yet it is patent that the great mass of drunkards and tipplers cannot be sent to asylums to be cured, and therefore they must perish in their vice and sin, unless they are induced to abstain, and surrounded by circumstances favorable to abstinence.* Multitudes who have been led to abstain have afterwards fallen by social temptations to drinking, and greater multitudes have fallen before the allurements of the drinking-house. And "the thing that has been will be," until the good of all classes earnestly resolve upon the adoption of the measures by which, while benefiting themselves, they will save others from "the snares of the destroyer."

And if the CURE of existing intemperance is hopeless without the exclusion of intoxicating drink from the diet, the hospitalities, and the traffic of the country, still more hopeless, were that possible, must be its future PREVENTION, unless such a method of defence is carried out. Alcohol will not lose its characteristic properties, nor human nature its susceptibility to its insinuating, seductive, and depriving power. The flowers of social courtesy and charms of social intercourse will not deprive alcoholic drink of its serpentine fascination and poisonous fangs. No mandate to the vendors of intoxicating drinks, to avoid dispersing the miasma of intoxication, will enable them to carry the mandate into effect. Who can doubt that ages must elapse before the bulk of men will be as able, as pure, as wise, as noble as many of those who, in the present age, have fallen victims to this "defrauder"? How, then, can it be imagined that, before that golden age is gained, alcoholic liquors will be rendered impotent for mischief, if incapable of good? May

* "It is the almost universal testimony of those connected with our criminal jurisprudence and the control of workhouses, and, indeed, of all who have looked deeply into the subject, that, in the case of persons addicted to intemperance, total abstinence from intoxicating drink is, under God, the only effectual remedy."—*Report of Convocation on Intemperance*, *pp.* 13, 14. *Also A. A. Appendix in the Report.*

it not rather be feared that no more certain means could be devised of hindering the arrival of a time when the body of the people will be well fed, well clothed, well educated, well ordered, well behaved, than to perpetuate a system which has been hitherto so fruitful in all misery and evil, and which, by its baneful influence on the bodies and minds of one generation, transmits some of its malignant marks, often by hereditary taint, to a posterity uncursed by heaven? It is important that no vain expectation should seize the social philanthropists and reformers of this day. If they permit the seed of strong drink to be sown, they will not, by any counter-contrivance, prevent the uprising of the old familiar crop of intemperance, disease, destitution, vice, and crime. What will be ensured besides this is the choking of much good seed that would otherwise come to fruition. "God will not be mocked" even by his servants when they act in ignorance of his laws. As are the seed and the sowing, so the harvest will be, as long as the sun gives light, and the rivers roll onward to the seas.

Objections.

1. It is objected that *the proposal of excluding intoxicating liquors from daily diet, social hospitalities, and from general commerce is, under existing circumstances, an extreme one; that there is already a gratifying advance made, as to public sobriety, upon former times; and that, whatever may be hereafter expedient, present effort should be limited to reforms of a more moderate description.*"

This threefold objection may be best examined in its separate parts:

(1.) *The charge of extremeness* is one well adapted to terrify those who are never more alarmed than when they are supposed to be going in advance of the opinion of their own social circle. But minds not enslaved by conventional fears and fetters will not be dissuaded by any cry of "extreme" from inquiring into its justice or error. It is palpably clear that the simple negative of what is worthless or injurious cannot be "an extreme" in any objectionable sense. But total abstinence is the negative of intemperance, and, on this account, entitled to the highest credit; and it is the negative of any use or sanction of the liquors by which intemperance is produced, and by which, before intemperance arises, damage is done to the interests of society. If, then, it be an extreme in this respect, it is not a measure in excess of what is fit, discreet, and good. It is no accusation against a man that he is extremely wise; nor against a woman that she is extremely chaste; nor against any one, that he keeps extremely distant from what is worthless and charged with peril. The total abstainer may be extremely sober, but sobriety admits of no excess; and if his principle is one that would render intemperance impossible, and would, in a thousand other ways, benefit the world, to call it "extreme" is to pass upon it the compliment of being *extremely efficacious* in preventing evil and in conferring good. The venerable maxims which warn against extremes, and recommend the middle as the safest course, can have no application against a measure which, if adopted, would make mankind extremely safe and happy. The physician is never blamed because he enables his patient to make an extremely rapid and complete recovery; nor would he be admired if he left the invalid half-way between prostration and health. To make these maxims applicable to total abstinence, it should be shown that it is followed by evils as severe and afflictive as those of intemperance; whereas, every recession from intemperance is a good, and "moderate drinking," when most moderate, derives its advantage over intemperance from the fact of its closer approximation to the abstinence standpoint. To speak, as some do, of "temperance" and "moderation" as a virtue opposed to total abstinence, is a proof how easily men are imposed upon by sounds. The essential idea in temperance is that of self-restraint; and temperance, as a virtue, is self-restraint carried to the point of excluding evil and needless risk of evil. Moderation is the regulation of the desires, so as to exclude their gratification in any injurious manner or degree. There is nothing in temperance or moderation thus understood incompatible with total abstinence from strong drink; on the contrary, the virtue of temperance finds its only complete exhibition, *in regard to strong drink*, in the total abstinence principle and practice.* The charge of "fanaticism" is another form of this "extreme" accusation; but great earnestness in a good work is not a vice, but a virtue; and in the sense of aiming at a chimerical result by impracticable means, temperance advocates are the opposite of "fanatics." Their means are most practicable, and the results, if the means are used, are inevitable. When will respectable speakers and writers have the good-sense to avoid using terms of reproach which simply betray their own fanatical prejudices or deficient discrimination?

(2.) *The claim to a great advance in public sobriety* is, to a certain extent, well founded; the gross convivial drunkenness once common in the higher circles is now discountenanced and has generally disappeared; but what is proved by these changes is the indisputable connection between drinking customs and drunkenness; and what is not proved is the non-necessity of a demand for the total exclusion of intoxicating drinks from diet, sociality,

*The word "temperance" is from the Latin *Temperantia*, the force of which is found in the Greek *temno*, "to cut off." Temperance, subjectively, is the cutting-off of the desire for what is improper in measure or kind; objectively, it is cutting off the things themselves. That *tèmperare* is used in the sense of entirely abstaining and restraining is known to every reader of the classics. Livy, the historian, once uses it in referring to wine, to express abstinence from that liquor (Book xl. sec. 14).

and ordinary trade. It by no means follows that, because after-dinner excesses are less common than they were, domestic and personal insobriety has decreased in a corresponding ratio; but, even if it had, and if drinking habits and the drinking appetite were less frequent among "respectable circles" than they are known to be, the proper inference would be that advantage should be taken of changes already induced—whether by fashion, refinement, enlightenment, or legislation—and a strenuous effort made to broaden the basis of reformation, and to carry it to the fullest extent, in order that all the evil still prevailing may cease, and the calamities so long and needlessly endured be for ever done away with.

(3.) The suggestion that "*present effort should be limitea to reforms of a description more moderate*" than those advocated in this essay, is one which, for reasons before indicated, cannot be admitted. Whatever might have been the duty of those who had less light than ourselves, it cannot be either just or expedient that those who have a fuller knowledge and a more extensive remedy should conceal the one and withhold the other. The expulsion of intoxicating drink is the one policy which, in proportion as it is practised by the private citizen, by the family, and, as an article of traffic (under legislative arrangement), by the district, will never disappoint, but will yield augmenting testimony to the wisdom which has inspired it, and the patriotism which has carried it to a happy consummation.

2. It is objected by some, that "*the temperance movement is itself a failure, since it has existed for forty years without removing drunkenness, while the sale and consumption of intoxicating drinks have continued to increase.*" But relatively to population, the sale and use of intoxicating liquors have not increased, though, in the consumption of many other articles, and in the general commerce of the country, the proportionate increase has been very great. The

temperance movement has acted, in a word, as the main check and drag on that development of drinking and the drink traffic which, but for its interposition, would have been terribly rapid and enormous. But to charge *it* with "failure" is one of the absurdities which it is difficult to believe are credited by those who coin them and add them to the current folly of the world. If it has failed to suppress the whole evil, it has done so because it has failed to be sufficiently supported, especially by those whose rank and influence would have given them the greatest power over social custom and the course of legislation. Yet how can the temperance system be blamed because such men failed to give it their valuable and necessary help? Is truth a failure because many are liars? or goodness, because many are base? or Christianity, because only a third of mankind are its nominal professors? or sobriety, because drunkenness is still extensive? Are sanitary laws failures because a fourth of those who die annually in our country are sacrificed by the neglect and violation of those laws? God demands human co-operation, in order to the full effect of his providential blessing; and where any evil is traceable—like this of intemperance—to man's own active wrong-doing, to expect its cessation until man ceases to do wrong is infatuation indeed. To go further than even this, and to ascribe the failure of relief to the system which urges man to forbear his wrong-doing, is to travesty every principle of common sense and common justice. Those who bring this charge will be fortunate if they can acquit themselves of contributing to the failure they discover, by withholding their own aid from the temperance reformation. Principles do not promulgate themselves, and movements are made up of co-operating minds; and those who censure either the one or the other for "failing" to do all that is needful, while they have been doing nothing to help or much to hinder, adopt the most conspicuous method of blazoning abroad their own unfaithfulness to the obligations they confess. What is practicable to each one and practicable at once is *to withdraw all his example and influence from the drinking system, and to transfer it to the side of total abstinence;* and, by doing this, he will both discharge his personal responsibility and render similar conduct more easy (and, therefore, more circumstantially practicable) to some others.

Parents, will you not take this step for your own benefit, and to enable you to train up your children more wisely in the way in which they should go, when they quit your roof to breast the storms and grapple with the trials of life?

Ministers of religion, to you many look up—and not least the young—for an exemplary guidance and prudent counsel; can you with a pure conscience recommend by your example the use of strong drink in preference to the total abstinence principle?

Teachers of youth, whether in the Sunday-school or day-school, will you not unite "wholesome doctrine" and the influence of a consistent practice in a course which must affect your youthful charge for good or evil, as long as their life shall last?

Medical practitioners, increase the honors of a noble profession by throwing your great social and scientific weight into the regimen which extends human life, and helps it to attain more fully its greatest ends.

Journalists and men of letters, myriads regard your words as oracles; is it too much to ask that you should employ your commanding influence not to stereotype old errors and bad habits, but to stimulate enquiry, circulate truth, and emancipate your country from the thraldom in which the drinking system holds her?

Philanthropists, add to your other works of benevolence this one, by which the value of the rest will be heightened and their permanence secured.

Citizens and legislators, your patriotism must be judged by your devotion to your nation's highest interests. Give not to party what is meant for the nation. In this reform you can co-operate, with the assurance that all that is politically good will be furthered by it.

Christians, your love of man, your concern for the advancement of religion, bring before you vividly the greatness of this duty and the glory of this privilege, by which you may at one and the same time assist in the reclamation of the lost and in defending the bodies and souls of men against the insidious enemy of both. Be not slack or weary in this species of well-doing: its reward is with it.

Young men and maidens, to you the temperance reform presents itself as a refuge against the most destructive of vices; and on your entrance into active life it may be of the utmost consequence whether you avail yourself of its protection or reject it. By enjoying its benefits thus early, you will possess them more fully than is possible with persons of riper years, and you may hope to employ them in your turn to the greater advantage of those with whom you may form intimacies of pleasure, of business, and of affection.

Reader, to you, be your position what it may, the counsel is affectionately and urgently given, to make the temperance reform your choice, and to promote it by every wise and worthy means. You will certainly find that, like "the quality of mercy," such influence as you can lend it will be

> "Twice blessed:
> "It blesseth him that gives and him that takes."

Make the trial, and trust in God for the result.

APPENDICES.

A.

Benjamin Franklin's Experience.

"At my first admission into the printing-house (Palmer's, Bartholomew Close, London), I took to working at press, imagining I felt the want of the bodily exercise I had been used to in America, where presswork is mixed with the composing. I drank only water; the other men, near fifty in number, were great drinkers of beer. On one occasion I carried up and down stairs a large form of types in each hand, when others carried but one form in both hands. They wondered at this and several instances that the Water American, as they called me, was stronger than themselves who drank beer. We had an alehouse-boy, who attended always in the house to supply the workmen. My companion at the press drank every day a pint before breakfast, a pint at breakfast with his bread and cheese, a pint between breakfast and dinner, a pint at dinner, a pint in the afternoon about six o'clock, and another when he had done his day's work. I thought it a detestable custom; but it was necessary, he supposed, to drink strong beer that he might be strong to labor. I endeavored to convince him that the bodily strength afforded by beer could only be in proportion to the grain or flour of the barley dissolved in the water of which it was made; that there was more flour in a pennyworth of bread; and, therefore, that if he would eat that with a pint of water, it would give him more strength than a quart of beer. He drank on, however, and had four or five shillings to pay out of his wages every Saturday night for that vile liquor—an expense I was free from. And thus these poor devils keep themselves under."—*Benjamin Franklin's Autobiography.* This had respect to London workingmen's love of ale in 1725. A quarter of a century previously, De Foe, in his "True Born Englishman," writing of the same class, had said:

> "In English ale their dear enjoyment lies,
> For which they'll starve themselves and families."

The same superstition still prevails, and with the same disastrous fruits.

B.

Waste in the Production of Fermented Drinks.

In the early stage of the temperance movement, Mr. Joseph Livesey, of Preston, rendered great service by the frequent delivery of a lecture on Malting and Brewing, This lecture, when printed, went through many editions, and Mr. Livesey has since enlarged and recombined the information there given in his essay on "Malt, Malt Liquor, Malt Tax, Beer, and Barley." Practical information of this kind is of great value, and if possessed by university scholars and writers for the press would prevent them speaking and writing the greatest nonsense on the nutritive properties of beer and ale. The process of perversion begins by steeping the barley in water for forty-eight hours, when it is taken out and laid in heaps upon a flag-floor; when it has germinated to a certain extent, it is spread to a depth of about six inches on the hot floor of the malt-kiln, and is there subjected to a uniform heat, by frequent raking and turning, for eight or nine days; thus necessitating a large amount of Sunday labor. What follows may be described in Mr. Livesey's words: "After crushing the malt, the next step is *mashing*. This consists, not in boiling the grain, but putting it into hot water at a temperature of 170 degrees, for the purpose of melting out the sugar or saccharine matter produced in malting. After mashing a sufficient length of time, the brewer draws off the liquor so long as it runs sweet, and rejects all the rest, which is sold to the farmers in the shape of 'grains.' The rejected parts of barley here are at least 2 lbs. out of 6 lbs. The sweet wort thus drawn off would not intoxicate, whatever quantity a person was to take. The next process, after mixing the liquor with hop-water, is to *ferment* it. It is here all the mischief is done. Carbonic acid gas and alcohol are here produced. The sugar becomes decomposed, and a recomposition (of its elements) takes place, forming these two. Sugar being nutritious and spirit not so, the loss of nutriment by this change and by the overflow of barm (which is part of the barley) is about 1 lb. The fourth process is that of *fining*. People don't like 'muddy' ale, and as some thick matter cannot be prevented coming over in mashing, the liquor is put to settle, and these settlings are disposed of as 'barrel bottoms.' These bottoms are really part of the barley, and the loss here again is at least ¾ lb. These are the losses during the four stages of beer-making :

We begin with barley................	6 lb.	
In Malting we abstract as 'Malt Combs'..		1½ lb.
In Mashing we dispose of in grains.......		2 "
In Fermenting we lose in sugar and 'barm'		1 "
In fining we reject as 'barrel bottoms'....		0¾ "
		5¼ "

So that when we come to examine the beer, we find that there is not more than 12 ounces, generally not more than 10 ounces in the gallon, of barley left, and this chiefly gum, the worth of which, when compared with other food, is less than a penny." Analysis shows that fermented liquors are as deficient in nutritive elements as the process of producing them would lead us to expect. An imperial pint of Bass's bitter beer showed on analysis the following constituents (exclusive of the acids):

Sugar...........................	52·5	grains.
Gum.............................	332·5	"
Bitter Extract...................	100·0	"
Alcohol, specific gravity ·794....	468·0	"
Water...........................	7,797·0	"
Total...............	8,750·0	

An imperial pint of Allsopp's ale was composed as follows (exclusive of the acids):

Sugar...........................	40·00	grains.
Gum.............................	263·75	"
Bitter Extract...................	93·75	"
Alcohol, specific gravity ·794....	477·50	"
Water...........................	7,875·00	"
Total.................	8,750·00	

London porter differs from the above in containing less bitter extract, less alcohol, and more water; the darker color is obtained by using malt dried at a high temperature, but as the same appearance is induced by drugs, adulterations are very common. In the South Kensington Museum, London, there may be seen two bottles, each containing an imperial pint of liquor, and each bearing an inscription testifying that they contain the following ingredients:—

	Pale Ale.		London Stout.	
	oz.	gr.	oz.	gr.
Water.......	17½	0..............	18½	0
Alcohol......	2½	0..............	1½	0
Sugar........	0	240..............	0	281
Acetic Acid..	0	40..............	0	54

C.

Adulterations of Intoxicating Liquors.

In the Report of the Committee of Convocation on Intemperance, the following paragraph occurs (p. 7): "Attention is loudly called by the clergy and coroners in their returns to the extent to which the adulteration of intoxicating drink prevails, with the effect, in many cases, of circulating a liquor—to use the words of one coroner—'which maddens and destroys.' It is to be observed that these adulterations generally arise out of the competition among rival dealers, and frequently supply the only margin of profit by which the trafficker is enabled to keep possession of his house as the tenant of some brewer or distiller." Appendix J to the Report presents a train of testimonies from the clergy and coroners to the prevalence of adulterations. Tobacco and salt are very commonly used in adulterating malt liquors; but there is evidence that in the manipulation of fermented and distilled liquors, among the substances used either to impart pungency, clearness, intoxicating fume, or some other property calculated to render the liquor more popular, are the following—nux vomica and its essential principle strychnine, henbane, cocculus indicus, grains of paradise, opium, arsenic, oil of vitriol, sulphuric ether, essential oil of almonds, oil of turpentine, alum, sulphur, sulphate of iron, aloes, quassia, cherry-laurel water, foxglove, wormwood, and "headings" (a mixture of powdered copperas and alum). Brewer's Guides and similar works have been written to reduce adulteration to a science, and one of these authors (S. Child), in his "Every Man his own Brewer," explains as the reason of this drugging that "malt, to produce [sufficient alcohol for] intoxication, must be used in such large quantities as would very much diminish, if not totally exclude, the brewer's profit." But the retailer, when a tenant of the brewer or distiller, has his own private and cogent reasons for making use of the druggist. In almost every ginshop and public-house the charge per gallon for malt liquor or ardent spirits is less than the wholesale price adding the duty! One of two things, therefore, either the retailer gets no profit, or his profit is obtained from dealings with the liquors before they pass into his customers' hands. Mere dilution with water, while a fraud upon the buyer, would not be objectionable in regard to the effect produced; but, as the buyers pay for excitement, and will have it, the seller is tempted to add further injury to fraud by adding from dark and occult sources to the poisonous potency of his measures. One of the worst effects of this practice is, that it enables so many drinksellers to remain in the business, and thus add to the public temptations to intemperance which the common sale of intoxicating liquors inherently presents.

D.

Nature of the Traffic in Intoxicating Drinks.

The difference between legitimate trade and the traffic in intoxicating liquors is not incidental but fundamental, residing in these two points, (1) that the articles sold are in other cases an improvement on the raw material, and that (2) an increase of trade is a *bona fide* increase in the national comfort and prosperity. In the traffic in intoxicating drinks these characteristics are not only absent, but the opposite are present in the most terrible forms. The drinks themselves have wasted in their manufacture the harvests of vast regions, and are not consumed for the little nutriment they retain. But in the place of food there is a poison. What the common sale of alcoholic compounds produces, the *Edinburgh Review* (July, 1854), may be left to describe: "The liquor traffic, and particularly the retail branch of it, is a public nuisance in all three respects, physically, economically, and morally. By its physical consequences it causes death to thousands, reduces thousands more to madness and idiocy, and afflicts myriads with diseases involving the most wretched forms of bodily and mental torture. Considered in its economical results, it impairs the national resources by destroying a large amount of corn which is annually distilled into spirits: and it indirectly causes three-fourths of the taxation required by pauperism and by criminal prosecutions and prison expenses; and, further, it diminishes the effective industry of the working-classes, thereby lessening the amount of national production. Thirdly, viewed in its social operation, it is the cause of two-thirds of the crime committed; it lowers the intelligence and hinders the civilization of the people, and it leads them to ill-treat and starve their families, and sacrifice domestic comfort to riotous debauchery."

E.

Responsibility for the Continuance of the Evils of Intemperance

[The following appeals are selected from the words of eminent men, who "being dead yet speak" to all who have ears to hear and hearts to feel.]

The late *Bishop of Norwich* (*Rev. Dr. Stanley*) said: "Few can bear more impartial testimony to the merits of teetotal societies than myself, since for some time I was opposed to them on the supposition that they were visionary and impracticable. I have, however, long since been a convert from conviction, founded on experience and observation, that they are most instrumental in raising thousands and tens of thousands from a degraded profligacy to virtuous and industrious habits, and converting sinners from the ways of vice to those of religion. I think every clergyman who has the welfare of his parishioners at heart ought to give them his support, and to take the lead."

Rev. John Wesley said (Works, vol. 7): "You see the wine when it sparkles in the cup and are going to drink it. I say there is poison in it, and therefore beg you to throw it away. If you add, It is not poison to me though it be to others, then I say, Throw it away for thy brother's sake, lest thou embolden him to drink also. Why should thy strength occasion thy weak brother to perish for whom Christ died?"

Ven. Archdeacon Jeffreys, of Bombay, has said: "Friends countrymen, and, above all, Christians! can you look upon this Golgotha, this Aceldama of human blood, and not stretch out a pitying hand to save? For it is in your power to stop the pestilence and arrest the march of the destroyer, if you will but be persuaded to take your censers in your hands, not filled with the unhallowed fire of intoxicating drinks, but with clear cold water from the spring, such as God gave to Adam in Paradise, and to stand between the living and the dead, and stay the plague. I say it is in your power to do it. A confederacy of all the sober and temperate of England and her colonies, to put away the instrument of intemperance out of their houses, and to declare that they will have nothing to do with the buying, selling, or using intoxicating drinks, would bring such disgrace upon their use, as positively to drive intoxicating drinks out of England, and to save your country! But nothing short of this will do it. If you would reap the blessing, if you have the noble ambition to save your country from her besetting sin, from the curse of intoxicating drinks, you must pay the price of it."

Rev. Dr. Potter (Protestant Episcopal Bishop of Pennsylvania) has said: "It was a glorious consciousness which enabled St. Paul to say, 'I take you to record this day that I am pure from the blood of all men.' May this consciousness be ours in respect, at least, to the blood of drunkards! May not one drop of the blood of their ruined souls be found at last spotting our garments! Are we ministers of Christ? Are we servants and followers of him who taught that it is more blessed to give than to receive? We can take a course which will embolden us to challenge the closest inspection of our influence as respects intemperance; which will enable us to enter without fear, on this ground at least, the presence of our Judge. May no false scruples, then, nor fear of man which bringeth a snare, no sordid spirit of self-indulgence, no unrelenting and unreasoning prejudice, deter us from doing that over which we cannot fail to rejoice when we come to stand before the Son of Man!"

The *Rev. William Jay*, of Bath, wrote: "I sincerely lament that many of my ministerial brethren in our severa denominations feel so little interest in this subject, especially as they know, or easily may know—First, the immensity of evil of every kind arising from the use of these liquors, and counteracting every means of doing good. Secondly, that the entire abstraction alone can preserve the mass from the malady and the curse. Thirdly, that their own example would have an extensive and powerful influence in their moral admonitions to sway others; and that influence is a talent for which we are responsible. Fourthly, that self-denial for the sake of usefulness is a species of benevolence the most noble, heroic, and Christian, enforced by Paul, and above all by him who "pleased not himself," but when "rich, for our sakes became poor, that we through his poverty might be rich." What! cannot we watch with him one hour? Fifthly, that though we cannot, and do not, deem this practice a substitute for religion, it amazingly promotes the temporal welfare of men, personally and socially. And as to religion—it is a preparation for it, and aids it in numberless ways, which must be obvious to every reflecting mind."

Rev. J. A. James: "I do most earnestly entreat you to abstain from all intoxicating liquors. You do not need them for health, and to take them for gratification is the germ of inebriety,

F.

The French Experiment in Alcohol.

Much interest in scientific circles was caused in the autumn of 1860 by the appearance of a French work, entitled *Du Rôle de l'Alcoöl et des Anestheniques dans l'Organisme, Recherches Experimentales* (Experimental Researches concerning the Procedure of Alcohol and of Anæsthetic Agents in the Animal System). This work, to which the prize of the French Medical Academy was awarded, was composed by Drs. Ludger Lallemand and Maurice Perrin, and detailed numerous carefully made experiments by those gentlemen, assisted by M. Duroy, a distinguished chemist.

The *Westminster Review,* which, in July, 1855, had published an article entitled "The Physiological Errors of Teetotalism," from the pen of Mr. G. H. Lewes, gave, in the number for January, 1861, an article on "Alcohol: What becomes of it in the living body," written by Dr. W. B. Carpenter, in which a retraction of Mr. Lewes's theorizings was offered, and a careful digest presented of the methods and results of the French experiments. By means of the test employed—a solution of bichromate of potass in sulphuric acid—it was found possible to detect alcohol in the breath and other emanations of persons who had taken even small doses of alcohol, which turned the red liquor to an emerald green, by decomposing the chromic acid and reducing it to the condition of green oxide of chromium. The experimentalists justly laid stress on the fact "that it is not the mere excess of alcohol which the system cannot profitably use up that finds its way into the excretions; for they detected alcohol in the urine of a man within half an hour after he had taken no more than 30 grammes (463 grains) of brandy; and the ingestion of only a litre, or ordinary bottle of weak wine, gave rise to a continued elimination of alcohol by the lungs during eight hours, and by the kidneys during fourteen hours. A very striking proof of the length of time during which alcohol remains unmodified in the system, after being ingested in any considerable amount, is afforded by the fact that it was found in abundance in the brains, liver, and blood of a vigorous man, who died of the remote results of alcoholic poisoning, thirty-two hours after drinking a litre of brandy, notwithstanding the early use of emetics and other remedial means." The *résumé* of the French writers is, literally translated, as follows:

A. Alcohol, taken into the stomach, applied by the skin, or inhaled by the lungs, is absorbed by the veins, and carried on by the blood into all the tissues.

B. The reception of alcohol causes, in animals, an intoxication which declares itself by a progressive series of functional disorders and alterations, whose intensity is in proportion to the quantity of alcohol absorbed.

C. It shows itself first in a general excitement; respiration and circulation are quickened; the temperature of the body is increased; afterwards, the respiration and circulation become slower, and the temperature falls.

D. Muscular power becomes enfeebled, and ultimately extinct; the loss commencing always in the posterior extremities.

E. Insensibility extends gradually from the circumference to the centre. The sensibility and motive power of the spinal cord and nervous trunks are abolished; mechanical irritation of these parts evokes no sign of either sensation or muscular contraction. However, the excitability of the nerves and spinal cord is still manifested under the action of electricity.

F. The respiratory movements cease before the pulsations of the heart; circulation continues after suspension of the other functions; the heart is the *ultimum moriens* (last to die).

G. The time which elapses between the beginning of the intoxication and its termination in death, has varied in our experiments from forty-five minutes to three hours.

H. When the dose of alcohol is not sufficient to cause death, the excitability of the spinal cord and the motive-power of the nerves reappear, after a suspension of variable duration. The sensorial and locomotive functions are not re-established in their integrity till after some considerable time—from fifteen to twenty hours.

I. The arterial blood continues of a bright color, and retains all its apparent qualities almost up to the moment of death.

J. The blood contains, both during life and after death, a great number of free globules of fat, recognizable even with the naked eye.

K. The anatomical and pathological changes are—an acute inflammation of the gastric nervous membrane; an accumulation of blood in the right cavities of the heart and in the large veins; congestion of the membranes of the brain. The lungs present no notable congestion.

L. All the fluids and all the solids contain alcohol, which is easily reproduced by distillation; or, by estimation, according to the method of volumes.

M. Alcohol accumulates in the liver, and in the cerebro-spinal nervous mass. The proportional distribution of the alcohol in the principal parts of the organism is represented, in some measure, according to our observations, by the following figures: In the blood, 1; in the cerebral substance, 1.34; in the substance of the liver, 1.48. The muscular, cellular, and other tissues retain a portion of alcohol very inferior to that which is found in the blood.

N. Alcohol, diluted and injected into the veins, produces the same phenomena as alcohol taken into the stomach; but they succeed each other more rapidly, and the animal succumbs in twenty minutes.

O. Alcohol, injected into the veins, spreads itself over all the tissues, but accumulates in the brain in a considerably larger proportion than in the liver, contrary to what takes place when it is administered by the stomach. This altered proportion is indicated by the following figures: In the blood, 1; in the substance of the brain, 3; in the liver, 1.75.

P. Death by alcoholic intoxication is due primarily to the special action which the alcohol exerts upon the cerebro-spinal nervous system.

Q. After the reception of a feeble dose of alcohol—say, twenty or thirty grammes of brandy—the blood, during several hours, contains alcohol, the presence of which can be demonstrated by tests.

R. During life, and after death, we do not find, either in the blood or in the tissues, any of the oxygenated derivatives of alcohol—such as aldehyde, acetic acid, etc.

S. The stomach, and the stomach only, contains a small quantity of acetic acid, formed at the expense of the ingested alcohol, by the action of the gastric juice, which operates in this case as a ferment.

T. The alcohol is rejected from the economy by different sources of elimination—by the lungs, by the skin, and by the kidneys. It is easy to recover the alcohol, in appreciable quantity, by distillation of the urine.

U. These sources of elimination reject the alcohol, not only after the ingestion of a considerable quantity of the substance, but even after the ingestion of very small doses of alcoholic liquors.

V. The elimination of the alcohol continues during several hours, even after very moderate ingestion. The elimination is continued by the kidneys for a longer time than by the skin and lungs.

X. Aldehyde introduced into the stomach is absorbed by and found in the blood; there is found there, at the same time, some acetic acid, due to the transformation of a portion of the aldehyde. But the aldehyde does not give place to the production of oxalic acid.

Y. Aldehyde introduced into the stomach is eliminated partially by the kidneys and by the lungs. After the ingestion of alcohol, aldehyde is not found either in the urine or in the products of the pulmonary exhalation.

Z. Alcohol has the same action, and produces the same effects, in man as in the lower animals.

G.

Medical Declarations on the Use of Intoxicating Liquors and Abstinence from Them.

Besides a great variety of collective statements, signed by medical men residing in the same town or district, three *certificates* of a national character have been published. The first of these was drawn up, in 1839, by Julius Jeffreys, Esq., himself one of the faculty, and the inventor of the well-known respirator. It was expressed in these terms: "An opinion handed down from rude and ignorant times, and imbibed by Englishmen from their youth, has become very general, that the habitual use of some portion of alcoholic drink, as of wine, beer, or spirit, is beneficial to health, and even necessary for those subjected to habitual labor. Anatomy, physiology, and the experience of all ages and countries, when properly examined, must satisfy every mind well informed in medical science that the above opinion is altogether erroneous. Man, in ordinary health, like other animals, requires not any such stimulants, and cannot be benefited by the habitual employment of any quantity of them, large or small; nor will their use during his lifetime increase the aggregate amount of his labor. In whatever quantity they are employed, they will rather tend to diminish it. When he is in a state of temporary debility from illness or other causes, a temporary use of them, as of other stimulant medicines, may be desirable; but as soon as he is raised to his natural standard of health, a continuance of their use can do no good to him, even in the most moderate quantities, while larger quantities (yet such as by many persons are thought moderate) do, sooner or later, prove injurious to the human constitution, without any exceptions. It is my opinion that the above statement is substantially correct." This important document was signed by Sir Benjamin Brodie, F.R.S.; Dr. W. F. Chambers, F.R.S., Physician to the Queen; Sir Jas. Clarke; Barnsby Cooper, F.R.S.; Dr. D. Davis, Physician to the Duchess of Kent; Sir J. Eyre, M.D.; Dr. R. Ferguson; Dr. Marshall Hall, F.R.S.; Dr. J. Hope, F.R.S.; C. A. Key; Dr. R. Lee, F.R.S.; Herbert Mayo, F.R.S.; R. Partridge, F.R.S.; Richard Quain, Professor of Anatomy in London University; Dr. A. T. Thomson; R. Travers, F.R.S., Surgeon Extraordinary to the Queen; Drs. Andrew and Alexander Ure, and, in all, by seventy-eight members of the medical faculty in London and the provinces, most of them men of distinction and authority in the profession.

In 1847, a second MEDICAL CERTIFICATE, in whose composition several London physicians of the highest eminence were concerned, was published by John Dunlop, Esq., who had taken an active interest in its preparation, and in securing signatures to it. These written adhesions amounted, in the course of a few years, to upwards of 2,000, and comprised the names of physicians and surgeons engaged in every branch of the profession, and acquainted with every detail, theoretical and practical, of the science of medicine in all its departments. This testimony was as follows:

"We, the undersigned, are of opinion—1. That a very large portion of human misery, including poverty, disease, and crime, is induced by the use of alcoholic or fermented liquors as beverages. 2. That the most perfect health is compatible with total abstinence from all such intoxicating beverages, whether in the form of ardent spirits, or as wine, beer, ale, porter, cider, etc., etc. 3. That persons accustomed to such drinks may, with perfect safety, discontinue them entirely, either at once, or gradually after a short time. 4. That total and universal abstinence from alcoholic liquors and beverages of all sorts would greatly contribute to the health, the prosperity, the morality, and the happiness of the human race."

Among the signatures to this valuable document were those of Dr. Addison, Senior Physician of Guy's Hospital; Dr. Niell Arnott, Physician to the Queen, and author of the "Elements of Physics"; Dr. B. G. Babington, F.R.S.; Dr. A. Billing, F.R.S.; Dr. John Bostock, F.R.S.; Dr. R. Bright, F.R.S., Physician to the Queen; Sir B. C. Brodie, F.R.S.; Sir W. Burnett, M.D., F.R.S., Physician-General to the Navy; Dr. W. B. Carpenter, F.R.S.; Sir J. Clark, M.D., F.R.S.; Dr. Copland, F.R.S., author of the "Dictionary of Practical Medicine"; Dr. A. Farre, F.R.S.; Dr. Robt. Fergusson, Physician to the Queen; Sir J. Forbes, M.D., F.R.S.; W. A. Guy, M.D., Professor at King's College; Sir H. Holland, M.D., F.R.S., Physician to the Queen; Dr. P. M. Latham, Physician to the Queen; Sir J. McGrigor, Bart., M.D., F.R.S., Director-General of the Army Medical Department; Dr. J. A. Paris, President of the Royal College of Physicians; Dr. J. Pereira, F.R.S.; Dr. W. Prout, F.R.S.; Dr. Forbes Winslow, Dr. A. Combe, Dr. P. Crampton, F.R.S.; and many others of equal or nearly equal eminence with the foregoing.

The latest MEDICAL DECLARATION CONCERNING ALCOHOL was issued in December, 1871, and is as follows:

"As it is believed that the inconsiderate prescription of large quantities of alcoholic liquids by medical men for their patients has given rise, in many instances, to the formation of intemperate habits, the UNDERSIGNED, while unable to abandon the use of alcohol in the treatment of certain cases of disease, are yet of opinion that no medical practitioner should prescribe it without a sense of grave responsibility. They believe that alcohol in whatever form should be prescribed with as much care as any powerful drug, and that the directions for its use should be so framed as not to be interpreted as a sanction for excess, or necessarily for the continuance of its use when the occasion is past.

"They are also of opinion that many people immensely exaggerate the value of alcohol as an article of diet, and, since no class of men see so much of its ill effects, and possess such power to restrain its abuse, as members of their own profession, they hold that every medical practitioner is bound to exert his utmost influence to inculcate habits of great moderation in the use of alcoholic liquids.

"Being also firmly convinced that the great amount of drinking of alcoholic liquors among the working-classes of this country is one of the greatest evils of the day, destroying, more than anything else, the health, happiness, and welfare of those classes, and neutralizing, to a large extent, the great industrial prosperity which Providence has placed within the reach of this nation, the UNDERSIGNED would gladly support any wise legislation which would tend to restrict, within proper limits, the use of alcoholic beverages, and gradually introduce habits of temperance."

George Burrows, M.D., F.R.S., President of the Royal College of Physicians, Physician-Extraordinary to the Queen; George Busk, F.R.S., President of the Royal College of Surgeons; and nearly three hundred of the most eminent members of the Faculty in London, subscribed the above.

INDIVIDUAL TESTIMONIES.

The following are but a few medical *dicta* culled from a large repertory of voluntary evidence, much of it given without any intention of aiding the temperance reform:

Abernethy.—"If people will leave off drinking alcohol, live plainly, and take very little medicine, they will find that many disorders will be relieved by this treatment alone." "Wine is neither food nor drink, but a stimulant."

Boerhaave.—"Food, not too fat or gross, and water as a drink, render our bodies the most firm and strong."

Dr. Brinton (St. Thomas's Hospital).—"Mental acuteness, accuracy of perception, and delicacy of the senses are all so far opposed by the action of alcohol as that the maximum efforts of each are incompatible with the ingestion of any moderate quantity of fermented liquid. The mathematician, the gambler, the metaphysician, the billiard-player, the author, the artist, the physician, would, if they could analyze their experience aright, generally concur in the statement, that a single glass will often suffice to take, so to speak, the edge off both mind and body, and to reduce their capacity to something below what is relatively their perfection of work."

Sir Benjamin Brodie.—"I cannot doubt that, on the whole, the condition of mankind would have been much better if alcoholic liquors had never been within their reach." "Stimulants do not create nervous power, they merely enable you, as it were, to use up that which is left, and then they leave you more in need of rest than you were before." "It is worthy of notice that opium is much less deleterious to the individual than gin or brandy."

Dr. Beddoes (1802).—"As the greatest authorities are against wine; as there are none worth regard on the other side; and, above all, as there is so little danger of being thought odd [in children abstaining], why risk the early destruction of that organ (the stomach) which may be regarded as the great regulator of the inward man?" "All considerations combine to show that fermented liquors, by their activity, class with the most powerful and, therefore, with the most hazardous drugs. In women the digestive organs may be as much injured by a glass (suppose two ounces) of wine as in a robust man by a pint."

Dr. W. B. Carpenter.—"My position is, that in the discharge of the ordinary duties of life, alcohol is not necessary, but injurious, in so far as it acts at all. Even in small quantities habitually taken, it perverts the ordinary functions by which the body is sustained in health."

Sir A. Carlisle, M.D.—"Long-continued experience in my profession has convinced me of the safety of a sudden transition from the daily employment of strong drink to a water diet, and that in the most inveterate habits. I have known the most emaciated and broken-down frames, both in body and mind, to spring up and become renovated after a total abstinence from strong liquors for only a few weeks."

Dr. T. K. Chambers.—"It is clear that we must cease to regard alcohol as in any sense an aliment."

Dr. George Cheyne, F.R.S. (1700).—"Without all peradventure, water was the primitive original beverage; and it is the only simple fluid fitted for diluting, moistening, and cooling—the code of drink appointed by nature. Happy had it been for the race of mankind if other revised and artificial liquors had never been invented! It has been an agreeable appearance to me to observe with what freshness and vigor those who, though eating freely of flesh meat, yet drank nothing but this element, have lived in health and cheerfulness to a great age."

Dr. Cheyne, late Physician-General of the Army in Ireland.—"The observation of twenty years in this city (Dublin) has convinced me that were ten young men, on their twenty-first birthday, to begin to drink one glass (equal to two ounces) of ardent spirits, or a pint of port wine or sherry, and were they to drink this supposed moderate quantity of strong liquor daily, the lives of eight out of the ten would be abridged by twelve or fifteen years. They represent themselves as temperate, very temperate."

Sir Astley Cooper.—"I never suffer ardent spirits to be in my house, thinking them evil spirits, and if the poor could witness the white livers, the dropsies, and shattered nervous systems which I have seen as the consequence of drinking, they would be aware that spirits and poisons are synonymous terms."

Dr. Copland (Authôr of "Dictionary of Practical Medicine").—"There can be no doubt that, as expressed by the late Dr. Gregory, an occasional excess is, upon the whole, less injurious to the constitution, than the practice of daily taking a moderate quantity of any fermented liquor or spirit."

Dr. Cullen (Edinburgh).—"Simple water, such as nature affords it, is, without any addition, the proper drink of mankind. The drinks which supply the necessary liquid (that is, for the support of the functions of the animal economy) do it only by the quantity of elementary water they severally contain."

Dr. Erasmus Darwin (1800).—"Under the names of

rum, brandy, gin, whiskey, wine, cider, beer, and porter, alcohol is become the bane of the Christian world."

Sir John Floyer.—"Water-drinkers are temperate in their actions, prudent, and ingenious; they live safe from those diseases which affect the head, such as apoplexies, palsies, pain, blindness, deafness, gout, convulsions, trembling, and madness. To the use of water children ought to be bred from their cradles."

Sir John Forbes, F.R.S.—"Men can do well without alcoholic drinks. It cannot be admitted that the most moderate quantity is, speaking generally, requisite for the maintenance of perfect vigor, under any ordinary circumstances of bodily labor. On the contrary, it seems proved that a proper allowance of good food, without any alcoholic drinks, is the best support of man."

Dr. W. T. Gairdner (Glasgow).—"I am strongly persuaded that to the young, in typhus and in most other fevers, stimulants are not less than actively poisonous and destructive, unless administered with the most extreme caution, and in the most special and critical circumstances."

Dr. Garnett (Author of "Lectures on Zoönomia," 1804).—"The most mischievous agent of all, and which contributes to bring on the greater number of nervous complaints, is wine. This I believe produces more diseases than all other causes put together. Every person is ready to allow that wine taken to excess is hurtful, because he sees immediate evils will follow; but the distant effects, which require more attentive observation to perceive, very few see and believe; and, judging from pleasant and agreeable feelings, they say that a little wine is wholesome and good for every one; and accordingly take it every day, and even give it to their children. The idea that wine or spirituous liquors will assist digestion is false. Those who are acquainted with chemistry know that food is rendered hard and less digestible by these means."

Dr. John Hope (inventor of the stethoscope).—"I have a strong conviction that drinking is the grand curse of this country, and more especially the notion almost universally prevalent among the lower classes, that a proportion of stimulating liquors is indispensable for the maintenance of health and strength, under which impression they take from two to four pints of ale per day, and think *that* moderation. I have hitherto taken no part in the cause of teetotalism, but if the question should ever become a strictly medical one, I shall feel it due to my country and to the cause of humanity to lend the aid of my feeble pen on the affirmative side."

Sir Henry Holland, F.R.S.—"We have not the less assurance that it (wine) is in numerous other cases habitually injurious in relation both to the digestive organs and to the functions of the brain. It is the part of every wise man once, at least, in life, to make trial of the effect of leaving off wine altogether; and this even without the suggestion of actual malady. To obtain them (the results) fairly, the abandonment must be complete for a time, a measure of no risk even where the change is greatest."

Dr. James Johnson.—"A very considerable proportion of the middling and higher classes of life, as well as the lower, commit serious depredations on their constitutions, when they believe themselves to be sober citizens and really abhor debauch. This is by drinking ale or other malt liquor to a degree far short of intoxication indeed, yet from long habit producing a train of effects that embitter the ulterior periods of existence,"

Professor Hoffman (Prussia).—"Drinkers of water, provided it be pure and excellent, are more healthy and longer-lived than such as drink wine or malt liquors. It generally gives them a better appetite, and renders them plump and fleshy."

Dr. Hufeland (Prussia, author of "The Art of Prolonging Life.")—"The best drink is water, a liquor commonly despised, and even considered as prejudicial. I will not hesitate, however, to declare it to be one of the greatest means of prolonging life."

Dr. Latham.—"There are whole classes of society in London who are never really sober for years together. The stimulus of spirits renewed day by day and hour by hour, gives them feelings and excitement which are unnatural; and, however they may be mistaken for those of health, do not in truth at all belong to it."

Dr. E. Lankester, F.R.S.—"So far as its physical action is concerned, I do not know that we can say anything good of alcohol at all; it may seriously interfere with the functions of absorption and injure the coats of the stomach; and, when taken injudiciously, even a long way short of producing any effect on the nervous system, may yet prevent the proper nutrition of the system, and insidiously lay the foundation of incurable disease."

Dr. Michel Levy.—"The influence of alcohol upon the nervous system, and particularly upon the brain, is manifest by a progressive but constant series of symptoms, which in different degrees of intensity are reproduced in all individuals. These constitute a true poisoning, and this morbid state is exhibited under three phases—viz., excitation, perturbation, abolition of the cerebro-spinal functions."

Dr. Macroire (late Physician to the Fever Hospital, Liverpool.)—"After having treated more than three thousand cases in the Town Hospital, Liverpool, I give it as my decided opinion that the constant moderate use of stimulating drinks is more injurious than the now and then excessive indulgence in them."

Dr. Markham (late editor of *British Medical Journal.*)—"We are in conscience bound to say that science has found that alcohol is not good, and that being simply a stimulant to the nervous system, its use is hurtful to the body of a healthy man."

Dr. B. W. Richardson, M.D.—"All alcoholic bodies are depressants, and although at first, by their calling injuriously into play the natural forces, they seem to excite, and are therefore called stimulants, they themselves supply no force at any time, but take up force, by which means they lead to exhaustion and paralysis of power."

Dr. Edward Smith, F.R.S.—"Alcohol is probably not transformed, and does not increase the production of heat by its own chemical action. It interferes with alimentation. Its power to lessen the salivary secretions must impede the digestion of starch. It greatly lessens muscular tone and power. Alcohol is not a true food; and it neither warms nor sustains the body by the elements of which it is composed. In from three to seven minutes [after a moderate dose taken in the morning by himself and friends], the mind was disturbed. Consciousness, the power of fixing attention, the perception of light, and the power of directing and co-ordinating the muscles, were lessened. After thirty minutes the effect diminished, as shown by increased consciousness and the perception of light, as if a veil had fallen from the eyes."

Dr. Trotter (Physician to the English Fleet in the French War, and author of an "Essay on Drunkenness," 1802).—"Intoxicating liquors in all their forms, and however disguised, are the most productive cause of disease with which I am acquainted."

Dr. S. Wilks (Guy's Hospital.)—"Alcohol, though an excitant, is a sedative to the nervous system—is, in fact, an anæsthetic. The argument, therefore, that a man feels better after his glass or two of grog would be equally applicable to the case of the Turk, who feels better for his opium. . . . Indeed, it may generally be assumed that whilst his feelings are benumbed, his organization is being injured."

Dr. Wood (late President of the Royal College of Surgeons, Edinburgh.)—" I have long been a practical abstainer, and fully sympathize with every movement calculated to put down the monster evil of intemperance."

Zimmerman (Physician to Frederick the Great of Prussia).—"Water is the most suitable drink for man, and does not chill the ardor of genius."

H.

Cases of Longevity in Connection with Abstinence from Intoxicating Drinks.

[The late Sir Cornewall Lewis was sceptical as to all cases of reputed longevity exceeding a hundred years. A tendency to exaggeration may be admitted in regard to extreme old age; but the following examples will be perused with interest, whatever allowance on the score of excess may be supposed necessary in the instances of extraordinary duration of human life. It is sometimes urged that persons who use intoxicating liquors sometimes live to very great old age, as occasionally those who indulge freely in them; yet the latter cannot be supposed to have escaped all injury from them. In not a few cases, as in those of Old Parr and Dr. Holyoke, of America, the use of intoxicating drink can be shown to have abridged even a term of life in itself of wonderful extent. Bishop Berkeley designated old topers who do not seem injured by their potations "the devil's decoy-ducks"; and that they are mere exceptions (if this can be claimed even for them) to a great physiological rule which connects shortened life with indulgence in strong drink, is strikingly illustrated in the anecdote told by Dr. Cheyne, of Dublin, of a gentleman far advanced in years, who boasted that he had drunk several bottles of wine every day for fifty years, and was as hale and hearty as ever. "Pray," asked a bystander, "where are your boon companions?" "Ah!" he quickly replied, "that's another affair; if the truth may be told, I have buried three entire generations of them."]

According to Herodotus, the ancient *Macrobians* ("long-livers") attained the age of a hundred and a hundred and twenty years; they used milk as their beverage.

The same longevity is stated to have been usual among the *North American Indians* when first discovered, and when they were ignorant of all intoxicating drinks.

The great age of the Hindoo *Brahmins*, and of the ancient philosophic and Christian *hermits*, is proved by indisputable evidence; and their avoidance of all inebriating drinks is equally well attested. *Kentigern*, known as St. Mongah, is said "never to have tasted wine or strong drink after arriving at the years of understanding." His years are recorded as 185. *Old Parr*, whose life extended to 152 years and 9 months, was of very abstemious habits. Taylor, the water-poet, says—

> "His daily swig,
> Milk, buttermilk, water, whey, and whig."

Having been invited to the Court of Charles I., his biographer says, "He fed high, and drank plenty of the best wines," and died the same year (1635). *William Aldridge* died in 1698, aged 114 years; he was remarkable for his sober habits. *I. Effingham*, of Cornwall, died in 1757, aged 144; in his youth he never drank strong liquor, and always lived very soberly. *Jonathan Harlop*, of Aldborough, Yorkshire, died in 1791, aged 138; his only beverage was milk and water. *Anne Maynard*, of Finchley, died very aged in 1756; she was exceedingly abstemious in her habits. *Seth Unthanke*, of Bath, was met by Dr. Baynard, and is described by him as 87 years, "a straight, upright man, and wonderfully nimble"; his drink, buttermilk and water; nothing stronger than "small beer." *John Bailes*, also seen by Dr. Baynard, reported himself as 128½ years, and said by very old people to have been old ever since they remembered; he had a very strong voice, and said "he had buried the whole town of Northampton, except three or four persons, twenty times over." "Strong drink," he said, "kills 'em all." Water, small beer, and milk were his drinks. Sir William Temple relates having met a beggar 124 years old, who, when asked what he drank, said, "Oh! sir, we have the best water in our parish in the whole neighborhood." The landlord of the inn which this "ancient man" visited, said he had got many a pound in his house, but had never spent a penny. *Francis Hongo* died 1702, aged 114 years and 10 months.

He was never sick, and drank only water. The venerable *Wesley*, who died at the age of 88, and performed labors almost unexampled for combined and continuous mental and corporeal effort, was very delicate in early life, but, by abstinence and careful diet, overcame very serious ailments and attained patriarchal years. Dr. A. Fothergill, in his essay on spirituous liquors, says: "My worthy friend, *Dr. B. Pugh*, of Midford Castle, having from early youth abstained from wines, spirits, and fermented liquors, declares that at this moment he not only enjoys superior health and vivacity, but feels himself as capable of every mental or corporeal exertion as he did at twenty-five, though now in the eighty-second year of his age." The late Earl Stanhope stated that his *grandfather* was a water-drinker, and at seventy-two devoted several hours a day to abstruse mathematical studies; and that his *grandmother*, who was the same, and enjoyed the use of her ordinary faculties to extreme old age, died at 93. *Thomas Winsloe*, who died in 1796, aged 146 years, was exceedingly abstemious in regard to his diet; as was also *John Wood*, who died in 1818, aged 122. *Thomas Laugher*, who died in 1813, aged 113, never drank strong beer, small beer, or spirits. *Mary Potter*, aged 106, died in 1839, at Larkhill, near Bath; she never drank beer or spirits. *Mr. Crossley*, of Uttoxeter, aged 100 years and 9 months, had used milk for many years as his principal beverage. *Mrs. Parker*, who died 1837, aged 109, had abstained from spirituous liquors all her life. *W. Dupe*, of Oxford, died at the age of 95, in 1843. He had never drunk alcoholic liquors, nor had his father and grandfather, who lived to the ages of 102 and 108. *Mrs. Cox*, of Bybrook, Jamaica, who died in 1831, and was reckoned to have attained 160 years, had drunk only water during her life. The *Jamaica Royal Gazette* contained the notice of an old black woman, who died 140 years old. She declared she never drank anything but water. She lived on

Holland Estate, the property of Mr. Gladstone (the present Premier). The *Stamford Mercury*, of 1853, contained the following notice: "There is now living a fine old man, 90 years old, who worked for many years as a journeyman fellmonger at Horncastle; he can carry twenty stone weight at the present time, can walk four miles in an hour, and he has drunk nothing stronger than water for the last forty years." *Mr. A. Johnson*, of Howden, died August 12, 1852, in his ninetieth year. He joined the Temperance Society December 15, 1840, and, up to the period of a fall some time before his death, enjoyed perfect health. The Liverpool newspapers, in 1859, contained a notice of a woman, by name *Elizabeth Roberts*, who stated that she was born in Northop, Flintshire, in June, 1749. She could (in 1859) walk three miles an hour, and ascribed her extended life to her simple natural habits, including entire abstinence from intoxicating drinks. In the same year, the wife of a captain in the navy recorded the fact that her grandmother married at fifteen, had fifteen children, and lived to her ninetieth year, without once tasting wine, spirits, or malt liquors. So, truly has Shakespeare put into the mouth of Old Adam, in "As You Like It":

> "Though I look old, yet I am strong and lusty,
> For in my youth I never did apply
> Hot and rebellious liquors in my blood:
> Nor did not, with unbashful forehead, woo
> The means of weakness and debility.
> Therefore my age is, as lusty winter,
> Frosty, but kindly."

I.

TESTIMONIES OF PHILOSOPHERS, POETS, DIVINES, PHILANTHROPISTS, GENERALS, TRAVELLERS, ETC.

Solomon.—"Wine is a mocker, strong drink is raging; and whosoever is deceived thereby is not wise. . . . Look not upon the wine when it is red, when it giveth his color (eye-bubble) in the cup, when it moveth itself aright (in straight lines); for at the last it biteth like a serpent, and stingeth like an adder."

Pythagoras.—"Pythagoras laid down such rules as he thought most conducive to maintain tranquillity of mind. He allowed no beverage but water."

Philo.—"The truly wise man aims to offer abstemious sacrifices, steadfastly setting himself, in the firmness of his mind, against wine and every course of folly."

Plato applauds the Carthaginian law against using wine in the camp, and considers it applicable to magistrates during their year of office, and to judges, and to those deliberating on any business of importance, and to persons generally during the daytime. "Many other cases a person might mention in which wine ought not to be drunk by those who possess understanding and a correct rule of action."

Pliny the Elder. (See extract on page 30.)

Among English philosophers of eminence, *Sir Isaac Newton, John Locke,* and *Robert Boyle* were examples of remarkable abstemiousness, amounting almost to total abstinence from all intoxicating drinks. When composing his treatise upon optics, Sir Isaac used water only as a beverage; and Locke, in his writings, strongly recommended abstinence, especially in the physical training of the young. *Dr. Smollett,* the historian and novelist, says (in his "Travels through France and Italy"), "The longer I live, the more I am convinced that wine and all fermented liquors are pernicious to the human constitution; and that, for the preservation of health, and exhilaration of the spirits, there is no beverage comparable to simple water." *Dr. Samuel Johnson* abstained for considerable periods from intoxicating drinks with great advantage to his mind and feelings, and always resolutely contended for the wisdom of this course.

Dr. Thomas Reid wrote: "Besides the appetites which

nature hath given us, for useful and necessary purposes, we may create appetites which nature never gave us. The frequent use of things which stimulate the nervous system produces a languor when their effect is gone off, and a desire to repeat them. Such are the appetites which some men acquire for the use of tobacco, for opiates, and for intoxicating liquors."

Jeremy Bentham wrote to a friend, "I am a single man, turned of 70, and as free from melancholy as man need be. Wine I drink none, being in that particular of the persuasion of Jonadab, the son of Rechab." *William Cobbett* wrote: "In the midst of a society where wine and spirits are considered of more value than water, I have lived two years with no other drink but water, except when I have found it convenient to obtain milk. Not an hour's illness, not a headache for an hour, not the smallest ailment, not a restless night, not a drowsy morning, have I known during these two famous years of my life."

Thomas De Quincey wrote in eulogistic terms of the modern temperance movement: "It has attained both at home and abroad a national range of grandeur." *Lora Brougham* highly commended temperance efforts, and was a Vice-President of the United Kingdom Alliance.

Homer represents Hector as refusing the cup of wine offered him by his mother Hecuba, as sure to relax his vigor; and *Pope*, in commenting on this passage, observes that "it is a vulgar mistake to imagine the use of wine either rouses the spirits or increases strength. The best physicians agree with Homer on this point, whatever modern writers may object to this old heroic regimen." *Pindar* opens his first Ode with the words, *Ariston men Hudôr*—"Water truly is the best!" *Milton*, in his "Paradise Lost," his "Samson Agonistes," his Sonnets, and particularly his "Comus," shows his appreciation of the strictest temperance, and his life corresponded with his doctrine. He rarely used any intoxicating liquors. These words of his are ever memorable: "Who can be ignorant that, if the importation of wine and the use of all strong drinks were forbid, it would both rid the possibility of committing that odious vice, and men might afterwards live happily and healthfully without the use of these intoxicating liquors?" *Shakespeare*, in several of his dramas, depicts the miseries of indulgence in strong drink, and puts into Cassio's mouth the celebrated words: "O thou invisible spirit of wine! if thou hast no name to be called by, let us call thee Devil!" *Waller*, one of the liveliest and wittiest poets of the Restoration period, was an inflexible abstainer from all intoxicating liquors. *William Cowper* and *Dr. Darwin*, very dissimilar in their religious sentiments and poetic gifts, yet agreed in their aversion to indulgence in strong drinks; and the latter was both a disciple and earnest advocate of abstinence.

Lord Lytton wrote (in 1846): "I agree in the main in the principles of the temperance society, and heartily wish it success, as having already done much good, and being calculated to do much more."

Lord Byron confessed: "The effect of wine upon me is to make me gloomy—gloomy at the very moment it is taken; but it never makes me gay."

St. Clement of Alexandria (A.D. 180) writes: "I admire those who desire no other beverage than water, avoiding wine as they do fire."

St. Jerome: "Whatever inebriates and throws the mind off its balance, fly in like manner as if it were wine. . . . If, without wine, my system is vigorous and well-strung, cheerfully will I abstain from the cup which is suspected to contain poison."

Dr. South: "Nothing is so great a friend to the mind of man as abstinence; it strengthens the memory, clears the apprehension, and sharpens the judgment, and, in a word, gives reason its full scope of acting; and, when reason has that, it is always a diligent and faithful handmaid to conscience." Among the most distinguished theologians and ornaments of the modern pulpit, there have been numerous adherents to the temperance movement in England and America.

Among the modern British statesmen, *Richard Cobden* holds a high and noble place. For many years he was entirely or almost a total abstainer, and the sum of his testimony may be expressed in his own words: "Every day's experience tends more and more to confirm me in my opinion that the temperance cause lies at the foundation of all social and political reform." *Earl Russell* said in Exeter Hall (1844): "This is no party, no sectarian question; and I am convinced that there is no cause more likely to elevate the people in every respect, whether as regards religious or political opinions, or as regards literary and moral culture, than this great question of temperance. It is the common and universal cause of all morality and of all religion." *John Howard*, the apostle of philanthropy, was a systematic abstainer, and attributed to this habit his remarkable immunity for many years from the diseases to which his prison labors exposed him. The venerable *Thomas Clarkson* said: "Total abstinence has been found to be an auxiliary to the promotion of Christianity and to the conversion of sinners." The late *Joseph John Gurney, Joseph Sturge, Rev. John Clay*, and Mr. Recorder *Hill*, and many of the most earnest of the social reformers of the present time, are zealous advocates of the temperance movement.

Charles XII., of Sweden, used no intoxicating drinks; and the same was true of the defender of Gibraltar, *General Elliot*, afterwards Lord Heathfield.

It is recorded of the Emperor *Napoleon* (Family Library, vol. ii. p. 246): "The labor he underwent at this period, when he was consolidating the administration throughout France, excited the astonishment of all who had access to his privacy. He exhausted the energies of secretary after secretary, and seemed hardly to feel the want of sleep; yet he sustained the unparalleled fatigue without having recourse to any stimulant stronger than lemonade." Napoleon's great rival, the *Duke of Wellington*, was accustomed to a very careful diet, and took but little wine for years preceding his death. The gallant General *Bem* was urged at the close of life to take a little wine. "Not a drop!" he said; "there are things enough in the world to send the blood to the head without strong drink." *Baron Larrey*, the eminent French surgeon under Napoleon, states that in the retreat from Moscow those soldiers who indulged in ardent spirits first fell victims to the cold; and the *Count de Linehulle*, one of the few officers who survived, ascribed his escape to his having drunk water and not spirits during that disastrous march. Marshal *Grouchy* ascribed his escape to his use of coffee instead of spirits. The illustrious *Havelock* took a warm interest in the promotion of temperance among the English soldiers in India from the time when he was a captain in the 13th Light Infantry. In his "Narrative of the War in Afghanistan," he relates the noble conduct of the troops engaged in the storming of Ghuznee, which he states may in "a great degree be attributed to the fact of the European soldiers having received no spirit ration since the 8th of July (the place was captured on the 23d), and having found no intoxicating liquor among the plunder of Ghuznee. Since then it has been found that troops can make forced marches of fifty miles, and storm a fortress in seventy-five minutes, without the aid of rum, behaving after success with a forbearance and humanity unparalleled in history. Let it not henceforth be argued that distilled spirits are an indispensable portion of a soldier's ration." Havelock continued to maintain his temperance principles, and though in the advance upon Cawnpore he ordered porter to be served to the troops after an exhausting march and long fast, and in the presence of a numerous foe, the circumstances were exceedingly peculiar, and the issue of the experiment was so little satisfactory that the order was not renewed. General Sir *W. F. Williams,* the hero of Kars, said, in a letter to the "Sons of Temperance," Nova Scotia: "I am indebted to a gracious Providence for preservation in very unhealthy climates; but I am satisfied that a resolution early formed, and steadily persevered in, never to take spirituous liquors, has been a means of my escaping diseases by which multitudes have fallen around me. Had not the Turkish army of Kars been literally 'a cold-water army,' I am persuaded they would never have performed the achievements which crowned them with glory." During the Crimean War the advantages of total abstinence were very conspicuous when practised. Colonel *Dacres,* who was in charge of the English artillery (now General Sir Richard Dacres), in writing from the camp, Jan. 17, 1855, said: "Since I have become a teetotaler I have gone through great fatigues in hot climates. I have crossed the Atlantic, come here, been exposed to disease and *some* discomfort (not much from my rank and situation), and I have never been sick or had even a short attack of diarrhœa. I ascribe this to water; but mind, I am a temperate eater also; never eat animal food more than once a day; no lunch but a piece of biscuit; am a very early man. Now, all these things combined enable me to do as much hard work at fifty-five as many men ten or fifteen years younger. What I began with, as an example, I now continue, as I consider I am much better without wine, beer, etc., both in a religious and worldly point of view; and I shall continue as I am, please God, to my life's end." General *Lewis Cass,* of the United States, said: "The more active portion of my life was passed in a country on the very verge of civilization, and much of it beyond, and I have had my full share of exposures, exertions, privations, in peace and in war. I have had, too, my full share of health.

I might almost say that I have enjoyed uninterrupted health; and I am, therefore, a living proof that ardent spirits are not necessary for physical endurance under any circumstances of toil and trial. It was this conviction which led me, when Secretary of War, to authorize the commutation of the ration of ardent spirits, previously issued to the troops, for the equivalent in coffee and sugar." During the sanguinary war between the Federal and Confederate armies (1861-5), some of the ablest commanders on both sides were those who carried the temperance principle most rigidly out by precept and example, as for instance, *Stonewall Jackson* and General *Stuart* among the Confederates, and General *Howard* among the Federals. The exclusion of liquor from the camps was found indispensable to sobriety, discipline, and military success.

James Bruce, the African traveller, 1768–73, states: "I lay down, then, as a positive rule of health, that spirits and all fermented liquor should be regarded as poisons, and, for fear of temptation, not so much as to be carried along with you, unless as a menstruum for outward application. Spring or running water, if you can find it, is to be your only drink."

Dr. Livingstone, writing from Kuruman, South Africa, Nov. 12, 1852, said: "I have acted on the principle of total abstinence from all alcoholic liquors during more than twenty years. My individual opinion is, that the most severe labors or privations may be undergone without alcoholic stimulus, because those of us who have endured the most had nothing else than water, and not always enough of that."

Mr. Charles Waterton, the eminent naturalist and author of "Wanderings in South America," writes: "I eat moderately, and never drink wine, spirits, or any fermented liquors in any climate. This abstemiousness has ever proved a faithful friend." Mr. Waterton, who died from the effects of an accident, in 1865, at the age of 83, had been an abstainer for sixty-two years.

Mr. James Silk Buckingham, the Eastern traveller and distinguished advocate of temperance, bore frequent testimony to the advantages of abstinence, and to his observation of these advantages in the people of the various countries through which he passed where total abstinence was practised. He describes himself as having been particularly struck with the sight of a band of Himalaya mountaineers, who "were indeed perfect Samsons," both as regards their feats of strength and abstinence from intoxicating drinks.

Mr. Keppel says, in his "Voyage up the Tigris (1820)": "We tried to content ourselves with water—an experiment which we found to answer so well that, while actually on the road, we entirely abstained from drinking anything else. To this circumstance we alone attribute our health during our long and fatiguing journey."

Mr. James Backhouse said: "I have travelled over hot sands, so hot that the very dogs howled with pain on treading upon it, the thermometer often at 116 degrees, and the water so bad that we had to conceal the taste with coffee; and I believe no journey of the same length was ever made with so little risk or danger. There is no single act of my life to which I look back with greater satisfaction than to the adoption of total abstinence."

Sir John Ross, the Arctic explorer, in an account of his career, states: "I was twenty years older [at the time of his four-years' voyage, April, 1829, to October, 1833] than any of the officers or crew, and thirty years older than all excepting three, yet I could stand the cold and fatigue better than any of them, who all made use of tobacco and spirits."

The *Rev. Dr. Scoresby*, in his evidence before the Parliamentary Committee of 1834 on drunkenness, said: "My principal experience has been in severely cold climates, and there it is observable that there is a very pernicious effect in the reaction after the use of ardent spirits. I did not use them myself, and I was better, I conceive, without the use of them."

J.

Effect of Abstinence in Prisons and Workhouses.

The venerated *Howard*, in his work on Lazarettos and Prisons (page 146), alluding to the Horsham County Gaol, states in a note: "The gaoler told me that he had a debtor who was so addicted to the use of spirits that he thought he should die if they were refused him; but after his discharge he had several times called to acknowledge the benefit he had received from entirely breaking him of that habit. The gaoler also asserted that the felons after a few weeks are evidently improved in health by their restriction from all spirituous and fermented liquors, and remained in prison perfectly well." One of Howard's suggestions was the exclusion of all intoxicating liquors from prisons, on which he observes "I am satisfied my ideas are contrary to the present fashionable mode of prescriptions, which I am persuaded confirms the habit of drinking strong liquors both in town and country; but may I not hope that the opinions of medical gentlemen will in time alter as much upon this subject as I have seen in their treatment of the small-pox?" *Mr. Henry Dunn* bears the following testimony: "From my position as surgeon to the West Riding of Yorkshire House of Correction, I have had thirty years' experience of all the prisoners being at once deprived of intoxicating liquors, and I cannot say with any prejudicial effect, but rather the reverse. Our committals have been for the last few years from 3,000 to 4,000 annually, so that the fact speaks volumes." In

Appendix "*S*" to the Report of the Committee of Convocation on Intemperance, there are eighteen pages of evidence on "Benefit to Health from Withdrawal of Intoxicating Liquors" from prisoners and inmates of workhouses. The testimonies from governors and chaplains of prisons are 56, and from masters of workhouses, 89. A very few extracts are all that need be given as samples of the rest. Governors and chaplains of prisons say: "I have not known one whose health was affected." "We are constantly hearing men say how well they can do without drink." "I am not a teetotaler; but I know of nothing that affords so good an evidence of the value of teetotalism as its results in the case of hundreds of prisoners on public works." "Prisoners come in very ill—they recover wonderfully when taken away from drink. I never saw one prisoner injured in his or her health by enforced abstinence, but the reverse. The women often recover their former good looks, even if they looked ugly and hideous on their admission." The masters of workhouses say: "The health of the paupers is greatly improved." "I believe, speaking from an experience of fifteen years as workhouse officer, that abstinence is beneficial to the general health of paupers." "A marked improvement is soon visible." "Twenty-four years' experience, I have not seen any injurious effects from total abstinence." "Thirty years' experience convinces me that total abstinence is not injurious to health." "We have scarcely ever any sickness or disease of any kind Out of 100 inmates we have 20 averaging 80 years, in perfect health, which speaks volumes in favor of abstinence." "No injury whatever, but benefit." "In some cases persons came in lunatics, and by abstaining from intoxicating liquors have been discharged sound in mind and body."

K.

Views of Archbishop Fenelon and the Duke of Orleans on Wine Production.

THE tale of Telemachus was written, it is well-known, by the pious *Fénelon*, Archbishop of Cambrai, for the benefit of the young Duke of Burgundy, heir-apparent to the French throne, in order that, in the attractive form of fiction, the young prince might be led to contemplate and admire the examples of virtue described in the story. As we may, therefore, consider that the author declares his own opinions where he paints scenes of happiness and manners conducive to the social welfare, it is interesting to notice that he makes Adoam say of the people of Bœtica: "They content themselves with eating grapes like other fruits, and dread wine as the corrupter of mankind. It is a kind of poison, say they, which inspires madness. It does not, indeed, kill a man at once, but it degrades him into a brute. Men may preserve their health and strength without wine; with it, they run the risk of ruining both their health and morals." So, Mentor (Minerva) in advising Idomeneus as to his government, is made to observe: "Wine is the source of the greatest evils among the people; it is the cause of disease, quarrels, sedition, idleness, an aversion to labor, and family disorders. Let wine, therefore, be reserved as a kind of restorative, or as a choice liquor only to be used in sacrifices, or for very extraordinary occasions; but do not expect so very important a rule to be observed, unless you set an example of it yourself." In his description of the effects of wine, Fénelon, there can be no doubt, painted from the life, as that life was presented to his view a hundred and fifty years ago. Fénelon, in his "Telemachus," strongly advocated free trade and the removal of all barriers to the commercial intercourse of nations, in things conducive to their true prosperity. When *Mr. E. C. Delavan* visited Paris in 1838, he waited upon the king, *Louis Philippe,* and his son, the *Duke of Orleans,* both of whom acknowledged that the intemperance of France was (then) upon wine, and that it would be an economical blessing to that country if the use of so large a portion of the soil in the growth of the vine for wine-making could be done away with, and if the industrial energies of the people were devoted to another purpose. The use of wine did not prevent the use of brandy and absinthe, and what wine, brandy, and absinthe have done for France, in both her military and civil estates, let history and the confessions of her wisest sons attest!

L.

Effects of No Liquor Traffic on the Social Condition of the People.

Jonas Hannay, in his work, "The Defects of Police the Cause of Immorality" (1775), alludes to "a certain parish in the North of England, where no public-house was licensed, and where there was no poors-rate, nor occasion for any such relief. At length three licenses were granted; and what was the consequence? Within thirty months the poors-rate amounted to eightpence in the pound. Upon this the justices withdrew the licenses, and the economy of the people reverted to its former channel, as no rate was necessary." In *Dr. Lees'* able "Argument for the Prohibition of the Liquor Traffic" (1856), and the "Condensed Argument" (1866), instances are given of the benefits arising from the suppression of the liquor traffic. The cases of *Saltaire* in England, and of *Besbrook* in Ireland, are illustrations of manufacturing places which are free from the sale of intoxicating liquors, and where the results are of the most pleasing description. The case of the agricultural district, 61½ miles square, in the *County Tyrone,* is an illustration of the similar good effect

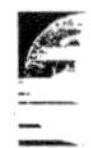

of the same rule applied to a rural population or upwards of 9,000 souls. Professor *Kirk*, in his "Progressive Legislation," shows how the absence of drink in Scotland operates in favor of sobriety and every social virtue. But the greatest body of evidence on this subject, in reference to the United Kingdom, is furnished in the *Appendices J. J. & K. K.* to the Report of the Committee of Convocation on Intemperance, where a list of 1,397 parishes, etc., without drinking-shops, in the Province of Canterbury, is given, with testimonies concerning the results as brought before the notice of resident clergy and constabulary. A few of these replies are quoted, but the reader is strongly advised to consult that admirable Report, with its invaluable supplemental synopsis of facts. "There being no public-house or beer-shop in the parish is a cause of unmitigated good, in so far as it removes temptation to some distance." "I attribute solely to this circumstance that there are no cases of habitual drunkenness within the parish, either of men or women." "I am glad to say that the people are very hale and temperate." "Having no public-house in the parish, intemperance is comparatively unknown to us." "I have been in the parish since 1844, and have not seen any one tipsy. We have had no case for the police since I have been here." "Magistrates never have a case from this parish, nor has there been a pauper in the Union for some time past." "Thank God there is no crime, no lunacy, no pauperism, beyond what comes occasionally of sickness!" "Intemperance does not exist." "No crime, pauperism, or lunacy." "It is a great blessing to the people that there is no public-house or beer-shop." From Chief Constables and Superintendents of Police there are some very interesting replies. "In parishes where there are neither public-houses nor beer-shops, the absence of crime is remarkable." "I may state, that from the above ninety-seven parishes,in which there are no public-houses or beer-shops, little or no crime comes." "From the permanent population of these parishes I have had no case of drunkenness or crime during the past five years and a half."

The evidence supplied by the States of the American Union where the prohibitory law is on the statute-book, bears a uniform relation to the degree in which the law is enforced in the respective districts. Where the local authorities do their duty, the effects are invariably seen in the reduction of intemperance and every social vice and burden. A crucial test is afforded by a district in New Jersey (not a Maine-law State) which is known as *Vineland.* The overseer, Mr. T. C. Curtis, reported as follows in 1869: "Though we have a population of 10,000 people, for the period of six months no settler or citizen of Vineland has required relief at my hands as overseer of the poor. During the entire year, there has only been one indictment, and that a trifling case of assault and battery, among our colored population. We, practically, have no debt, and our taxes are only one per cent. on the valuation. The police expenses amount to $75 (£15) per year; the sum paid to me. I ascribe this remarkable state of things—so nearly approaching the golden age—to the industry of our people and the absence of King Alcohol." At the last annual vote on the question of "license or no license," the vote was *unanimous*—electors of all politics concurring to sustain so desirable a state of things. The remarkable colony so long residing on *Pitcairn's Island,* in the South Seas, and some years ago removed to *Norfolk Island,* have, as one of their code of laws, a provision that no intoxicating liquors shall be imported, and none sold except for medicinal purposes. A number of such settlements exist in various parts of the globe, and the results are so uniformly beneficial as to constitute an argument, irresistible to the impartial mind, in favor of the extension of the same policy throughout the civilized world.

Aunt Dinah's Pledge. 12mo, 318 pages. By Miss MARY DWINELL CHELLIS, author of "Temperance Doctor," "Out of the Fire," etc., ... **$1 25**

Aunt Dinah was an eminent Christian woman. Her pledge included swearing and smoking, as well as drinking. It saved her boys, who lived useful lives, and died happy; and by quiet, yet loving and persistent work, names of many others were added who seemed almost beyond hope of salvation.

The Temperance Doctor. 12mo, 370 pages. By Miss MARY DWINELL CHELLIS, ... **$1 25**

This is a true story, replete with interest, and adapted to Sunday-school and family reading. In it we have graphically depicted the sad ravages that are caused by the use of intoxicating beverages; also, the blessings of Temperance, and what may be accomplished by one earnest soul for that reform. It ought to find readers in every household.

Out of the Fire. 12mo, 420 pages. By Miss MARY DWINELL CHELLIS, author of "Deacon Sim's Prayers," etc., ... **$1 25**

It is one of the most effective and impressive Temperance books ever published. The evils of the drinking customs of society, and the blessings of sobriety and total abstinence, are strikingly developed in the history of various families in the community.

History of a Threepenny Bit. 18mo, 216 pages, ... **$0 75**

This is a thrilling story, beautifully illustrated with five choice wood engravings. The story of little Peggy, the drunkard's daughter, is told in such a simple yet interesting manner that no one can read it without realizing more than ever before the nature and extent of intemperance, and sympathizing more than ever with the patient, suffering victim. It should be in every Sunday-school library.

Adopted. 18mo, 236 pages. By Mrs. E. J. RICHMOND, author of "The McAllisters," . . . **$0 60**

This book is written in an easy, pleasant yle, seems to be true to nature, true to itself, and withal is full of the Gospel and Temperance.

The Red Bridge. 18mo, 321 pages. By THRACE TALMAN, . . **$0 90**

We have met with few Temperance stories containin- so many evidences of decided ability and high literary excellence as this.

The Old Brown Pitcher. 12mo, 222 pages. By the Author of "Susie's Six Birthdays," "The Flower of the Family," etc., **$1 00**

Beautifully illustrated. This admirable volume for boys and girls, containing original stories by some of the most gifted writers for the young, will be eagerly welcomed by the children. It is adapted alike for the family circle and the Sabbath-school library.

Our Parish. 18mo, 252 pages. By Mrs. EMILY PEARSON, . . **$0 75**

The manifold evils resulting from the "still" to the owner's family, as well as to the families of his customers, are truthfully presented. The characters introduced, such as are found in almost every good-sized village, are well portrayed. We can unhesitatingly commend it, and bespeak for it a wide circulation.

The Hard Master. 18mo, 278 pages. By Mrs. J. E. McCONAUGHY, author of "One Hundred Gold Dollars," and other popular Sunday-School books, ... **$0 85**

This interesting narrative of the temptations, trials, hardships, and fortunes of poor orphan boy illustrates in a most striking manner the value of "right principles," especially of honesty truthfulness, and TEMPERANCE.

Echo Bank. 18mo, 269 pages. By ERVIE, ... **$0 85**

This is a well-written and deeply interesting narrative, in which is clearly shown the suffering and sorrow that too often follow and the dangers that attend boys and young men at school and at college, who suppose they can easily take a glass or two occasionally, without fear of ever being aught more than a moderate drinker.

Rachel Noble's Experience. 18mo, 325 pages. By BRUCE EDWARDS. **$0 90**

This is a story of thrilling interest, ably and eloquently told, and is an excellent book for Sunday-school libraries. It is just the book for the home circle, and cannot be read without benefiting the reader and advancing the cause of Temperance.

Gertie's Sacrifice; or Glimpses at Two Lives. 18mo, 189 pages. By Mrs. F. D. GAGE, ... **$0 50**

A story of great interest and power, giving a "glimpse at two lives," and showing how Gertie sacrificed herself as a victim of fashion, custom, and law.

Time will Tell. 12mo, 307 pages. By Mrs. WILSON, ... **$1 00**

A Temperance tale of thrilling interest and unexceptionable moral and religious tone. It is full of incidents and characters of everyday life, while its lessons are plainly and forcibly set before the reader. The pernicious results of the drinking usages in the family and social circle are plainly set forth.

Philip Eckert's Struggles and Triumphs. 18mo, 216 pages. By the author of "Margaret Clair," **$0 60**

This interesting narrative of a noble, manly boy, in an intemperate home, fighting with the wrong and battling for the right, should be read by every child in the land.

Jug-Or-Not. 12mo, 346 pages. By Mrs. J. McNAIR WRIGHT, author of "John and the Demijohn," "Almost a Nun," "Priest and Nun," etc., ... **$1 25**

It is one of her best books, and treats of the physical and hereditary effects of drinking in a clear, plain, and familiar style, adapted to popular reading, and which should be read by all classes in the community, and find a place in every Sunday-school library.

The Broken Rock. 18mo, 139 pages. By KRUNA, author of "Lift a Little," etc., ... **$0 50**

It beautifully illustrates the silent and holy influence of a meek and lowly spirit upon the heartless rumseller until the rocky heart was broken.

Andrew Douglass. 18mo, 232 pages, **$0 75**

A new Temperance story for Sunday-schools, written in a lively, energetic, and popular style, adapted to the Sabbath-school and the family circle.

Vow at the Bars. 18mo, 108 pages. **$0 40**

It contains four short tales, illustrating four important principles connected with the Temperance movement, and is well adapted for the family circle and Sabbath-school libraries.

Job Tufton's Rest. 12mo, 332 pages, ... **$1 25**

A story of life's struggles, written by the gifted author, CLARA LUCAS BALFOUR, depicting most skilfully and truthfully many a life-struggle with the demon of intemperance occurring all along life's pathway. It is a finely written story, and full of interest from the beginning to the end.

Frank Oldfield; or, Lost and Found. 12mo, 408 pages, ... **$1 50**

This excellent story received the prize of £100 in England, out of eighty-three manuscripts submitted; and by an arrangement with the publishers we publish it in this country with all the original illustrations. It is admirably adapted to Sunday-school libraries.

Tom Blinn's Temperance Society, and other Stories. 12mo, 316 pages, ... **$1 25**

This is the title of a new book written by T. S. ARTHUR, the well-known author of "Ten Nights in a Bar-room," and whose fame as an author should bespeak for it a wide circulation. It is written in Mr. ARTHUR's best style, composed of a series of tales adapted to every family and library in the land.

The Harker Family. 12mo, 336 pages. By EMILY THOMPSON, **$1 25**

A simple, spirited, and interesting narrative, written in a style especially attractive, depicting the evils that arise from intemperance, and the blessings that followed the earnest efforts of those who sought to win others to the paths of total abstinence. Illustrated with three engravings. The book will please all.

Come Home, Mother. 18mo, 143 pages. By NELSIE BROOK. Illustrated with six choice engravings, ... **$0 50**

A most effective and interesting book, describing the downward course of the mother, and giving an account of the sad scenes, but effectual endeavors, of the little one in bringing her mother back to friends, and leading her to God. It should be read by everybody.

Tim's Troubles. 12mo, 350 pages. By Miss M. A. PAULL, . . **$1 50**

This is the second Prize Book of the United Kingdom Band of Hope Union, reprinted in this country with all the original illustrations. It is the companion of "Frank Oldfield." written in a high tone, and will be found a valuable addition to our Temperance literature.

The Drinking Fountain Stories. 12mo, 192 pages, ... **$1 00**

This book of illustrated stories for children contains articles from some of the best writers for children in America, and is beautifully illustrated with forty choice wood engravings.

The White Rose. By Mary J. Hedges. 16mo, 320 pages, . . **$1 25**

The gift of a simple white rose was the means of leading those who cared for it to the Saviour. How it was done is very pleasantly told, and also the wrongs resulting in the use of strong drink forcibly shown.

Hopedale Tavern, and What it Wrought. 12mo, 252 pages. By J. WILLIAM VAN NAMEE, . **$1 00**

It shows the sad results which followed the introduction of a Tavern and Bar in a beautiful and quiet country town, whose inhabitants had hitherto lived in peace and enjoyment The contrast is too plainly presented to fail to produce an impression on the reader, making all more desirous to abolish the sale of all intoxicants

Roy's Search; or, Lost in the Cars. 12mo, 364 pages. By HELEN C. PEARSON, ... **$1 25**

This new Temperance book is one of the most interesting ever published—written in a fresh, sparkling style, especially adapted to please the boys, and contains so much that will benefit as well as amuse and interest that we wish all the boys in the land might read it.

How Could He Escape? 12mo, 324 pages. By MRS. J. NCNAIR WRIGHT, author of "Jug-Or-Not." Illustrated with ten engravings, designed by the author, ... **$1 25**

This is a true tale, and one of the writer's best productions. It shows the terrible effects of even one glass of intoxicating liquor upon the system of one unable to resist its influences, and the necessity of grace in the heart to resist temptation and overcome the appetite for strong drink.

The Best Fellow in the World. 12mo, 352 pages. By Mrs. J. MCNAIR WRIGHT, autnor of "Jug-Or-Not," "How Could He Escape?" "Priest and Nun," **$1 25**

"The Best Fellow," whose course is here portrayed, is one of a very large class who are led astray and ruined simply because they are such "good fellows." To all such the volume speaks in thrilling tones of warning, shows the inevitable consequences of indulging in strong drink, and the necessity of divine grace in the heart to interpose and save from ruin.

Frank Spencer's Rule of Life. 18mo, 180 pages. By JOHN W KIRTON, author of "Buy Your Own Cherries," "Four Pillars of Temperance," etc., etc., . **$0 50**

This is written in the author's best style, making an interesting and attractive story for children.

Work and Reward. 18mo, 183 pp. By Mrs. M. A. HOLT, . **$0 50**

It shows that not the smallest effort to do good is lost sight of by the all-knowing Father, and that faith and prayer must accompany all temperance efforts.

The Pitcher of Cool Water. 18mo, 180 pages. By T. S. ARTHUR, author of "Tom Blinn's Temperance Society," "Ten Nights in a Bar-room," etc., ... **$0 50**

This little book consists of a series of Temperance stories, handsomely illustrated, written in Mr ARTHUR'S best style, and is altogether one of the best books which can be placed in the hands of children. Every Sunday-school library should possess it.

Little Girl in Black. 12mo, 212 pages. By MARGARET E. WILMER, ... **$0 90**

Her strong faith in God, who she believes will reclaim an erring father, is a lesson to the reader, old as well as young.

Temperance Anecdotes. 12mo, 288 pages, ... **$1 00**

This new book of Temperance Anecdotes, edited by GEORGE W. BUNGAY, contains nearly four hundred Anecdotes, Witticisms, Jokes, Conundrums, etc., original and selected, and will meet a want long felt and often expressed by a very large number of the numerous friends of the cause in the land. The book is handsomely illustrated with twelve choice wood engravings.

The Temperance Speaker. By J. N. STEARNS, ... **$0 75**

The book contains 288 pages of Declamations and Dialogues suitable for Sunday and Day-Schools, Bands of Hope, and Temperance Organizations. It consists of choice selections of prose and poetry, both new and old, from the Temperance orators and writers of the country, many of which have been written expressly for this work.

The McAllisters. 18mo, 211 pages. By Mrs. E. J. RICHMOND, . **$0 50**

It shows the ruin brought on a family by the father's intemperate habits, and the strong faith and trust of the wife in that Friend above who alone gives strength to bear our earthly trials.

The Seymours. 12mo, 231 pages. By Miss L. BATES, . . . **$1 00**

A simple story, showing how a refined and cultivated family are brought low through the drinking habits of the father, their joy and sorrow as he reforms only to fall again, and his final happy release in a distant city.

Zoa Rodman. 12mo, 262 pages. By Mrs. E. J. RICHMOND, **$1 00**

Adapted more especially to young girls' reading, showing the influence they wield in society, and their responsibility for much of its drinking usages.

Eva's Engagement Ring. 12mo, 189 pages. By MARGARET E. WILMER, author of "The Little Girl in Black," **$0 90**

In this interesting volume is traced the career of the moderate drinker, who takes a glass in the name of friendship or courtesy.

Packington Parish, and The Diver's Daughter. 12mo, 327 pages. By Miss M. A. PAULL, . . . **$1 25**

In this volume we see the ravages which the liquor traffic caused when introduced in a hitherto quiet village, and how a minister's eyes were at length opened to its evils, though he had always declared wine to be a "good creature of God," meant to be used in moderation.

Old Times. 12mo. By Miss M. D. CHELLIS, author of "The Temperance Doctor," "Out of the Fire," "Aunt Dinah's Pledge," "At Lion's Mouth," etc., . **$1 25**

It discusses the whole subject of moderate drinking in the history of a New England village. The incidents, various and amusing, are all facts, and the characters nearly all drawn from real life. The five deacons which figure so conspicuously actually lived and acted as represented.

John Bentley's Mistake. 18mo, 177 pages. By Mrs. M. A. HOLT, **$0 50**

It takes an important place among our temperance books, taking an earnest, bold stand against the use of cider as a beverage, proving that it is often the first step toward stronger drinks, forming an appetite for the more fiery liquids which cannot easily be quenched.

Nothing to Drink. 12mo, 400 pages. By Mrs. J. MCNAIR WRIGHT, author of "The Best Fellow in the World," "Jug-or-Not," "How Could He Escape?" etc., ... **$1 50**

The story is of light-house keeper and thrilling adventures at sea, being nautical, scientific, and partly statistical, written in a charming, thrilling, and convincing manner. It goes out of the ordinary line entirely, most of the characters being portraits, its scenery all from absolute facts, every scientific and natural-history statement a verity, the sea incidents from actual experience from marine disasters for the last ten years.

Nettie Loring. 12mo, 352 pages. By Mrs. GEO. S. DOWNS, **$1 25**

It graphically describes the doings of several young ladies who resolved to use their influence on the side of temperance and banish wine from their entertainments, the scorn they excited, and the good results which followed.

The Fire Fighters. 12mo, 294 pages. By Mrs. J. E. MCCONAUGHY, author of "The Hard Master," **$1 25**

An admirable story, showing how a number of young lads banded themselves into a society to fight against Alcohol, and the good they did in the community.

The Jewelled Serpent. 12mo, 271 pages. By Mrs. E. J. RICHMOND, author of "Adopted," "The McAllisters," etc., ... **$1 00**

The story is written earnestly. The characters are well delineated, and taken from the wealthy and fashionable portion of a large city. The evils which flow from fashionable drinking are well portrayed, and also the danger arising from the use of intoxicants when used as medicine, forming an appetite which fastens itself with a deadly hold upon its victim.

The Hole in the Bag, and Other Stories. By Mrs. J. P. BALLARD, author of "The Broken Rock," "Lift a Little," etc. 12mo, **$1 00**

A collection of well-written stories by this most popular author on the subject of temperance, inculcating many valuable lessons in the minds of its readers.

The Glass Cable. 12mo, 288 pages. By MARGARET E. WILMER, author of "The Little Girl in Black," "Eva's Engagement Ring," etc., ... **$1 25**

The style of this book is good, the characters well selected, and its temperance and religious truths most excellent. The moral of the story shows those who sneer at a child's pledge, comparing its strength to a glass cable, that it is in many cases strong enough to brave the storms and temptations of a whole lifetime.

Fred's Hard Fight. 12mo, 334 pages. By Miss MARION HOWARD, ... **$1 25**

While it shows the trials which a young lad endured through the temptations and enticements offered him by those opposed to his firm temperance and religious principles, and warns the reader against the use of every kind of alcoholic stimulant, it points also to Jesus, the only true source of strength, urging all to accept the promises of strength and salvation offered to every one who will seek it.

The Dumb Traitor. 12mo, 336 pp. By MARGARET E. WILMER, **$1 25**

Intensely interesting, showing how the prospects of a well-to-do New England family were blighted through the introduction of a box of wine, given in friendship, used as medicine, but proving a dumb traitor in the end.

Miscellaneous Publications.

Forty Years' Fight with the Drink Demon. 12mo, 400 pages. By CHARLES JEWETT, M.D., . **$1 50**

This volume comprises the history of Dr. Jewett's public and private labors from 1826 to the present time, with sketches of the most popular and distinguished advocates of the cause in its earlier stages. It also records the results of forty years' observation, study, and reflections upon the use of intoxicating drinks and drugs, and suggestions as to the best methods of advancing the cause, etc. The book is handsomely bound, and contains illustrated portraits of early champions of the cause.

Drops of Water. 12mo, 133 pages. By Miss ELLA WHEELER, **$0 75**

A new book of fifty-six Temperance Poems by this young and talented authoress, suitable for reading in Temperance Societies, Lodge Rooms, Divisions, etc. The simplicity of manner, beauty of expression, earnestness of thought, and nobleness of sentiment running through all of them make this book a real gem, worthy a place by the side of any of the poetry in the country.

Bound Volume of Tracts. 500 pages, ... **$1 00**

This volume contains all the four, eight, and twelve page tracts published by the National Temperance Society, including all the prize tracts issued the last two years. The book comprises Arguments, Statistics, Sketches, and Essays, which make it an invaluable collection for every friend of the Temperance Reform.

Scripture Testimony Against Intoxicating Wine. By Rev. WM. RITCHIE, of Scotland, . . **$0 60**

An unanswerable refutation of the theory that the Scriptures favor the idea of the use of intoxicating wine as a beverage. It takes the different kinds of wines mentioned in the Scriptures, investigates their specific nature, and shows wherein they differ.

Alcohol: Its Place and Power, by JAMES MILLER; and **The Use and Abuse of Tobacco,** by JOHN LIZARS, ... **$1 00**

Zoological Temperance Convention. By Rev. EDWARD HITCHCOCK, D.D., of Amherst College, **$0 75**

This fable gives an interesting and entertaining account of a Convention of Animals held in Central Africa, and reports the speeches made on the occasion.

Delavan's Consideration of the Temperance Argument and History, **$1 50**

This condensed and comprehensive work contains Essays and Selections from different authors, collected and edited by EDWARD C. DELAVAN, Esq., and is one of the most valuable text-books on the subject of Temperance ever issued.

Bible Rule of Temperance; or, Total Abstinence from all Intoxicating Drinks. By Rev. GEORGE DUFFIELD, D.D., ... **$0 60**

This is the ablest and most reliable work which has been issued on the subject. The immorality of the us , sale, and manufacture of intoxicating liquors as a beverage is considered in the light of the Scriptures, and the will and law of God clearly presented.

Alcohol: Its Nature and Effects. By CHARLES A. STOREY, M.D., **$0 90**

This is a thoroughly scientific work, yet written in a fresh, vigorous, and popular style, in language that the masses can understand. It consists of ten lectures carefully prepared, and is an entirely new work by one amply competent to present the subject.

Four Pillars of Temperance. By JOHN W. KIRTON, . . . **$0 75**

The Four Pillars are, Reason, Science, Scripture, and Experience. The book is argumentative, historical, and statistical, and the facts, appeals, and arguments are presented in a most convincing and masterly manner.

Communion Wine; or, Bible Temperance. By Rev. WILLIAM M. THAYER. Paper, **20** cents; cloth, **$0 50**

An unanswerable argument against the use of intoxicating wine at Communion, and presenting the Bible argument in favor of total abstinence.

Laws of Fermentation and Wines of the Ancients. 12mo, 129 pages. By Rev. WM. PATTON, D.D. Paper, **30** cts.; cloth, . . **$0 60**

It presents the whole matter of Bible Temperance and the wines of ancient times in a new, clear, and satisfactory manner, developing the laws of fermentation, and giving a large number of references and statistics never before collected, showing conclusively the existence of unfermented wine in the olden time.

The National Temperance Society's Books.

Pamphlets.

John Swig. A Poem. By EDWARD CARSWELL. 12mo, 24 pages Illustrated with eight characteristic engravings, printed on tinted paper, ... **$0 15**

The Rum Fiend, and Other Poems. By WILLIAM H. BURLEIGH. 12mo. 46 pages. Illustrated with three wood engravings, designed by EDWARD CARSWELL. . . . **$0 20**

Suppression of the Liquor Traffic. A Prize Essay, by Rev. H. D. KITCHELL, President of Middlebury College. 12mo, 48 pp., **$0 10**

Bound and How; or, Alcohol as a Narcotic. By CHARLES JEWETT, M D. 12mo, 24 pp., . . . **$0 10**

Scriptural Claims of Total Abstinence. By Rev. NEWMAN HALL. 12mo, 62 pp., ... **$0 15**

Buy Your Own Cherries. By JOHN W. KIRTON. 12mo, 32 pp., **$0 20**

National Temperance Almanac and Teetotaler's Year Book for 1874, **$0 10**

Illustrated Temperance Alphabet, **$0 25**

The Youth's Temperance Banner

The National Temperance Society and Publication House publish a beautifully illustrated Monthly Paper, especially adapted to children and youth, Sunday-school and Juvenile Temperance Organizations. Each number contains several choice engravings, a piece of music, and a great variety of articles from the pens of the best writers for children in America. It should be placed in the hands of every child in the land.

TERMS—IN ADVANCE.

Single copies, one year, - - - - $0 25	Thirty copies, to one address, - - $3 75
Eight copies, to one address, - - - 1 00	Forty " " " - - 5 00
Ten " " " - - - 1 25	Fifty " " " - 6 25
Fifteen " " " - - - 1 88	One Hundred " " - 12 00
Twenty " " " - - - 2 50	

The Total Abstainer's Daily Witness and Bible Verdict. 75 Cents.

This is a series of Scripture Texts printed on thirty-one large sheets, arranged so that one can be used for each day in the month. The size of each sheet is 19 by 12 inches, all fastened together with roller and cord, so as to be easily hung up in room, office, workshop, etc.; and turning over a sheet day by day as required.

New Temperance Dialogues.

The First Glass; or, The Power of Woman's Influence.
The Young Teetotaler, or, Saved at Last. 15 cents each. Per dozen, . $1 50
Reclaimed; or, The Danger of Moderate Drinking. 10 cents. Per dozen, ... 1 00
Marry No Man if he Drinks; or, Laura's Plan and How it Succeeded. 10 cents. Per dozen, ... 1 00
Which Will You Choose? 36 pages. By Miss M D. Chellis. 15 cents. Per dozen, ... $1 50
Aunt Dinah's Pledge. Dramatized, . 0 15
The Temperance Doctor. Dramatized, 0 15
Wine as a Medicine. 10c. Per dozen, . 1 00
The Stumbling-Block. 10c. Per dozen, 1 00
Trial and Condemnation of Judas Woemaker. 15 cents. Per dozen, . . 1 50
Temperance Exercise, ... 0 10

Band of Hope Supplies.

Band of Hope Manual. Per dozen, $0 60
Temperance Catechism. Per dozen, 60
Band of Hope Melodies. Paper, 10
Band of Hope Badge. Enamelled, $1 25 per dozen; 12 cents singly. Plain, $1 per dozen; 10 cents singly. Silver and Enamelled, 50 cents each.
Juvenile Temperance Speaker. - - $0 25
Illuminated Temperance Cards. Set of ten. - - - - 35
Juvenile Temperance Pledges. Per 100, 3 00
Certificates of Membership Per 100, - 3 00
The Temperance Speaker, - - - 75
Catechism on Alcohol. By Miss Julia Colman. Per dozen, - - - 60

Sent by mail, post-paid, on receipt of price. Address

J. N. STEARNS, Publishing Agent,

58 READE STREET, NEW YORK.

www.ingramcontent.com/pod-product-compliance
Lightning Source LLC
LaVergne TN
LVHW050527100826
845148LV00002B/461

* 9 7 8 1 4 2 5 5 1 9 5 9 9 *